2

IN SEARCH OF WHITE CROWS

IN
SEARCH OF WHITE
CROWS
Spiritualism, Parapsychology, and American Culture

R. Laurence Moore

New York
Oxford University Press
1977

Library of Congress Cataloging in Publication Data

Moore, Robert Laurence.
  In search of white crows.

  Bibliography: p.
  Includes index.
  1. Spiritualism—United States—History.
2. Psychical research—United States—History.
I. Title.
BF 1242.U6M66   133   76-51720
ISBN 0- 19-502259-9

"If I may employ the language of the professional logic-shop, a universal proposition can be made untrue by a particular instance. If you wish to upset the law that all crows are black, you must not seek to show that no crows are; it is enough if you prove one single crow to be white."

"If there is anything which human history demonstrates, it is the extreme slowness with which the ordinary academic and critical mind acknowledges facts to exist which present themselves as wild facts, with no stall or pigeon-hole, or as facts which threaten to break up the accepted system."

William James,
"What Psychical Research Has Accomplished" (*1897*)

FOR MY MOTHER AND MY FATHER

Acknowledgments

I choose first to wish the people mentioned in the dedication a happy forty-fifth anniversary. I believe enough in the importance of genetic endowment and early education to think that they deserve considerable credit for whatever intelligence is revealed in the pages that follow.

A number of colleagues (past and present) helped me in one important way or another to write this book. These people include Sydney Ahlstrom, Steven Ozment, R. Hal Williams, Michael Kammen, Mary Beth Norton, and Frank Turner. For his many vivid portrayals of peculiar happenings in California, I wish to thank Joseph C. Friedman. Several students provided valuable assistance and suggestions, especially John Siliciano, Ron Denson, and David Miller. Susan Rabiner was at every stage of publication a superior editor, and I owe her and Sheldon Meyer a considerable debt. Norman Kolpas, a "professional American" living in London, corrected and typed the final version of the manuscript.

Every historian depends on librarians and archivists. In particular I would like to acknowledge the help given to me at the American Society for Psychical Research; the Society for Physical Research, London; the American Antiquarian Society; the Institute for Historical Research, London, the State Historical

Society of Wisconsin; the New York Public Library; and the university libraries at Yale, Harvard, Cornell, Brown, and Duke.

The American Philosophical Society, the National Endowment for the Humanities, and the Yale University Morse Fellowship Fund provided generous financial support for my research and writing.

Several years ago I was invited by Loma Linda University to deliver a lecture on the origins of American spiritualism. That lecture appeared in Edwin Gaustad, ed., *The Rise of Adventism* (Harper and Row, 1974) and is the basis for Chapter 2 of the present study. Earlier versions of Chapters 1 and 4 appeared in the *American Quarterly*.

I have reserved two names to mention last. They are William R. Taylor and Elizabeth Anne Moore. I really don't know how to adequately acknowledge their assistance. But some day, when we again gather ourselves and others at San Frediano, I shall try.

Preface

This is a book about people who believe in white crows. Presumably most educated Americans (and certainly most historians) don't spend any more time thinking about white crows than they do about unicorns. Skepticism with respect to the reality of such oddities has generally outweighed William James's plea that we keep an open mind about reports of stray and strange facts.

However, there are signs that in one important way James's particular sort of curiosity has recently been gaining in influence. Over the past decade and a half a growing academic interest in the "irrational" has prompted (or accelerated) a reevaluation of a whole range of historical subjects. In many instances the reevaluation has forced us to think again about what we mean by such words as "science," "reason," and "irrationality." We no longer regard Newton's interests in the occult as somehow superfluous to his scientific discoveries. Nor in present historical studies do we locate Anton Mesmer in the fringes of Enlightenment thought. Things that we once treated as monstrous delusions (witchcraft) or meaningless superstitions (astrology) have become the subjects of important studies. Many once-ignored "delusions" and "superstitions" are now seen as crucial aspects of the beliefs of past cultures. Understood in their historical context, they have often ceased to strike us as irrational. Indeed, we have discovered surprising connections between them and the ideas of people we had commonly portrayed in our histories as walking the high road toward modernism.

Spiritualism (a belief in communication with spirits through human mediums) and psychical research (the investigation of a variety of alleged mental powers that supposedly defy normal explanation) deserve much more careful historical assessment than they have received. During the nineteenth and twentieth centuries in the United States, both drew enormous audiences made up of people from every social and educational level. For many decades (including the 1970s), American readers have supported an extraordinary number of publications concerned with spirit communication and extrasensory perception. Surely that public curiosity has a cultural meaning beyond the interpretation suggested by some commentators that spirits and ESP satisfied a yearning in the popular mind for mystification. Briefly, in this book I have argued that over the past 175 years spiritualism and then psychical research have offered Americans a "reasonable" solution to the problem of how to accommodate religious and scientific interests. Whether or not Americans believed in spirit communication and telepathy, they discussed the possibility with considerable enthusiasm. And in their discussions they revealed a great deal of what was then on their minds.

In analyzing the reasons for the appeal of spiritualism and psychical research to the American public, I do not want to be misunderstood as saying that the particular claims of either one made it into what historians are wont to call the mainstream. They did not, and that fact had an important effect on the behavior of people who became vigorous advocates of "supernormal" phenomena. Historical mainstreams, however vague, do exist, and in the course of their careers people do come to believe that they are more or less in or out of them. In conducting my research, however, I have found many reasons to be cautious about using the word "mainstream." For all its demonstrable importance to analysis, the mainstream is a societal invention that has no necessary relation to an actual consensus of values. Labeling something mainstream can be a political act, and all political acts depend on power to make them stick. Need one add that even in egalitarian democracies power is not necessarily backed up by majority opinion? Spiritualists and psychical researchers may have been placed outside the mainstream, but their views on many issues came as close to representing a numerical majority as did the views of those who wished to deny legitimacy to their endeavors.

The concept of a mainstream can lead to an especially blinding historical myopia if we assume that whatever is outside it is a cultural anachronism and doesn't quite belong in the particular time and place under study. That attitude surely accounts for the neglect of the subjects of this book. Yet even deviant behavior and belief reflect significant aspects of a culture. In fact, what is regarded as normal in any particular historical period only takes on meaning when it is related to what is regarded as deviant. Analyzing the reciprocal influence between the two may well be a more important task for the cultural historian than, for example, locating points of contact between high and low culture. In any case, the limits on the things that can be said (as well as on the forms of saying them) in a historical period ensure that no expression of belief can be devoid of cultural meaning. Since spiritualists and psychical researchers reached large audiences, one must assume that what they were saying was easily grasped and in fact resembled a great many other things in the same historical milieu. If the opponents of spiritualism had been right in claiming that only a sixteenth-century mind would see anything in it, they would have had much less to worry about. As it was, the ideas of spiritualism, its vocabulary, and its modes of demonstration were all well suited to nineteenth-century listeners.

The "familiarity" of spiritualism and psychical research to their contemporaries was based on many things I have discussed in the text. Spiritualists drew their language from popular tracts on scientific empiricism. Everything they said and wrote echoed a widespread nineteenth-century secular optimism that stemmed from a faith in evolutionary progress and temperate reform. Spiritualists spread their ideas in unexceptional ways, in the same manner that other ideas were disseminated: books, pamphlets, newspapers, and public lectures. While some writers have argued that the séance ritual was a bizarre practice within the context of nineteenth-century American society, I would maintain that the reputed bizarreness was largely the fabrication of spiritualism's critics. Professional mediums were really rather skillful in adopting common forms of public entertainment and religious worship to their own purposes. The homely, down-to-earth spirit messages came mostly from family members and patriotic heroes, and they immediately created a feeling of rapport between the sitters and the purported spirit. Most visitors to séances remarked on how little sense of strangeness or astonishment they felt, and there were good reasons for that impression. In many ways spiritualism could claim to being the quintessential expression of the age of the common man.

Psychical researchers in the twentieth century organized their activities differently from nineteenth-century spiritualists and relied on somewhat different rhetorical justifications. But they too expressed themselves in ways and categories perfectly familiar to an American audience. Many of them were almost obsessive imitators of what they took to be the established procedures of scientific investigation. They modeled their journals on existing scientific publications and designed experiments to meet the requirements of the general scientific community. I do not argue that spiritualists and psychical researchers managed to satisfy everyone about the seriousness of their scientific attitude or that they were totally free of arcane interests. They did and said things that struck many of their contemporaries as unusual. All I mean to emphasize is that their unusualness did not negate important ties which they had to cultural norms. Both their unusualness and their normality can doubtless be used to explain the widespread interest they provoked, and I have made reference to both factors in the text. Yet in accounting for the size of their audience, I have stressed the degree to which spiritualists and psychical researchers were able to tailor their beliefs and practices to fit then-popular concerns and conventions.

I would even push my point to an ironic conclusion. Spiritualists and psychical researchers were so totally absorbed by the forms of their culture that the potentially most innovative aspects of their point of view were bound to fall short of general acceptance. Their attempts to convince the scientific community to acknowledge the occurrence of events were doomed to fail because spirit communication and ESP could not be proved with the means of scientific verification spiritualists and psychical researchers had at their disposal. About this point, there is much more to follow. It is a conclusion we can reach only by examining the long history of frustrations that spiritualists and psychical researchers encountered in their work.

Before beginning, I should make it clear that I have not written a complete history of spiritualism and psychical research. In Part I, I have organized the discussion of spiritualism around the topics which seem to me of most importance in placing it within a proper historical context. Chapter 1 concentrates primarily on the rise of the spiritualist movement in the 1850s. The other three chapters on spiritualism move rather generally through the years from 1850 to 1875—the period in which spiritualism had its greatest influence in America. I have also taken up the subject of spiritualism's decline during the last quarter of the nineteenth-century—a decline that should make clear to the reader why I have not dealt with spiritualism in the twentieth century except insofar as the impulse behind it was redirected into psychical research. I have not omitted consideration of the institutions that were formed to promote spiritualism. But since I do not believe that the institutional forms of spiritualism defined the movement, I have not let them dictate the arrangement of the text.

Compared to Part I, Part II is chronologically arranged and focuses on the activities of the most important societies devoted to psychical research. Unlike spiritualism, the historical issues raised by psychical research are relatively easy to discuss with reference to the work of a few key individuals and the organizations they formed. This is partly a consequence of the fact that in the twentieth century America became a more specialized society, a trend that forced the institutionalization of any endeavor that sought scientific recognition. The consolidation of inquiries into "supernormal" happenings, however, should not necessarily suggest that psychical research had a less general cultural impact than nineteenth-century spiritualism. In the twentieth century science quickly became more important than theology in intellectual circles, and the American people were dramatically affected by scientific advances. Scientific revolutions appear to have had ramifications for every aspect of human life. Popular audiences were time and again exposed to debates about whether scientific discoveries implied a godless, materialistic, and mechanistic universe. To many Americans who were fearful that they might, psychical research seemed crucial. It won a limited academic following and yet remained an area of scientific inquiry fully comprehensible to a lay audience. It was a perfect subject for what some historians have called "middle culture." Books about extrasensory perception have had tremendous sales at various times during the past eight decades. Therefore, whatever the difference in approach followed in Parts I and II, the story of psychical research is a fascinating sequel to the themes laid out in Part I.

Let me close this preface with a warning about bias. Nothing in these pages is meant to suggest that anything like spirit communication or mind reading is an established or a likely phenomenon, but I have every intention of persuading the reader that a belief in the "supernormal" is frequently compatible with sensible human behavior and that the opposite attitude does not guarantee wisdom. No society has an obligation to encourage the popular dissemination of nonsense, but the opponents of spiritualism and psychical research have not always acted as disinterested seekers of truth. For my part, I rather doubt that either spiritualists or psychical researchers will ever achieve the scientific standing they have sought. I would even predict that psychical research will soon go the way of nineteenth-century spiritualism and become much less visible in our culture. If it disappears, however, it will not be because it is mere foolishness. It will be because it has gone stale using tools that were never up to the task it set for itself. Besides, if foolishness is what is in question, we had better recognize with respect to proponents and opponents of these movements that foolishness has not been the exclusive attribute of anyone.

Contents

I
Spiritualism

1

Nineteenth-Century Spiritualism: The Foundation of Its Appeal

Beginning in 1850, spiritualism became vastly popular in this country and the rage spread quickly to the countries of Europe.[1] Americans in astounding numbers studied the reputations of a growing roster of professional mediums and crowded into the séance rooms of those they judged the best. Even at séances conducted by the less adept, ardent believers in spirit communication almost always caught a word of encouragement from some departed and dearly beloved relative. Many other investigators, well aware of repeated disclosures of fraud, treated mediums with considerable skepticism; yet the great bulk of favorable personal testimony stimulated their curiosity and drew them time and again into darkened parlors to await the spirits.

It was not just the half-baked, the uneducated, and the credulous who appeared at séances or spirit circles. The number of prominent people who attended spiritualist meetings in the 1850s is impressive. Harriet Beecher Stowe and her husband Calvin followed with great interest the many reports that circulated about the proliferating variety of spirit manifestations. So to one degree or another did William Lloyd Garrison, George Ripley, Benjamin Wade, Horace Greeley, Rufus W. Griswold, Lydia Maria Child, William Cullen Bryant, Nathaniel P. Willis, James Fenimore Cooper, David Ames Wells, William Torrey

Harris, and John Roebling.[2] George Bancroft was so impressed with the mediumship of Daniel Douglas Home that he put the attractive young man on display as after dinner fare for the visiting author William Thackeray.[3] When the Society for the Diffusion of Spiritual Knowledge was founded in 1854 to spread the truth of spirit communication, it counted among its organizers a former U. S. senator, four judges, two military officers, and several successful businessmen.[4]

Scarcely another cultural phenomenon affected as many people or stimulated as much interest as did spiritualism in the ten years before the Civil War and, for that matter, through the subsequent decades of the nineteenth century. Theodore Parker, one of America's best-known religious thinkers, repeatedly expressed his doubts about spiritualist claims. However, mindful of the widespread and literate attention focused on the movement, he admitted that "in 1856, it seems more likely that spiritualism would become the religion of America than in 156 that Christianity would be the religion of the Roman Empire, or in 756 that Mohammedanism would be that of the Arabian population." Evidence of it, he continued, was more plentiful than that of "any historic form of religion, hitherto." [5]

George Templeton Strong, a prominent New York City lawyer, was distressed by the popularity of the movement. Like many other critics of spiritualist claims, he too had attended a number of séances and had been unable to explain how many of the things he had witnessed had occurred. Yet he found the acceptance of a spiritualist explanation by many educated and otherwise level-headed people inexplicable. He confided his perplexity to his famous diary:

> What would I have said six years ago to anybody who predicted that before the enlightened nineteenth century was ended hundreds of thousands of people in this country would believe themselves able to communicate daily with the ghosts of their grandfathers?—that ex-judges of the Supreme Court, senators, clergymen, professors of physical sciences, should be lecturing and writing books on the new treasures of all this, and that others among the steadiest and most conservative of my acquaintance should acknowledge that they look on

the subject with distrust and dread, as a visible manifestation
of diabolic agency? [6]

Despite the public interest spiritualism as a movement at one
time generated, historians have only recently begun to take
serious interest in it. The bulk of sensible scholarship tends to
treat the movement simply, as yet another expression of a restless, troubled society. As such, these scholars have placed it in
the same category as Mormonism, Shakerism, Millerism, and
Grahamism—antebellum movements that Alice Felt Tyler has
described as the unstable products of "freedom's ferment."
Geoffrey K. Nelson, in a more recent study, has linked the
growth of spiritualism more specifically to unsettling social conditions prevailing in America at midcentury—namely, to a high
degree of social mobility, a sudden influx of immigrants with
different cultural experiences, and an accelerating rate of indus-
trialization. [7] Communion with spirits was, according to these
scholars, one way in which the generations whose social patterns were most shaken by the changes wrought by science and
technology reanchored themselves; at the same time, spiritualism made the very real miracles of science and technology less
incredible. In fact, the professional medium appeared in
America at about the moment Thoreau heard a locomotive
whistle penetrate the woods around Walden Pond.

To be sure, many economic and cultural factors combined to
make the vogue of spiritualism possible. The movement began
in a rapidly changing section of western New York that in the
early nineteenth century had produced more than its share of
deviant behavior. Second, séances attracted a great many el-
derly people, those who stood fearfully at the end of life, as well
as countless bereaved parents and lovers. The common need of
these groups to be consoled, a need that traditional churches
did not always satisfy, turned these individuals too often into
the victims of spiritualism's outrageous trickery. [8] And most certainly the simplest explanation of spiritualism's appeal is that
mediums could be good theater. Often in the public eye during
the nineteenth century, they were another source of entertainment for at least two generations of Americans who liked to

explore puzzling situations and gathered to witness anything
billed as out of the ordinary.[9]

None of this, however, entirely explains the favorable reception of spiritualism by people who were not easily fooled, and
the degree to which it raised passions among partisans and
critics for over twenty-five years. Historians have not found it
easy to reconcile the flowering of an interest in spirits at the
same time that empirical and scientific thought was supposedly
gaining in influence and have thus left the matter to stand as a
paradox. Likewise, biographers of "respectable" Americans
have consistently shown embarrassment upon discovering their
subjects in a darkened room waiting expectantly for a table to
rise off the floor or a dew-dropped bouquet of lilies to drop into
a lap. An aberration? An uncharacteristic capitulation to the irrational in this one area? A lapse of taste? Each of these explanations, though they suggest examples of what Leon Festinger has
called cognitive dissonance, misses the point.[10]

In the twentieth century, psychology has taught us a good
deal about shared psychopathology and has given us some understanding of how sensible people upon entering a séance
room become victims of hallucinations. There are extensive
writings on mediumistic trances in the literature of abnormal
psychology. Nevertheless, it is not at all evident, as some psychologists have argued, that nineteenth-century spiritualism
spread as a reaction to the world view of scientific naturalism.
Those accounts have dismissed spiritualism as a modern-dress
revival of magic and witchcraft and have attributed its popularity to man's eternal craving for mystification.[11]

The historical record is complicated. Down through the years
spiritualism has found allies among genuine occultists, those
persons who through secret and ancient rites sought to recover
lost knowledge about the universal mysteries of cosmic order
and oneness. One thinks immediately of Madame Blavatsky,
who launched the Theosophical Society in 1875, as well as of a
number of modern literary figures from William Butler Yeats to
Malcolm Lowry. A belief in spirit communication has, without
question, started many people off on a search for wisdom that
cannot be attained with the tools of modern science.[12]

There have also been instances of links between spiritualism and religious mysticism. While it is easy enough to make a verbal distinction between trance mediumship and mystic illumination (the entranced spiritualist medium receives unreliable information from nondivine sources and undergoes no inward transformation as a result of the experience), in practice the demarcation line sometimes grew hazy. For example, Emanuel Swedenborg, who as we shall see was an important figure to early leaders of the American spiritualist movement, was both a mystic and a medium.

However, in noting these important and obvious connections, we risk losing sight of spiritualism's connections with the dominant cultural values in the nineteenth century. Any interpretation of spiritualism's impact must begin with what has appeared to many as an anomaly. Spiritualism became a self-conscious movement precisely at the time it disassociated itself from occult traditions of secrecy. It appealed not to the inward illumination of mystic experience, but to the observable and verifiable objects of empirical science. There was little new in the spirit manifestations of the 1850s except this militant stance, which proved to be exactly the right position to gain the attention of an age that wanted to believe that its universe operated like an orderly machine. For most of the nineteenth century, leading spiritualists held a childlike faith in empirical science as the only approach to knowledge. They tried to emulate the scientific method; more important, they copied and helped popularize scientific language. Certainly no others tried so hard to borrow science's prestige, and as a consequence, probably no one else benefited as much as they did from the great interest in science awakened in that century. A movement that eschewed all interest in the marvelous and sought to erase "supernatural" from the categories of human thought may still in some sense have appealed to people's superstitious fears—but it appealed just as much to their desire to make religion rational.

Histories of "modern spiritualism" usually date the beginning of the movement from March 31, 1848, when Margaret and Kate Fox professed to having discovered an intelligent force behind the unexplained rappings that had disturbed their family in its small cottage in Hydesville, New York since the end of 1847.[13] The fraudulence, whether conscious or unconscious, of the mediumship of the Fox girls has been demonstrated time and again.[14] Moreover, their "momentous" discovery took an unaccountably long time to get any recognition. One small pamphlet was published almost immediately, but local newspapers did not follow up on the report.

Not until many months later did the girls find a suitable press agent in E. W. Capron, who staged a public exhibition of the rappings in Rochester in November 1849. Admission was a quarter. The sisters (there were three by this time, an older sister who quickly developed mediumistic powers having joined Margaret and Kate) spent most of the summer of 1850 at Barnum's Hotel in New York City, and only after Horace Greeley's *New York Tribune* had given favorable notice to the séances the girls conducted there did they emerge to any degree as leading figures of a new profession.[15]

The spirits had had to wait over two years for widespread recognition of their first marvelous work, but once mediumship appeared to be a paying proposition, a host of men and women stepped forward to claim priority over the Fox girls. Many did so legitimately. After all, the tradition of spirit communication stretched back into biblical times and to the oldest known civilizations.[16] Nineteenth-century Americans scarcely needed to rummage back that far or even as far as the Renaissance for their ghost stories. The eighteenth-century poltergeist who upset the childhood home of John Wesley also bore an unmistakable likeness to the Fox family's spirit. Of course, no one during Wesley's time dared argue that the poltergeist was up to any good, whereas the murdered man who disturbed the Hydesville cabin was, despite the protests of local ministers, able to convince many of his good intentions. Even more recent than the Wesley story was an 1845 English translation of Justinus Kerner's *Die Seherin von Prevorst*. The book relates a scientific experiment with a girl whose clairvoyant powers opened up channels of communication with a supermundane sphere. There were also stories of mediums in American Shaker communities who received, beginning in the 1830s, a steady stream of spirit messages.[17]

The Prevorst story and to a certain extent the reports from the Shaker communities were linked in the minds of many Americans with other well-publicized demonstrations of mesmerism or animal magnetism. In the late eighteenth century, Anton Mesmer had tried to convince the French Academy that the instillation of a superfine, hitherto unidentified, fluid by a healer (using his hands or some substance rich in the fluid) into his patient could produce remarkable cures.

With many variations mesmerism became for the first fifty years of the nineteenth century a widely exhibited procedure in Europe and America.[18] The press carried reports about extraordinary cases of extrasensory vision and clairvoyance; mesmerized young men and women, it was claimed, often identified objects held before them even with their eyes tightly blindfolded. Some subjects even perceived events happening at a great distance away or could look back into the past or forward into the future. Mesmerized persons, especially those who attributed their powers to the inspiration of guardian spirits, were indistinguishable in their actions from many of the later trance mediums of the spiritualist movement.[19]

In the United States in the 1840s the writings of Emanuel Swedenborg also prepared the way for spiritualism. In the middle of his life, this Swedish philosopher turned away from a distinguished scientific career to pursue the paths of enlightenment open only to religious mystics. Over the course of several decades, Swedenborg was visited by God, Christ, and a host of minor spirits, including the souls of departed human beings. His death in 1772 did not diminish his disciples' interest in his detailed revelations about Heaven and Hell. In antebellum America, Swedenborg's ideas became known through the teachings of the Church of the New Jerusalem (a small denomination that treated Swedenborg's published volumes as sacred texts) and the commentaries of such distinguished literary men as Ralph Waldo Emerson and Henry James, Sr.

Yet it was spiritualism that proved to be the single most important vehicle for the popularization of Swedenborgianism in

America. The Swede's teachings about a hierarchical series of
spiritual spheres surrounding the earth turned up in many of
the spirit messages in the 1850s. The plagiarism horrified
members of America's Church of the New Jerusalem, but there
was little they could do about it. The ability to contact the
spirits of dead humans, which had been one of the special divine powers imparted to Swedenborg, became in this democratic country a widespread gift among common folk.

Andrew Jackson Davis provided the most direct link between
the teachings of Swedenborg and those of spiritualism.[20] The
"Poughkeepsie Seer" never became as well known to the American public as the Fox sisters, although his own channel to the
spirit world opened several years before theirs. In fact, his mediumistic talents never commanded the journalistic attention
paid to many less interesting nineteenth-century mediums.
That was the penalty he suffered for playing down the importance of the visible manifestations of the spirits in an attempt to
turn the movement toward philosophy. Even though, as will be
discussed later, his efforts went against the major thrust of
American spiritualism, insofar as spiritualist leaders were able
to develop a set of teachings beyond the mere claim that the
dead return, Davis deserved the major share of the credit.

His beginnings were not promising. A sickly and nervous
boy, Davis passed through several apprenticeships without im-
pressing anyone. The boy seemed to lack both wit and physical
strength. Just as he seemed about to succumb to total indolence,
a lecture on animal magnetism gave Davis a career. Proving to
be a good subject for mesmerism, he began to fall at regular in-
tervals into a trance state and to have visions.

In 1844 the spirits of Swedenborg and the Greek physician
Galen paid a visit to the mesmerized Davis. The former told
him that he would become a conduit for the influx of truth and
wisdom. The latter announced to him his mission as a clairvoyant healer and gave him a magic staff. The advice proved to be
profitable. A year later his reputed success in visualizing the
inner organs of ailing persons and prescribing cures brought
him to the attention of Dr. Silis Lyon and two Universalist ministers, Samuel Byron Brittan and William Fishbough. Under

their influence, Davis's career again took a new turn. On November 28, 1845, with Lyon as operator (mesmerizer) and Fishbough as scribe, the nineteen-year-old Davis commenced a series of public lectures delivered while in a trance state. This series of inspired utterances terminated on January 25, 1847. A wealthy lady, Mrs. Silone Dodge, furnished the money for publication of the lectures.

The Principles of Nature, Her Divine Revelations, and a Voice to Mankind, By and Through Andrew Jackson Davis, the 'Poughkeepsie Seer' and 'Clairvoyant' appeared in 1847 to largely skeptical newspaper notices, but there were notable exceptions. Davis's messages, or at least the manner of their transmission, impressed Albert Brisbane, George Ripley, and Parke Godwin.[21] George Bush, a professor of Hebrew language and literature at New York University and America's foremost Swedenborgian, examined Davis at length. Davis, he certified, dictated in Hebrew, Arabic, and Sanskrit, languages he could not possibly know. Bush wrote to the poet Sarah Helen Whitman that having read Davis's published lectures, he now regarded Davis "as the most astonishing prodigy the world has ever seen next to Swedenborg's oracles." Swedenborg remained in Bush's opinion "seven heavens above Davis;" but Davis, who was "very handsome and most fascinating from the simplicity of his manner and a certain guileless grace," was destined to be a "world's wonder." Davis, Bush conceded, probably did receive messages from Swedenborg just as he had claimed.[22]

Following the publication of Davis's book, S. B. Brittan began with Lyon and Fishbough to edit a journal called *The Univercoelum and Spiritual Philosopher,* of which the first issue appeared in December 1847. The journal was published for two years, just long enough for the final issue to contain a brief account of the Hydesville rappings. Most of the group who wrote for *The Univercoelum* were either ex-Universalist ministers or Swedenborgians. They included Robert Carter, an editor and author; Thomas Holley Chivers, a poet and Poe's close friend; Luther R. Marsh, a New York lawyer engaged in various reform movements; and Thomas Lake Harris, a Universalist clergyman who broke with his church and established independent credentials as a mystic and spiritual leader.[23] The circle treated Davis's revelations seriously but never asked readers to regard them as infallible.[24] They had come to loathe what they regarded as the dogmatism of American churches and were not about to let the attention showered on Davis turn him into a Joseph Smith. What Davis said was inspirational and a basis for further reflection, but it did not define a new sect.

While undogmatic, the contributors to *The Univercoelum* did share some assumptions they had derived in roughly equal parts from Davis, Swedenborg, the Universalist Church, and American Transcendentalism. They believed in the importance of Brittan's quest for an "interior or spiritual philosophy, comprehensively explaining the character and operations of natural laws, accounting for their exterior phenomena and results, and showing the tendencies of all things to higher spheres of existence." [25] The writers accepted Swedenborg's "science of correspondence," an attempt to reveal the universal relationship between the material and spiritual world. In pursuit of that science, according to Brittan, man must attempt "to interpret the mystic manuscripts wherein Deity has written his great thoughts—the revelations in the earth, and seas, and skies, and above all in the human soul." [26] The reverence for nature reflected the influence of Transcendentalism, as did the emphasis on the inward divinity of human beings. According to Harris, the goal of life was to discover "the Divinity within. To believe in God is but to believe that the spiritual which we feel flowing into ourselves, flows from an Infinite Existing Source." [27] Davis labeled the body of his teachings Harmonial Philosophy. To the staff of *The Univercoelum,* harmony meant above all the underlying unity of science and theology. They argued that only those who penetrated the full set of relationships that existed between the spiritual and material world would understand that both realms operated according to the same principles of natural law. A divine immanence that sustained universal order made all things knowable to those individuals who developed their internal (spiritual) and external (bodily) senses together.

Because these men believed in spirit communication, they were strongly impressed by the sensation the Fox sisters created

in New York City during their presence there in the summer of
1850. In fact because their own journal had not been a commercial success, they were eager to capitalize as best they could on
the strong wave of popular interest in the rappings. Davis and
Fishbough were among the first outside the Rochester area to
endorse the Fox girls. Brittan caught the drift of the times so
neatly that in the early 1850s he became the leading publisher of
works heralding the new movement. In partnership with
Charles Partridge, a wealthy New York match manufacturer, he
brought out the most important volumes of spirit messages in
that decade. Brittan edited both a quarterly journal called the
Shekinah, and the most widely circulated spiritualist newspaper
of the period, the *Spiritual Telegraph,* which he and Partridge
launched in 1852; the paper did not flounder until 1860.
Hundreds of other spiritualist periodical publications emerged
during the 1850s, but most were ephemeral. For example,
LaRoy Sunderland, a former Methodist minister and abolitionist, managed to keep the *Spiritual Philosopher* going for just over
a year. From October 1850 to December 1851, Sunderland conducted it "under the direct supervision of hosts of friends in the
first, second, third, fourth, fifth, sixth, and seventh spheres
above." [28] Titles of other publications included the *Spirit Messenger,* the *Messenger of Light,* the *Christian Spiritualist* and the
Spirit World. Only when Luther Colby founded the *Banner of
Light* in 1857, however, did spiritualism gain a more important
newspaper than the one Brittan edited. Toward the end of the
nineteenth century, the *Banner of Light,* which was published in
New York and Boston, and the *Religio-Philosophical Journal,*
which began publication in Chicago in 1865, surpassed the
record of longevity set by the *Spiritual Telegraph.*

Ernest Isaacs has shown that the words spiritualist and spiritualism did not come into common usage until 1852. [29] In the
preceding several years the nation's press had reported a lot of
strange things, but it was not entirely clear what these happenings had in common. People in the 1850s spoke of spiritualism,
and public lectures on the subject drew thousands in major
American cities. As a movement, however, spiritualism lacked
an institutional definition. By the end of the 1850s, organiza-

tions of spiritualists had sprung up in most states. So had a few regional societies, such as the New England Spiritualist Association, founded in Boston in 1854. There were also spiritualist churches and an uncountable number of local societies and private circles. But none of them provided unified direction to the movement. The only attempt at national organization during the 1850s, known as the Society for the Diffusion of Spiritual Knowledge, was a flop. Horace Day financed it, and a handful of self-styled Christian spiritualists tried to run it. They quite misunderstood the independence and anti-Christian feelings of many others who also claimed to represent the movement.

Lacking coherence, most gatherings that claimed to explore the truths of spiritualism simply made diversity a virtue. The leaders identified most closely with the new movement emphasized unrestricted investigation rather than institutional loyalty or public commitment. Since only a minority of those Americans interested in the spirit manifestations belonged to an organization dedicated to "spiritual philosophy"—a fact that applied with special force to prominent people—it is simply not possible to know how many Americans counted themselves as spiritualists at any point in the nineteenth century. Estimates made during the 1850s ranged from under a million to eleven million (the latter estimate made by an alarmed Catholic). There was no basis for these figures, although indirect evidence suggests that the number was significant. Belief in spirit communication ran high enough to call forth thousands of published works on the subject and to trouble those who regarded the well-attended demonstrations of the medium's art as the greatest folly of the age.

Subsequent chapters will have more to say about the range of beliefs found within the spiritualist movement. At least one attitude was shared by all those who took the spirit rappings at face value. Regardless of how much time they spent reading the spiritualist press or studying the substance of the messages emanating from the spirit world, nineteenth-century séance goers believed they were making an important contribution to empirical science. Through an appeal to what they felt was objective data, they hit upon a unifying theme which they hoped would make the movement respectable. Mesmerism and phrenology had also appealed to empiricism, but not with the same success. Spiritualism outlasted both these earlier movements by many decades.

While the Fox sisters rarely said anything about the significance of their performances, they were accidentally responsible for the directions the spiritualist impulse took in the 1850s. The impressive rappings produced in their presence encouraged an emphasis within the movement on empirical tests and objective verification. However impressive one might have found Davis's trance statements to be, there was no obvious way to test their authenticity as spirit communications. People could appraise the value of their moral teachings, but could say nothing definite about their origin. In contrast, the guardian spirits of the Fox sisters held themselves available to answer test questions put to them by an investigative audience. Using one of several common codes, the summoned spirits proved their supermundane powers to members of the circle by rapping out messages containing trivial information known only to the sitters around the table. The setting for public mediumistic displays was usually quite ordinary. Nathaniel Hawthorne was no friend of the spiritualists, but the narrator of *The Blithedale Romance* did comment on the "simplicity and openness of scientific experiment" that marked the public performances of spiritualist mediums. By contrast, the appearances of the Veiled Lady in *Blithedale* had, in the decade prior to the rise of spiritualism, been carried out in an atmosphere of artfully designed mystification.[30]

After the triumphs of the Fox sisters in New York City, the variety of spirit manifestations increased with amazing rapidity. For example, during the summer of 1850, some one hundred mediums blossomed in Auburn, New York, a town near Hydesville.[31] Most of the spirits were rappers, but already some had learned to do other things. Aside from making rapped replies to questions, spirits could rely on automatic writing, slate writing, and control of the medium's voice to get their message through—or they could skip the message altogether and depend entirely on physical effects. Table-raising remained an impressive display throughout the nineteenth century, as did the playing of untouched musical instruments. Sometimes spirits levitated the body of the medium or of one of the sitters. After the Civil War, spirit photography and materialization séances considerably expanded the medium's repertoire. Throughout the 1850s various mediums continued to publish volumes of spirit teachings that had been imparted to them in private. These books, however, which resembled Davis's spirit volumes, became less pretentious in the years just before the Civil War and virtually disappeared as a genre during the latter part of the nineteenth century.[32] Published messages grew shorter and more straightforward in accordance with the needs of newspaper editors.

Moreover, mediums became more numerous as the art of mediumship became a source of profit. Spirits relied less on sanctified vessels to serve as their agents, and the vocation of the medium included many of more dubious personal reputations. Spirits in the 1850s discovered that they had to tailor their manifestations to the demand for public demonstrations. Séances were almost always designed to give the audience a full sense of participation. Amidst ringing bells and flying objects the medium played a passive role, acting only as a vehicle through which spirits worked their effects. In or out of trance, the medium typically saw or heard nothing beyond what everyone present could witness for himself. In fact, mediums who entered unconscious states claimed to remember nothing of what had gone on. Raucous spirit concerts (complete with trumpet, accordion, and assorted percussion instruments) such as those heard at Koonses' Spirit Room in Athens County, Ohio, may not have been soul-inspiring, but they could be performed before a crowd. Such dignified and saintly spirits as George Washington or Jesus proved in the long run to be less frequent guests at séances than rambunctious ones. Spiritualists concluded from this fact that the great leaders of history had progressed so far out in the hierarchy of heavenly spheres that travel back to earth was very difficult. In fact, however, séance goers found that noisier, earthbound spirits put on a more convincing show.

One can get some idea of the sort of manifestations that were most impressive to regular séance attendants in the early years of spiritualism from a letter William Lloyd Garrison wrote in 1867. At one séance conducted by a twelve-year-old girl, he witnessed:

> bells ringing over the heads of the circle, floating in the air, and dropping upon the table; a spirit hand seen to extinguish the light; spirit hands touching the hands or garments of all present; pocket books taken out of pockets, the money abstracted, and then returned; watches removed in the same manner; the contents of one table conveyed by an invisible power from one end of the parlor to another; the bosoms of ladies partially unbuttoned, and articles thrust therein and taken therefrom; powerful rappings on the table and floor; . . . a basket, containing artificial oranges and lemons, emptied, and its contents distributed around the circle, and the basket successfully put upon the head of every one present in a grotesque manner; striking and tickling of persons by spirit hands—etc., etc.[33]

The early critics of the spiritualist movement failed to see anything spiritual in the average séance, and this was a complaint raised within the movement as well. Too often sitters ordered the heavens down to earth, never encouraging their own souls to soar any higher than the furniture flying around the room. LaRoy Sunderland was one of the first to complain about the movement's emphasis on public displays. The mediumship of his own daughter convinced Sunderland that there were more sublime truths to discover than those forthcoming from the usual spirit manifestations.

Andrew Jackson Davis, though he never doubted their occurrence, also regretted the attention given to external physical phenomena. In the 1870s he disassociated himself from the other major leaders of the movement and complained that "Modern Spiritualism is summed up in the one word 'manifestation.' "[34] Thomas Lake Harris connected the movement's misplaced emphasis on externality with its democratic style. Mediumship, he felt, should be practiced only by consecrated vessels such as he. Otherwise, spiritualists gave all their attention to the spirits of departed men and lost interest in the "spirit of Christ, which descends to be immanent in the heart." [35]

Swedenborg's Church of the New Jerusalem rejected an alliance with spiritualism for roughly the same reasons. In spirit séances one spoke only to dead human beings, never with non-human spirits. No medium claimed a direct infusion of divine intelligence. Swedenborg had warned against casual spirit intercourse because of the deception practiced by evil demons. Henry James, Sr., one of Swedenborg's most important American admirers, also expressed concern about the perverse influence of low-minded spirits. Spiritualism, according to James, completely overlooked the fact that a true and proper faith had preceded the experience that had been opened to the Swedish theologian. [36] Despite these warnings, leaders of the Church of the New Jerusalem were to witness defections by their members to the new movement and were of course upset by these losses.

Prior to 1850 almost all the literature about spirit communication had been cautionary. Spirit communication, it was believed, might lead to insanity and suicide. Presentiments and clairvoyance had long been associated with disease and abnormal mental states. Utterly unconcerned about possible terrors lurking in the universe, spiritualists refused to entertain such cautious attitudes about the spirit world.

Giles Stebbins, a man who was active in many antebellum reform movements and who did successfully combine Transcendentalism and Swedenborgianism with an enthusiastic espousal of spiritualism, summed up his dual faith in a sentence of his autobiography: "The transcendentalist would say immortality is a truth of the soul; the spiritualist would grant that, but would verify that truth by the testimony of the senses." [37] That balanced formula satisfied Stebbins, but insofar as the emphasis of spiritualism fell heavily on the latter half of his statement, often explicitly rejecting the former half, spiritualists made a substantial contribution to what John Higham has characterized as a retreat in the 1850s from a mental attitude embracing boundlessness. [38] The importance that the editors of *The Univercoelum* had assigned to awakening the inward senses to the presence of God did not carry over into popular writings about spiritualism.

In the interest of science and in the service of a population excited by scientific discovery, spiritualists proposed a religious faith that depended upon seeing and touching. Transforming a concern for man's inward spiritual nature into an empirical inquiry into the nature of spirits, they built a belief in an afterlife upon such physical signs as spirits from another realm could muster. What, after all, as one spiritualist inquired with a characteristic lack of any sense of the sublime, was the difference between the "spiritual world" and the "world of spirits?" [39]

In their early pamphlet on the Fox sisters, Eliab W. Capron and Henry D. Barron denied any wish "to feed the popular credulity, or to excite the wonder loving faculties of the ignorant and superstitious." [40] From that time on, most leading spiritualists, in their efforts to make spirit communication credible, never wavered from four principles: a rejection of supernaturalism, a firm belief in the inviolability of natural law, a reliance on external facts rather than on an inward state of mind, and a faith in the progressive development of knowledge. In upholding such principles, they struck a responsive chord among many Americans who had earlier rejected orthodox Christian theology partially because they wanted to believe that life posed a limited set of questions with rational, discoverable answers.

While there is no typical spiritualist of the 1850s or of any other time, the case of John C. Edmonds does illustrate in more concrete form the attitude partisans adopted. Edmonds was a respected lawyer who had been elevated by the Democratic party to the New York State Supreme Court. He had gained a reputation as an able, reform-minded judge with a particular interest in improving conditions of penal servitude. He was also a scholar whose legal writings were widely admired both before and after his fall from political favor. Spiritualists hailed Edmonds as their most important convert in the early 1850s, and he remained a prolific publicist of the movement until his death in 1874. In losing his place on the Supreme Court because of his activity in behalf of spiritualism (his enemies charged that he consulted spirits about his decisions), he also became the movement's first martyr.

Edmonds's conversion to spiritualism followed a common pattern. The death of a relative, in Edmonds's case his wife, preceded his first visit to a séance in January 1851. Although he was depressed and withdrawn at the time of his visit, Edmonds later insisted that his investigative abilities were not impaired. As he mentioned in his every account of the story, he went to the sitting without enthusiasm, at the invitation of a friend. He expected to see nothing he could not easily explain or expose as fraud. As a skeptic in daily affairs and as an exponent of an open-minded Christianity, he could not, he felt, be fooled. Yet on that first occasion he saw things that puzzled him, and he went back. Four months of intensive investigation followed, during which he took extensive notes, dictated arrangements so as to facilitate careful observation, and badgered everyone with "his obdurate skepticism." After long weeks, evidence accumulated to the point that he could no longer doubt the presence of spirits. Edmonds simply accepted what he thought was the only possible explanation of the plain facts before him.[41]

The unconvinced will have difficulty reading the spirit messages Edmonds collected (he quickly developed into a medium after his conversion) without entertaining doubts as to the critical sharpness of his mind. Edmonds received these long spirit messages through visions and automatic writing. In one of these visions Benjamin Franklin revealed, before a host of applauding spirits, how his discoveries in electricity had made possible the communication they now had with their still-living relatives. In another, Newton admitted to an error in his work on gravity—one which Edmonds had suspected for some time.

No matter how suspicious one might be of the information Edmonds drew from his visions and writings, there was no doubt about the desire of the author to make a scientific presentation. In his books, pamphlets, and letters, Edmonds adhered to the stylistic principle of describing the sensational spirit manifestations in a matter-of-fact way. One of his admirers wrote: "His narratives were told with such straightforward simplicity, that, though unprecedented, the reader might accept them with all confidence. Expressions of wonder and astonishment never marred his testimony, which was sober and subdued—free from extravagant adjectives, and couched in the chaste, poetical style, which led the reader with an attraction which could not be resisted." That appraisal was not accurate in all respects. Edmonds was no poet, and his "straightforward simplicity" made him marvelously easy to parody. A "chaste" style could not turn fantasy into science, as Edmonds himself discovered to his embarrassment when he touted a piece of fiction about a talking corpse (modeled after one of Poe's stories) as a genuine report of spirit activity. Nonetheless, Edmonds's "sober" and "subdued" tone satisfied many Americans as to the seriousness of his scientific intentions. And that was exactly the impression Edmonds wanted to create.[42]

Edmonds's soberness was especially evident when he described his own receipt of spirit messages. He was careful to emphasize that the spirit visions granted to him were quite humdrum affairs. No trace of saintly rapture dulled his mind, nor did he, like Davis and some other mediums, profess to enter a different level of consciousness and utter things he could not later recall. In describing his own mediumship, Edmonds was careful to avoid the word "possession." He wrote that his visions neither severed his contact with reality nor led him to abandon reason and self-control. While having a vision, he could concurrently talk about other things with friends and associates. Often he interrupted the spirits to look after pressing business. "Let us ever bear in mind," Edmonds wrote, "that spiritual intercourse is not supernatural, but in compliance with fixed laws affecting the whole human family."[43] By his own lights, in whatever he did, he worshiped devoutly at the shrine of reason erected by Tom Paine, who, not incidentally, became a favorite spirit voice.

One can offer other reasons for the ease with which Edmonds's tracts became associated in the popular mind with science. The very format in which the spirit messages were printed helped to create the impression of scientific investigation. The first large volume of spirit messages Edmonds and Dr. George Dexter published in 1854 was largely made up of long didactic messages from Bacon and Swedenborg on the subject of progress. But these "elevated" spirits encouraged sitters to pose questions, and they said over and over that no statement should be regarded as true on their authority alone. The question-and-answer format was even more pronounced in Edmonds and Dexter's second volume (published in 1855), and the appearance of "lower" spirits at the recorded sittings served to lessen the intellectual distance between sitters and their spirit mentors. That equality plus the ignorance that spirits professed on many matters encouraged readers to attach more importance to their own intellectual resources. Human knowledge, these volumes made clear, did not advance by revealed expressions of divine will, but by a process of searching out facts and assessing their significance with the sole aid of human reason.

There were other styles and formats in spiritualist literature than the ones Edmonds used, but in all cases the strategy of spiritualism was to sell itself by language and by deed as a scientific endeavor. Spirit messages consistently flattered human abilities. In the mid-nineteenth century that was most easily accomplished by praising technological advance, which in the popular mind was the same thing as scientific advance. Nineteenth-century spirits equated the uplifting of man's spiritual nature with the building of locomotives and the laying of railroad tracks. As spiritualists said many times, they intended no attack on the mechanical order of the universe, which science had constructed and which literate Americans took for granted in the mid-nineteenth century. Indeed, by urging science to recognize an extension of the laws of physics and engineering into unseeable worlds, they went most mechanists one better. Spiritualist journals were full of mechanical images. The telegraph was a favorite choice of those trying to explain how something once considered marvelous might be reduced through science to a completely understandable accomplishment. A symbol of long-distance communication as well, it suggested a model of how spirit communication might take place. Spirits themselves demonstrated a mechanical aptitude by handing down inventions for riving shingles, milling, and net-weaving.[44]

Spiritualists also acted as adamant champions of openness. They had no esoteric formulas or mysterious rites of initiation. Séances carried out under proper test conditions were merely public disclosures of fact. Claiming their adherence to the Baconian procedures that had guided American science in the first half of the nineteenth century, they professed to let their conclusions emerge naturally from the observed data. To them it appeared that scientists who scoffed at their labors violated empirical principles by ruling out their facts "not for the want of testimony in their favor, but because they presume, beforehand, that nature has no power to produce them." [45] In fact during the 1850s the spirit of Francis Bacon sent many messages of consolation to spiritualist circles because of the hostility these groups encountered among professional scientists, and he reminded them of the persecution and eventual vindication of Galileo and Copernicus.

According to spiritualists, scientists ignored their claims only because the attitudes of the latter were biased by the assumptions of philosophical materialism (sometimes referred to in spiritualist publications as French materialism). Against the belief that nothing existed in the universe but matter, spiritualists waged a steady, though confused, battle. They took up the struggle to demonstrate the independent existence and endurance of spirit, which usually boiled down to an attempt to prove that there was some life beyond this one.

However, critics of the movement again stepped in and expressed doubt that a real victory over materialism could come about by merely talking about the presence of spirits. In major spiritualist publications the rescued spirit looked suspiciously like the matter out of whose jaws it presumably had been wrested. It required little wit to ridicule a spirit realm whose inhabitants lived in elegant houses, ate enormous meals capped by fine cigars, and carefully put money away in savings accounts for a rainy day in Heaven. Many spiritualists seemed to be greatly relieved to learn that spirits wore clothes.

Spiritualists had some difficulty clarifying their views about the nature of spirit. Most agreed that "immaterial substance" could not exist. The two words in that phrase, according to

Thomas Gales Forster, a popular trance medium, contradicted each other.[46] The spirit teachers seemed to concur that soul and spirit should not be considered something discontinuous from matter, but rather a higher, perfected form of matter.[47] A Mr. Levi found spiritualism required only minor adjustments in his former materialistic outlook: "The whole universal creation, unimaginable even to our highest conceptions, is entirely, and without exception, composed of matter in thousands and tens of thousands of different shapes, figures, and forms, more or less refined, rarefied, and elevated." [48] Spiritualism's war on materialism consisted totally in getting science to recognize the existence of a matter "too refined, subtil, and sublimated for our vision," [49] although its proponents involved themselves in a contradiction by also insisting on the proposition, stated in its most naïve form, that seeing is believing.

In trying to convince science to apply its instruments of measurement to things that lay beyond earthly horizons, spiritualists wound up reinvesting spirits with all the qualities of matter. Spirit matter—which was the term they employed and which did not differ in concept from Thomas Hobbes's definition of spirit as "a physical body refined enough to escape the senses" [50]—somehow had to demonstrate its existence to the senses or go begging. There were those who interpreted this position as a capitulation to materialism. For example, later in the century Wilhelm Wundt, the German psychologist who was himself wrongly accused of materialism, reached a harsh conclusion after examining various mediumistic phenomena: "I see in Spiritualism . . . a sign of the materialism and barbarism of our time. From early times . . . materialism has had two forms; the one denies the spiritual, the other transforms it into matter." Modern spiritualism, according to Wundt, had fallen into the latter trap.[51]

One of the claims spiritualists were proudest of was that they rejected the distinction between natural and supernatural. In an attack on Horace Bushnell's book *Nature and the Supernatural, as Together Constituting the One System of God,* Andrew Jackson Davis said that Bushnell's desire to distinguish a supernatural realm whose laws were superior to human "reason, argument and judgment" reflected "the uneducated mind that yearns for the romantic . . . and the incomprehensible." [52] Davis had completely missed Bushnell's point: the theologian was worried about an age "which had become fastened to, and glued down upon nature; conceiving that nature, as a frame of physical order, is itself the system of God; unable to imagine anything higher and more general to which it is subordinate." [53] Given his own concerns about the movement, Davis might well have wondered whether the loss of the supernatural to the imagination did not account for spiritualism's overemphasis on the strictly physical.

Spiritualists derived their attitude toward the supernatural from American Transcendentalists, who also rejected the theistic concept of miracles. As Barbara Novak has shown, several important midcentury American painters regarded spiritualism and Transcendentalism as complementary movements. Spiritualism's assertion that spirit was a tangible presence in the everyday world lent support to attempts by these artists to represent on canvas the point of contact between the infinite and the finite—or, as Emerson would have it, the point where spirit became manifest in visible creation. However, despite the influence of Transcendentalism upon spiritualism, the terminology used by spiritualists altered the Romantic point of view in crucial ways. In joining Emerson's attack on miracles, most spiritualists forgot to balance such a potentially mundane doctrine with the Transcendentalist's concern for inward illumination (or "internal evidences"). "Natural" for the spiritualists meant observable, and the realm of nature they observed (the séance room) had little in common with Walden Pond. The regularity in life perceived by the five senses became the standard against which to measure all divine activity. Not surprisingly, Emerson regarded the whole spiritualist affair as trite. "No inspired mind," he said, "ever condescends to these evidences." They comprised "the rat hole of revelation." [54]

The many charges against spiritualism did overlook one important point. When spiritualists of the 1850s accused the science of their day of materialism, they really had in mind something other than the doctrine that nothing exists except matter and its movements and modifications. In employing that definition, they would have been hard pressed to find many materialists during the first half of the nineteenth century, especially among American scientists. The materialism they spoke of posed a more practical danger, for it grew not from some formal philosophical denial of spirit, but from a lost interest in it.

Spiritualists feared that anything science would not investigate would in the modern world become a matter of indifference. The implications of the great prestige science had won by the mid-nineteenth century were not lost on spiritualists, and they therefore could not remain satisfied with an understanding between science and theology whereby science, without denying the existence of God and the soul, merely ignored them.[55] That settlement was tantamount to the most thoroughgoing materialism, for what scientists took for the measurable world would in time define the limits of man's aspirations. To leave the great questions of life to speculative metaphysics guaranteed their trivialization within a generation. The insistence that there was a spirit world that was measurable, although invisible, proved to be no solution to this dilemma. But the spiritualists did not address themselves to an unreal problem.

The appeal of spiritualism in the 1850s can be better understood when something more is said about the considerable opposition spiritualism aroused. As Collingwood once said, "An intense polemic against a certain doctrine is an infallible sign that the doctrine in question figures largely in the writer's environment and even has a strong attraction for himself." [56]

From the beginning of the movement, spiritualists complained about their treatment by the scientific community. Their claims, they charged, were dismissed in a summary and indefensible way. That is not exactly true. What is true is that in the 1850s the American Association for the Advancement of Science did firmly turn aside Robert Hare, a distinguished American chemist, in his attempts to present to their meetings his research in spiritualism. Further, scientific journals did refuse to recognize the legitimacy of the subject. And in 1854, Congress did table a petition with 13,000 signatures urging an impartial national inquiry.[57]

But the argument that scientists put forth—that séances, whether held in the dark or in brilliantly lighted rooms, could not meet acceptable laboratory conditions—was a reasonable one and one that was based on principles applied not only to investigations of spiritualism but also to investigations of all unfathomable phenomena. Their training in observation, scientists rightly noted, left them no better equipped than anyone else to detect the art of the conjurer. As had been demonstrated time and again, mediums did get away with fraud in settings where all present had sworn to the strictness and absolute reliability of the test conditions. Fraud was so common that even convinced spiritualists came to expect the best mediums now and again to mix trickery in with their genuine demonstrations.

Moreover, beginning with a trio of doctors from the University of Buffalo who attributed the rappings of the Fox sisters to crackings of their knee joints, a number of scientists in the 1850s *did* investigate spiritualist claims.[58] The British physicist and chemist Michael Faraday, for example, performed several experiments with tables that moved in hopes of discovering a new physical force. His investigation resulted in his adopting a hostile stance toward spiritualism, but he did not, as spiritualists charged, dismiss the reported phenomena as a priori impossibilities.[59]

On the other hand, much of the early criticism of spiritualism, whether it came from inside or outside the scientific community, looks in retrospect as foolish as any of the spiritualist claims. Important newspapers crusaded against mediums, preachers denounced them, and politicians ridiculed them with thunderous rhetoric. From the 1850s to the end of the nineteenth century, the *New York Times* regularly condemned spiritualism for its "subversion of all respect and devotion to the only true faith."[60] Washington's *National Intelligencer* suggested legislation against the practice of holding séances after it became clear (or so the paper bemoaned in language typical of the period) that levity and contempt had proved ineffective weapons: "However absurd and despicable it may appear to men of sound reason and resolute conviction, it is spreading itself like a pestilence through our borders, carrying with it the madness of infidelity, of sensuous materialism if not actual atheism, and distracting the minds of the nervous, the feeble-witted, and the timid into actual insanity." [61]

The intensity of the opposition is somewhat surprising, especially since many of the opponents of spiritualism were willing to accept that the phenomena had actually occurred as reported. If those in the antispiritualist camp had all cried fraud and turned away, they would have killed the movement. Like George Templeton Strong, however, they themselves had witnessed puzzling things that needed explanation.[62] Many persons who thought it nonsense to speak of spirits still accepted the fact that tables rose off the floor in some unaccountable manner. Many fervent antispiritualists were at the same time ardent believers in clairvoyance and second sight. Spiritualism was only one of several explanations of the manifestations associated with mediums, and it was not the most improbable entry.

In an address given in 1853, the Reverend Charles Beecher, one of Lyman Beecher's many children, conceded both the genuineness of many of the reported manifestations and their spirit origin. The Bible, as he pointed out, contained abundant testimony to the reality of spirit communication, and many other pages out of history indicated that spirit voices had not been silenced with the close of the biblical era. But God, having ordained certain channels of communication between Himself and His creatures, had strictly prohibited communication with spirits, who, it was believed, wandered through space furthering the Devil's mission of deception and destruction. Clearly, according to Beecher, the spirits that had been so vocal in recent years were agents of Satan.[63]

The idea of diabolic intervention was not original with Beecher, and he was only one among many to use it in the 1850s to inveigh against spiritualist practices.[64] Writers blamed these evil spirits for broken marriages, for ruined businesses—even for the outbreak of the Civil War.[65] Protestant clergymen warned their parishioners to stay away from séances, for if the manifestations were real, participation in a circle violated di-

vine commandment. Horace Bushnell adopted this safe position, although he hastened to add that he had only indirect
knowledge of what happened at a séance.[66] The Roman Catholic
church went further and issued a ban against consulting with
mediums.

No matter what the Scriptures said, many clergymen and laymen thought Beecher and the others who took his line as be-
nighted as the most enthusiastic spiritualist. These clergy and
laymen felt that belief in bad spirits was just as superstitious as
belief in good spirits, and it seemed incredible to them that
Beecher and the others should dip back into the language of the
seventeenth century to accuse mediums of witchcraft. Explanations, they thought, had to rest on known physical laws.

During the mid-nineteenth century no force in nature was
more intriguing to the popular mind than electricity. Professional scientists did not know exactly what it was despite the
work of Franklin, Galvani, Coulomb, Ampère, Faraday, and
other distinguished researchers. Its effects remained curious
enough to lend believability to a variety of theories, and scientists and occultists alike invoked its name to explain otherwise
mysterious occurrences. When confronted with reports of lifted
tables, mysteriously rung bells, clairvoyance, pencils moving
independently across slates, and materializations of human
forms, the American public of this period listened sympa-
thetically to theories attributing all these strange happenings to
electrical currents.

John Dods, whose writings on electrical psychology and animal magnetism won him a following and who is remembered
for his influence on Mary Baker Eddy,[67] was among the first
writers to suggest electricity as an alternative explanation for
those things attributed by spiritualists to unseen intelligent
agents. In a book seeking to strip the "mystery" from spiritual
phenomena, he wrote: "The entire passivity of the voluntary
powers of the mind and of the voluntary nerves is the cause of
unduly charging the involuntary powers with too great an
electro-nervous force, and the result is those singular manifestations that are so confidently attributed to the agency of
spirits." [68] That is about as close to the core of Dods's argument

as one can get; and however much one might like to credit him for at least searching for answers in the little-understood depths of the human mind, he offers no adequate explanation of the phenomena he admitted to be genuine.

A more widespread explanation of spiritualist phenomena originated in Germany. In the mid-1840s, after several years of research, Karl, Baron von Reichenbach, announced his discovery of a new imponderable force. (Some scientists at that time still referred to electricity, heat, magnetism, and light as imponderable fluids—that is, forces without weight or extension but with measurable properties and observable physical effects.) According to Reichenbach, this force behaved similarly to electricity and magnetism in some ways and before this point had been confused with them; it emanated to a greater or lesser degree from all objects. He thought that it explained all the perplexing problems of animal magnetism and mesmerism. The German baron had first noticed that when a magnet was passed before certain sensitive persons, they felt a physical sensation as if something in the magnet had reached out and touched them. They could, he further found, see light streaming from the poles of a magnet in a darkened room. He concluded that this force resided in all mass and could be perceived by anyone under the right conditions. He called it "Odyle" or "Od," so people usually referred to it as the Odic force.[69]

Reichenbach's work received scant attention from German scientists, but this cool reception did not prevent translations of his book into English, first in Britain, then in America. While no attention was paid to Reichenbach's findings in American scientific journals, Od managed to get tremendous amounts of publicity in the press and elsewhere. Even spiritualists believed in Od until in 1853 E. C. Rogers identified Od as the natural force behind all the phenomena previously traced to spirits. In doing so, he invested Od with much livelier qualities than even the imaginative Reichenbach had come up with. For example, to explain some of the things he had witnessed, Rogers had to turn Odyle into a material agent affecting the muscles, one which could operate upon bodies at a considerable distance from it and could even work through walls. Moreover, it was an emanation by which thoughts in one mind might be directly transferred to another. Rogers's assertions were as preposterous (or as logical) as any claim of spirit communication, and the people who took his side did so for reasons that had little to do with science.[70]

Stubborn Asa Mahan, a Presbyterian minister, militant abolitionist and the first president of Oberlin College, joined other respected Americans in accepting and supporting Rogers's conclusions; in fact Mahan added two large books to the spiritualist controversy.[71] Abel Stevens, who as editor of the *National Magazine* (a Methodist journal that competed with popular general periodicals) had condemned Beecher's theory as "unfortunate and preposterous," leaped at this "scientific explanation" and expressed pleasure that the whole affair of spiritualism—which according to him had severely damaged Christianity—had at least uncovered a "new scientific agent of untold interest."[72] Such statements at one point led William Lloyd Garrison to write, after admitting to some discrepancies and absurdities in the spirit manifestations, "nothing do I find so puerile, or so preposterous, as the various theories which are stated to account for them, short of a spiritual origin."[73]

Christianity, not science, prompted most of the early opposition to spiritualism. That held true even among scientists. When Robert Hare, after ending a distinguished career at the University of Pennsylvania, began to mix research into spiritualism with his work in chemistry, soon announcing his conversion, an old and close associate of his expressed dismay. From New Haven, Benjamin Silliman, one of America's most respected scientists and the editor of its most prestigious scientific journal, sent Hare a small volume entitled *The Christ of History*. With it he enclosed a letter written in an attempt to dissuade Hare from his folly. He made a theological argument, defending the divine origin of the Scriptures. "I cannot desert my Saviour," Silliman wrote, "Him who spoke as never man spake, while he knew what was in man; who has paid my debt when I was bankrupt; and who sustained in my stead the penalties of a violated law;—I cannot desert him, and repose my confidence in the visions of so-called mediums."[74]

Hare demonstrated the mental infirmities of advanced age when he turned to spiritualism. He felt persecuted by former colleagues who made light of his conversations with Franklin, Washington, and Jesus. Charles Partridge and Samuel B. Brittan, who published Hare's writings about spirits, found Hare extremely difficult to handle and complained that in his communications to the *Spiritual Telegraph* he neglected to discuss (of all things) the *scientific* aspects of spiritualism. Having gained in Hare an important convert from the scientific community, Brittan urged Hare in 1857 to consider spiritualism "so far as it may be convenient for you. . . . in its relations to science and natural law—instead of mainly regarding its theological bearings." [75] Partridge agreed entirely: spiritualist readers preferred to take their stand "in the eternal now" and not "know anything that is not tangible to [their] natural senses or has been made so to the natural senses of somebody else." Partridge characterized himself to Hare as "a matter of fact man" who had "no sympathy with the popular pretensious [sic] philosophy which disregards facts." [76]

However, no matter what mental vagaries may result when one has made it a "primary object of daily exertion for three years" to talk to the other side,[77] Hare was certainly able to construct a sensible case against Silliman's argument. In his reply to the Yale scientist, Hare called attention to his own initial skepticism about the rappings and related phenomena. He had originally agreed with Faraday that electricity accounted for any unaided movement of furniture at a séance.[78] A nominal Episcopalian, he had remained skeptical about religion all his life, and only irrefutable proofs had overcome lifelong biases and forced him to believe in voices from the beyond. In contrast, Silliman had always clung to an orthodox faith, which Hare called "bigotry in disguise," and now used that faith to excuse himself from investigating reported facts. Hare thought it contradictory for Silliman to accuse him of being too skeptical with respect to Christianity and not skeptical enough when confronting the spirits. He tried to persuade Silliman that the only hope for Christianity lay in the empirical proof of an afterlife furnished by the spiritualist demonstrations; religious beliefs based on the "internal evidence" of Christianity could not survive in the nineteenth century.[79]

There is no record of a reply from Silliman. He didn't attempt to counter Hare's "facts," nor did he discuss the scientific propriety of Hare's research. Silliman had apparently rested his argument on other grounds.

Another famous confrontation during this period between the men of science and the spiritualists ended in a stalemate, with the moral victory, as judged by Theodore Parker, going to the latter.[80] In 1857, Henry Lawrence Eustis, a professor of engineering at Harvard, called Frederick Willis, a Harvard School of Divinity student, before the faculty to answer charges of fraud. Willis, Eustis asserted, had passed himself off as a medium, had conducted séances, which Eustis and other Harvard faculty had attended, and had been caught cheating. Willis pleaded not guilty but was expelled anyway. The incident, by the way, did not keep Eustis and his colleagues away from later séances with other mediums.[81]

The ousted Willis picked up some defenders. Thomas Wentworth Higginson, a Unitarian minister and an abolitionist (who also befriended John Brown), took Willis into his home and testified to the genuineness of his mediumship. During the summer the *Boston Courier,* a paper Parker called the "wickedest" in New England,[82] decided to capitalize on the controversy to boost circulation, hoping at the same time to make a public mockery out of spiritualist claims. It offered $500 to any medium who could convince a committee of distinguished Harvard scientists that spirits communicated. Benjamin Peirce, Louis Agassiz, E. N. Horsford and Dr. B. A. Gould consented to serve as the impartial committee.[83]

H. F. Gardner accepted the challenge on behalf of spiritualism and arranged for the appearance of, among others, Kate Fox and the Davenport brothers. (The latter performed Houdini-like escapes with the aid of spirits.) Different accounts of what happened did not agree on much except the poorness of the manifestations. Gardner's side claimed plenty of raps, which they said baffled Agassiz, but they admitted to an overall disappointing show. They attributed the weak display to the overt

hostility of the committee members, who had created an un-
cooperative atmosphere for spirit demonstrations.[84] The results
as reported by a friendlier group of newsmen from the *Boston
Post, Traveler,* and *Journal,* whom Gardner summoned after the
Harvard group walked out, were very impressive.[85] Spiritualists
have never resolved the question of whether spirits will communicate with a largely unbelieving group of observers. According to Gardner, spirits did at the very least insist on receptive, open minds, which he felt the Harvard scientists lacked to
a high degree.

The *Courier* had not intended to elicit anything more than an
exposé of spiritualism as a way of defending an orthodox proclamation of man's "legitimate relations with heaven." [86] What
the Harvard scientists had in mind when they decided to partic-
ipate in this investigation and to contribute their time and prestige to the project is not so clear, for even though they had originally promised to publish a report of their findings, they never
did. They did sign a joint statement that in conclusion read: "It
is the opinion of the committee, derived from observation, that
any connection with spiritualistic circles, so called, corrupts the
morals and degrades the intellect. They therefore deem it their
solemn duty to warn the community against this contaminating
influence, which surely tends to lessen the truth of man and the
purity of women." [87]

Gardner had arranged the proceedings in collaboration with
Allen Putnam and Dr. Luther V. Bell. Bell was a respected doctor who for twenty years had acted as a very effective superintendent of the McLean Hospital for the Insane. He believed that
thought transference rather than spirits explained how mediums acquired the information they then imparted to as-
tonished sitters at séances, but that belief made him tremen-
dously interested, as a psychologist, in further investigation.
Nothing indicates that these men knowingly perpetrated fraud;
they welcomed the *Courier* proposal as "an opportunity to investigate the phenomena upon scientific principles." [88] No matter what the committee decided, the rappings would gain the
status of a serious scientific question—a status scientific organizations in America had been careful not to award them. How-

ever, to the dismay of Gardner, Bell, and Putnam, the spiritualist displays elicited from the Harvard group the same moral outrage they brought forth from the pulpit. Opposition to spiritualism in the 1850s usually concluded in support of the Bible and Christianity.

Orestes Brownson joined the Roman Catholic church in 1844. When the spirits began to move across America, he followed the lead of his church in seeing the footprints of Satan. He did not on that account remain detached from the subject; in 1854 he published a novel entitled *The Spirit Rapper: An Autobiography*. The plot may be summarized as the protagonist's successful attempt to overcome his Faustian urge to know everything. The hero of the book gets deeply involved in a conspiracy to overthrow Christianity along with the whole social order. Finding a strictly secular ideology lacking in mass appeal, he latches onto spiritualism as a suitable "religion" to further his revolutionary principles. Finally recognizing that spiritualism is Satanically inspired, he pulls back. From a character called Merton, who speaks for Brownson in the book, he learns that spirits are real despite the settled opinion of most scientists. But he also realizes that one cannot walk among them without losing one's soul.

The narrator of *The Spirit Rapper* stopped just short of self-destruction. The theme of the scientist who dared to find out too much had considerable currency in mid-nineteenth-century America. Hawthorne and Poe used it in their stories. Traditional religious doctrine dealt with it in explicit, unambiguous terms. The evil of spiritualism, according to the *Boston Courier*, lay in its reckless tampering with areas "beyond the plain revealed path of human duty." [89] In 1856, John P. Fairbanks, "a young man of amiable repute and irreproachable life" who was for a time an assistant editor of the *Scientific American*, leaped to his death. The *New York Times* blamed the suicide on the influence of spiritualism (Fairbanks had become an obsessed investigator), and warned readers not to "yield to the presumptuous curiosity that tries to peer across the gulf dividing us from God's undiscovered world." [90]

Totally committed to change and progress, spiritualists could not believe that man would lose his soul by advancing his knowledge. In their estimation science erred because it dared too little. Most scientists of that period in America would have agreed with James Dwight Dana, an American geologist, when he stated that no form of investigation could penetrate all mysteries, for "the ultimate nature of matter or life" is beyond investigation.[91] Spiritualists dissented vigorously. When in the opening of Brownson's story the narrator declares his rebellion against heaven, he speaks for the spiritualists: "I was resolved to push my scientific investigations to the furthest limits possible. I would, if I should be able, wrest from nature her last secret, and avail myself of all her mysterious forces—I am freeing the world from the monster superstition, and delivering the people from their gloomy fears and terrible apprehensions."[92] According to Adin Ballou, a Universalist minister and the spiritualist who founded the Hopedale community, only our ignorance kept the world in dread of "evil spirits, ghosts, goblins, and witches."[93]

The war between science and religion had not yet been declared in America in the 1850s. Most scientists did not even dream of one. But had a declaration been made, spiritualists would have declared themselves in intent and method on the side of science. They were eventually disappointed in finding no comfortable place in either camp. But it would be churlish to fault them, however pedestrian their phrasing, simply for believing that the world had for too long been afraid of the dark.

In the decade of the 1850s, the notions of American spiritualists strained human credulity no more than did the ideas of most of the embattled defenders of revealed religion. Moreover, their view of popular science had some plausibility. In what way, for example, did the hazily defined ether, which scientists used to fill space, differ from the spirit matter they believed in? The spiritualists' outlook encompassed what seems in retrospect to have been the most liberal, progressive, and liberating intellectual currents of their generation.

However, in the area where they most expected to succeed, they failed in many ways. In their craving for scientific respectability, they neglected philosophy. Had all their supposedly indisputable evidence been authenticated, they would have filled the world with spirits without having at all revealed a spiritual dimension in man. Spiritualists wanted to demonstrate that communication could occur, that some insignificant fact spelled out on Robert Hare's "spirit-scope" could only have come from a spirit who had once lived on this earth. Later spiritualists would try to make the very triteness of the messages received the most persuasive argument of their authenticity. Spiritualists argued that the spirits discussed small details of their earthly life because they believed that the public required such specific facts to be convinced of the reality of communication with the former-living.[94] Here was a tortured logic that reduced spirituality to man's most trivial activities. No amount of moralizing about the courage to confront truth could repair that kind of damage to human imagination.

Spiritualists, despite their professed interest in spiritual things, offered no corrective to the matter-of-fact attitude toward all endeavors that predominated in the expanding, and torn, commercial society of America in the 1850s. Paradoxically, then, they preserved spirit only by extending the realm of matter and offered evidence that proved more dull than marvelous. The American congressman Robert Dale Owen did experience a "strange, soul-stirring emotion" the first time he witnessed a spiritualist phenomenon. But one suspects that the agnostic Owen, like many of his countrymen, had lived for too long on a diet of the ordinary.[95] Horace Bushnell had no trouble pinpointing the country's spiritual undernourishment as the reason for spiritualism's popularity:

> The secret of this greedy, undistinguishing haste of delusion is the sharpness of the previous appetite; and that was caused by the abstinence of long privation. We had so far come into the kingdom of nullities—calling it the kingdom of God—we had become so rational, and gotten even God's own liberty into such close terms of natural order, that the immediate, living realities of religion, or religious experience, were under a doom of suppression. . . . Which hunger, alas! they are thinking to feed by a superstitious trust, in the badly written, silly oracles of our new-discovered, scientific necromancy.[96]

Hawthorne found it impossible to get interested in spiritualism, although the spirit demonstrations that he saw in 1858 did
seem genuine:

> But what astonishes me is the indifference with which I listen
> to these marvels. They throw old ghost-stories quite in the
> shade: they bring the whole world of spirits down amongst
> us, visibly and audibly; they are absolutely proved to be sober
> facts by evidence that would satisfy us of any other alleged
> realities, and yet I cannot force my mind to interest myself in
> them. . . . My inner soul does not in the least admit them;
> there is a mistake somewhere.[97]

If the raps indicated the quality of a future life, Thoreau promised to "exchange my immortality for a glass of cold beer."[98]
Another bored listener to the raps kept thinking of a line he had
often heard at Woods and Christy's Minstrels: "Who's dat
knockin' at de door?"[99] Spiritualism was at once a reaction to
what it conceived of as materialistic science and the most absurd product of the set of assumptions we call positivism. That
mixture resulted in an ambiguous legacy that has not yet been
straightened out.

Spiritualism successfully framed a theory that brought forth a
very positive response from a population who liked its marvels
packaged in machines or put into one of P. T. Barnum's cages.
Its claims gained acceptance in the same way that electrical phenomena did. While never quite achieving respectability, the
spiritualists clearly attracted everyone's attention. Important
men of business, politics, the arts, and journalism discussed the
implications of spiritualism's claims with dead earnestness.
Many were persuaded that they had been offered valid evidence
of a world beyond this one. Others began to inquire into the
possible existence of yet-unfathomed powers of the human
mind. Virtually everyone conceded that spirit communication
was at least a possibility. And because that possibility was associated in the popular mind with other questions concerning
science, Christianity, progress, and democracy, even the opponents of spiritualism found it too central an issue to be ignored.

The next two chapters deal with the influence of spiritualism
upon American religion and American reform; and in so doing,

clarify some of the ways people related the spirit rappings to other issues of public concern. What must always be kept in mind is that spiritualism reached its greatest audiences in nineteenth-century America when it adopted a language of plain common sense and spoke to the everyday interests of ordinary people. Like other Americans in the 1850s, spiritualists never stopped to ask if anything vital would be cast away in a world where people, having lost their capacity for reverence and awe, no longer felt those still moments of the soul when they struggled toward some incomprehensible Wonder and called it Holy. In Howells's novel *The Undiscovered Country*, a Shaker warned a visiting spiritualist guest within the community: "They are not miracles if you follow them up to see them a second time. We must beware how we make the supernatural a commonplace." [100] Spiritualists sought no more than the commonplace. The Americans of the 1850s who labored to make spirit communication respectable were not waiting, as Lawrence Ferlinghetti said for a later generation, "for lovers and weepers to lie down together again in a new rebirth of wonder." [101]

2

Spiritualism and the Complaint of Christian Orthodoxy

Early in the 1850s, the leaders of America's largest church denominations mustered considerable moral force to combat the spreading influence of spiritualism.[1] Ecclesiastical opposition, in fact, did not abate until the last two decades of the nineteenth century, and even then it did not disappear entirely. It merely subsided, as did the wave of public interest in spiritualism after the 1870s. Spiritualism's decline after the 1870s, though certainly made somewhat quicker by this earlier ecclesiastical opposition and various other challenges, was paradoxically a consequence of its success as a liberalizing influence. A good part of what had seemed blasphemous about spiritualism in the antebellum years would by the end of the century take on the role of a new orthodoxy. A lessening controversy over spiritualism's religious teachings made the movement less visible in American culture.

There is respected testimony to the fact that in the third quarter of the nineteenth century a good many American churches had reason to fear the influence of spiritualism. Octavius Brooks Frothingham, whose religious beliefs owed a great deal to Massachusetts Transcendentalism, was one of the first to describe the impact of the new movement. Before spiritualism became popular in America, he noted, "the theological atmosphere was . . . still. . . . The people looked stupidly acquiescent in the doctrines that were taught them by their clergy. . . . Unitarianism and Universalism were unpopular." Then mediums began to materialize all over the country, and "all on a sudden the 'rappings' are heard, tables begin to tip, mahogany vibrates, and one whole side of the calm mountain of the common mind comes down in a fierce avalanche, and rushes across the continent depopulating churches, desolating homes of faith, scattering communions, burying shrines, and covering the fair gardens of religion with heaps of ruin." [2]

While on the one hand, Frothingham personally saw only fraud in the spiritualist demonstrations, he was willing to look favorably upon it and all other movements that contributed to the woes of nineteenth-century American Calvinism. Spiritualism, he noted, had provided him with many valuable fellow travelers in his own campaign against religious orthodoxy.

Another well-known opponent of Calvinism put the matter more facetiously. Oliver Wendell Holmes referred to Margaret and Kate Fox together as the "Nemesis of the pulpit." "With the snap of a toe joint," they had begun a theological revolution that ended "with such a crack of old beliefs that the roar of it is heard in all the ministers' studies of Christendom." [3]

Allowing for their intentional irony, Frothingham and Holmes do suggest that very solid bones of contention lay between spiritualism and most Christian churches. What were they? The persistence of the theological opposition to spiritualism had its puzzling side. After all, spiritualism was a diffuse movement with no official philosophy other than the claim that spirit communication was a scientific fact. It was not even entirely clear—even among its own partisans—as to who counted as a spiritualist. In anything like an organized church form, it remained a small sect, never numbering more than 50,000 members, although those who attacked spiritualism as a threat to Christianity reckoned the actual number of believers in spiritualism into the millions. (Certainly if you included everyone who had ever heard of spirit communications and who expressed the thought "there was something in them," the movement did seem enormous.) But why public interest in these novel proofs of human survival after death should have been perceived as a threat to established religion is a question requiring more specific comment than anything to have yet been said.

If Emma Hardinge was right in claiming that most of spiritualism's nineteenth-century American adherents regarded it "as a religion separate in all respects from any existing sect," the religious opposition to spiritualism would be easier to understand.[4] At least the doctrinal disputes, to which Frothingham and Holmes correctly attributed much of the opposition, would be clear. But the evidence leads us to believe that Hardinge, although her role as a leading public medium gave her reason to know, was making a statement about spiritualism as she wished it to be. Her later unhappiness with the movement came about, in fact, when she realized how inaccurate her earlier assessment had been.[5]

It simply is not true, as George Lawton has argued in his 1932 study of spiritualist religion, that "spiritualism presents as elaborate, definite and as nearly articulated a system of religious beliefs and practices as can be found anywhere in the history of thought." His mistakes begin with his erroneous identification of the beliefs and practices of spiritualists with the writings of Andrew Jackson Davis.[6] Samuel B. Brittan, editor of *The Spiritual Telegraph*, noted in one of his many articles during the eight years of existence of this paper that it was dangerous to generalize about the religious beliefs of the average nineteenth-century spiritualist. Americans intrigued by spiritualist claims, he wrote, would go anywhere to see a table turned for the fortieth time; but "they would neither occupy an hour in a rational effort to comprehend the philosophy of the fact, nor invest a single dollar in the practical application of the truth to any human interest." [7]

This attitude, which Brittan lamented, struck other believers in spirit communication as perfectly justified. At any rate they clearly regarded as premature any effort to treat spiritualism as an organized set of religious teachings. In 1854 the New England Spiritualist Association expressed an attitude that was shared by most other nineteenth-century spiritualist organizations. It declared itself against the idea of trying to codify a set of beliefs: "Spirits do communicate with man—that is the creed. . . . All else that spiritualists may believe and do, belong to them as individuals, and not necessarily as spiritualists." [8]

As but another example, in a letter to the *Banner of Light,* Thomas Wentworth Higginson wrote: "Undoubtedly the facts of Spiritualism are the most important yet launched upon the history of humanity. . . . But the philosophy of Spiritualism is not yet born, and the more boldly one talks about it, the less attention it deserves." [9] Even Judge Edmonds, who took the substance of spirit messages far more seriously than Higginson, discounted the value of public spiritualist meetings. No more than one in ten spiritualists, he said approvingly, bothered to attend such functions regularly.[10] Most of them stuck to the private investigation of mediums.

People attended séances for consolation, for entertainment, and for assurance of a purpose behind life. All these satisfactions blended with the usually expressed scientific aim of penetrating nature's mysteries. The motives of the spirit investigators were mixed; and clearly many of them emphasized only in a very general way the religious implications of spirit communication. Either they remained uninterested in the traditional questions of Western Christian theology, or they took the major part of their religious beliefs from outside the spiritualist movement.

Some churches of course saw sufficient danger in the séance itself. They warned against any enterprise—independent of whether it was promoted as scientific or religious—that sought out the company of disembodied spirits. Roman Catholics, Swedenborgians, and Seventh-Day Adventists all viewed the movement with horror because of their particular interpretation of mediumistic phenomena. Satan, they said, was behind the strange happenings, and the men and women who attended these séances were debasing their spiritual natures beyond all hope of salvation.

These religious groups resented spiritualism as they would have resented any other set of beliefs that challenged their own teachings about who could communicate with the dead and how. They feared, with some cause, an overlapping appeal.

Moses Hull, for example, an early leader of the Adventist Church, defected to the spiritualist camp and in time began to edit a free-love journal.[11] The Church of the New Jerusalem was virtually torn apart by the challenge of spiritualism.[12]

Roman Catholics, comprising a larger group, had much less to fear. But still there were interesting conversions from Roman Catholicism to spiritualism and back the other way throughout the nineteenth century. For example, Margaret Fox and D. D. Home, the two most famous nineteenth-century mediums, made celebrated conversions to Catholicism and then lapsed back into infidelity.[13] Two other American spiritualists, Thomas Low Nichols and his wife Mary Gove Nichols, made permanent switches to Catholicism—significantly at the urging of spirit voices.[14] There is no way to estimate the number of American Catholics who at one time or another fell under the sway of spiritualism in the nineteenth century, but one official of the National Spiritualist Association estimated that half of its members in the twentieth century were formerly Catholic.[15]

For a variety of reasons, the major Protestant churches were less inclined to make the presence of evil spirits the sole basis for their attack. Many Protestant ministers themselves believed in the Devil. In the many pamphlets they put together to counter the claims of mediums, they cited the same scriptural injunctions Catholics had, those forbidding intercourse with familiar spirits, but when someone as prominent as Charles Beecher flat-footedly opted for a diabolical explanation of spiritualism, Protestant clergymen were made clearly uncomfortable.[16] In branding spiritualism superstitious, they had to be wary lest the charge come back too easily. Most, therefore, in accounting for the witnessed reports of spirit communication, much preferred to keep evil spirits at the bottom of the list of possibilities. Sensitive already to the claim that faith and science conflicted, they found it infinitely preferable to explain lifted tables and raps by Reichenbach's Odic force or by fraud. Their theological opposition, they argued, grew not from the fear that people were actually trafficking with the Devil but because of their concern that spiritualist delusions were encouraging, even among people only slightly affected, some unhappy trends in American religious beliefs.

For Protestant ministers, spiritualism represented a serious threat only because it added yet another element to a religious imbroglio that was already underway at the time of the Fox rappings. The intensity of the Protestant campaign therefore conveyed not only the extent of the threat posed by spiritualism as a heretical movement but the confused state in which Protestantism had been left by the weakening of Calvinist orthodoxy in the early nineteenth century and by the sectarian fever that had swept the country. While the proliferation of new religious denominations in antebellum American may have increased overall church membership, ministers of once-dominant denominations feared that the splintering of congregations would render church authority a less effective agent of social control. Protestant clergymen in 1850 expressed concern about the possible undermining of social morality with the weakening in the popular imagination of such orthodox concepts as Hell. They argued further that the spiritualists' version of a revelation, dispensed as it was promiscuously across all social classes, could only add to the problem of social disruption.

Most spiritualists, of course, also abhorred a sectarian spirit and consistently made no more than minimum statements at their conventions about their beliefs. From the viewpoint of the ministers of the largest Protestant denominations, however, the noncreedal aspects of spiritualism were just as harmful to social unity as the church schisms caused by John Murray, William Miller, or Joseph Smith. The net effect, they argued, of investigation into important theological questions without the guidance of the Scriptures or of any church was the diminishing of established church authority. Several years after his own interest in séances had cooled, Thomas Low Nichols referred to spiritualism as "a segregating or scattering force." It led people away from their churches without providing a common bond that might lead to effective regroupment.[17]

Spiritualism's challenge to the authority of existing churches was especially resented because spiritualist practices seemed to denigrate, even mock, traditional forms of religious worship. Casual visitors to nineteenth-century spiritualist meetings often expressed surprise at the complete absence of any devotional atmosphere. A Southern woman who attended a spiritualist gathering in 1870 at Apollo Hall in New York City observed none of the trappings she associated with a church service: "I was struck with the hum of conversation and the lack of gravity which befits a house of worship. . . . It was good so far as it went but there was no religion there. . . . That night there was no prayer offered, no invocation made. The audience, I cannot call them a congregation, dispersed without a blessing and applauded frequently as at any other lecture." [18]

Spiritualist meetings did vary. For example, many spiritualists remained in their Christian churches and demanded the singing of Christian hymns at séances they attended. But what Mrs. Thomas witnessed in Apollo Hall was not unusual. Such spiritualist churches as were formed (and these did appear by the end of the 1850s) held weekday and Sunday meetings that differed little from the large public demonstrations conducted by commercial mediums. They normally met in auditoriums rather than in buildings attempting to re-create the arrangement of a church. Depending on whether the members felt some nominal attachment to Christianity or none, religious icons might or might not be displayed. Most services included music, a prayer, and a lecture. Again, the Christian elements in these components depended on the congregation. But without doubt, the most important part of the meeting was that part of the service given over to the receipt of spirit messages. To hostile observers the inordinate attention given to human spirits trivialized the true point of a religious service, which was to worship God.

By the mid-nineteenth century the authority of the Christian Scriptures was running into even more trouble. The Transcendentalist emphasis on intuitive evidence posed one of many new problems for evangelical Protestants, but Transcendentalism was at least a geographically limited threat. (The Unitarians at Harvard, who deserved their trouble, could worry about the Transcendentalists.) On the other hand, Protestant theologians across the country were under pressure to reconcile those parts of the Scriptures in conflict with new critical evidence about the age and development of the earth. They had the difficult task of defending biblical authority when it appeared that parts of their Scriptures were either mythical or merely wrong.

Obviously, as the nineteenth century wore on, it became increasingly difficult for Protestant ministers to go on as they had been, certifying biblical miracles while falling over one another to insist on the absolute orderliness of natural law in modern times. Hiram Corson, a professor of English at Cornell University who over many years had communicated with spirits in the Ithaca area, posed a slightly different version of the dilemma. "Strange, indeed," he wrote, "is the attitude the Christian Church now takes, in regarding the exhibitions in these days of the very spiritual gifts which especially characterized primitive Christianity, as the work of the Devil." [19] Merely to deny the possibility of modern miracles (diabolical or otherwise) was no answer to Corson. He simply asked the embarrassing question of why Divine Providence had been so much more bountiful with miracles in biblical times than today.

The affront to the Bible, then, more than anything else represented that part of spiritualism most troubling to spiritualism's opponents. It compounded all the aforementioned problems. Of course, spiritualist mediums did not claim to be the recipients of infallible revelation. Under different circumstances, the writings of Andrew Jackson Davis might well have become the foundation of an entity as distinct as the Mormon church; but his early sponsors thwarted that possibility from the beginning.

Of the famous commercial mediums—Margaret and Kate Fox, J. V. Mansfield, Anna Fay, and the Davenport brothers, for example—none pretended to receive messages containing anything so elevated as God's word. Some of them even refused to certify the spirit origin of the things that went on in their presence, and almost all balked at guaranteeing the good character of the spirit communicators. Dr. Charles Main, a healing medium, reminded an audience of spiritualists that "many in the Spirit-world are even below our level, both intellectually and morally." [20] Main turned the spiritualist practice of receiving messages on its head. He gave daily lectures to hundreds and thousands of spirit pupils on the subject of moral improvement. The trivialities and the contradictions in the messages, not to mention the bad grammar and deliberate lies, never put off true spiritualist believers. They themselves did not deny that many of the manifestations emanated from disreputable spirits. According to Judge Edmonds, who was a steady recipient of long spirit messages, there was reason to be grateful for the imperfections of the communications. They forced the recipient to think and to discriminate. A perfect revelation, he argued, would leave the human mind with nothing further to do. It "would come to us 'with authority' and we should be encouraged to render obedience and not judgment." [21]

However, even when spirit messages did not claim to compete with the Bible, they inevitably worked to weaken arguments for reliance on scripture. Some spiritualists, including such popular writers as Robert Dale Owen and Epes Sargent, maintained that the materialization of spirits in the nineteenth century gave new credibility to biblical stories about the miracles of Jesus.[22] In actuality, however, the constant emphasis spiritualists placed on the fallibility of spirit messages cast into doubt the credibility of biblical writing as well. Biblical prophets had relied on the same sorts of spirits that controlled nineteenth-century mediums. If Judge Edmonds got only garbled messages, who then was to say that Moses had done any better?

Perhaps many supposedly divine commandments delivered in biblical times were really forms of practical advice on the order of the spiritual information given in modern times to E. J. French. According to the latter's testimony before a weekly conference of spiritualists at Clinton Hall in New York City, he had by following spirit direction, kept himself from being in a railway accident, subdued a vicious dog, and healed the paralytic ailments of his mother and grandfather. His daughter, using a similar ability to hear spirit voices, relieved herself of a toothache. The spirits were useful but not in most cases indispensable. French did find it convenient to communicate with his brother in California by "spiritual telegraphy," but failing that, he had the U.S. mail service to fall back on.[23]

It was one thing to say, as did many orthodox Christian ministers, that the Bible did not reveal everything and that many of its passages should not be taken literally. But it was quite another to suggest, as Judge Edmonds had, that no gulf existed between God and man that could not be bridged by reason. With a little ingenuity, Edmonds had suggested, human beings could figure out what lay beyond the known universe. This immodesty quite outshot the goals of most antebellum American scientists, who never imagined that their discoveries would render revelation irrelevant. To anyone who believed in the necessity of revelation Judge Edmond's attitude had to be chastised as damnable arrogance. His statements, in effect, dismissed revelation as both unnecessary and undesirable.

According to most other believers in spirit communication, the spirit messages were important because they offered tangible evidence of an afterlife. But any other truths that they purported to contain had to be weighed by the "individual consciousness—which is always the final standard of judgment." [24]

Thus in spite of its diffuseness, and in part because of it, spiritualism spoke to the interests of many Americans who sought a rational theology. While the movement taken in its widest sense could not in the nineteenth century be designated a church or a denomination, its meaning in terms of America's religious past was clear enough. The people who began the first publicity boom on behalf of the spirits came in the largest proportionate numbers from the Universalist Church and from the ranks of non–church members. Unitarians contributed a fair share, including men as well known as Thomas Wentworth Higginson, James Richardson, and John Pierpont. Many Christian spiritualists of one sort or another did complain about what they regarded as the infidel drift of the movement. For example, William Fishbough, one of Davis's early supporters, was by 1853 thoroughly disillusioned with the anti-Christian attitude of many of those he had formerly worked with. "New York," he reported, "is eminently a superficial, sensual, and practically infidel place, and . . . there are comparatively few spiritualists here who acknowledge the Lord and his providential rule, either in theory or practice." [25]

Gerrit Smith, the Liberty party leader, also warned "that spiritualism is fraught with great evil to those who are foolish enough to welcome it as a new religion, and a substitute for Christianity." [26] However, self-styled Christian spiritualists opposed Calvinism as strongly as those spiritualists who regarded the basis of spiritualism as something "separate and different from that of the Christian Church, or of any Church extant." [27] The nineteenth-century Americans who were the most strongly attracted to spiritualist practices—whether they belonged to a church or not, were Christian or non-Christian, religious or profane—shared an aversion to what they called Christian orthodoxy. They did not believe in the Trinity, human depravity, predestination, vicarious atonement, or a final judgment.

The religious liberalism that influenced spiritualist publications throughout the nineteenth century has been easy to overlook. Historians have found it difficult to see how a belief in heavenly realms filled with thoroughly human spirits could encourage a rationalistic trend in theology. Christian liberalism is under enough clouds without adding spiritualism to its heritage.

Of course, in many ways spiritualism was simply another religious movement that spread through New York's "burned-over district," and those characteristics that made it recognizable as akin to already familiar movements contributed to its success. It shared with Millerism and Mormonism, for example, a religious imagination that was graphic and literal. The plain people of western New York responded to visual, exactly measured detail; and whether the subject was Hell, the Second Coming, the New Jerusalem, or the spirit world, really did not matter all that much to them. Mormons and spiritualists alike had a passion for collecting witnesses to certify the facts of their faith. Both in their own way strove after a religion whose evidences, however strange they seemed on first telling, fell entirely within the domain of advancing science.

A comparable interest in outward physical signs was evident in other ways in the successive waves of Protestant revivals that gave the "burned-over district" its name. A saint rolling in the dust gave evidence of spiritual presence as surely as a symphony of raps. All such phenomena attested to the daily intrusion of the invisible world into the visible.

In addition, Christian revivalism and spiritualism both fell under the influence (though with different emphases) of notions of human perfectionism, and spiritualism surely owed aspects of its anticlericalism and antidenominationalism to the revivals. Since the forms of revivalism evinced themselves everywhere in antebellum America, some spiritualist camps inevitably caught the contagion of religious excitement.

Nonetheless, while parallels between revivalism and spiritualism in the antebellum period were abundant enough (both contributed, after all, to the decline of Calvinism), the emphasis of the revivals upon conversion was alien to spiritualism. Countless stories circulated about spiritualism driving people insane or to suicide. Doubtless some were true. The atmosphere at many séances most certainly elevated the blood pressure of those present. The fact remains, however, that the aim of spiritualism was not to arouse religious emotion but to calm passions by making things rational and understandable.

Spiritualism appealed, with good reason, to many temperance advocates. It arose too late to reflect the enthusiastic pietism that had earlier been so evident in the cities and towns of antebellum America. It rejected outright the Evangelical Protestantism that had furnished the theology of the revivals.[28] Men and women who actually left other churches to become spiritualists no longer paid much attention to the sovereignty of God, the depravity of man, or the doctrine of divine grace.

Despite the reluctance of spiritualists to make more than brief statements about religious belief, spiritualist publications over the course of the nineteenth century did speculate about many theological questions. About some matters there even arose a consensus—most of it simply following outlines of speculation set by the dissatisfaction of many with traditional Christian accounts of life after death.

Salvation was a theological subject that fascinated spiritualists. The discussions of God, Christ, and Heaven contained in the spiritualist press and in books written by spiritualists did not define articles of faith for everyone who believed in spirit communication. However, the teachings that got repeated with the most regularity deserve attention. These were ideas to which many spiritualists informally subscribed, and these commonly held antiorthodoxy beliefs served to widen the gap between denominational Christianity and spiritualism.

From the standpoint of orthodoxy, one of the most irksome characteristics of religious discussions among spiritualists was the lack of attention given to God. If there were Christian spiritualists, there were also atheistic spiritualists. E. W. Capron, the first business manager of the Fox sisters, held that the existence of spirits did not compel belief in the existence of God. "On the subject of the existence of a great first cause," he wrote, "we have no new proofs or revelations. The probability is that spirits generally know but little, if any, more about how, where, or in what form the Deity exists, than we mortals. I see nothing in the new revelations that would, of necessity, lead an atheist to change his views." [29]

Most spiritualists professed not to be atheists, but most spiritualist publications played down or opposed any view of a personal God who had made the world and planned its destiny. According to one, "A belief in a personal God, as above Nature, is the cause of all error." [30] Religious opponents charged spiritualists with teaching pantheism. Spiritualists usually denied the charge, but it fit many of them well enough. "God is not a person," read a quote from the *Banner of Light*, "but a principle, permeating all things." [31] In the words of F. L. Wadsworth, a spiritualist lecturer, "Nothing is outside of God, and God is not outside of anything. Every particle that exists, every human soul, possesses within itself that which is absolutely and essentially divine." [32]

Spiritualists were not dogmatically pantheistic, however. Had they been so, pantheism would have led to a greater emphasis on a religion of the heart than most of them were inclined to follow. To be sure, S. B. Brittan and those other leaders of the spiritualist movement who borrowed from Transcendentalist philosophy trusted intuition. Their belief in the immanence of

God and the divine spark within each person led them to conclude that certain truths were written in the human soul.[33]

In the main, however, spiritualists were inclined to give only marginal epistemological status to intuition; a survey of their literature reveals that they rarely addressed themselves to a discussion of it in any systematic way. The truth of a spirit message might in many cases have to be weighed by nonempirical standards of individual conscience, but mediumistic practices were intended generally for the outer rather than the inner eye.

In emphasizing divine immanence, spiritualists wished to prove that the world was in its entirety open to scientific investigation. To them, pantheism was the intellectual consequence of one's having rejected the distinction between natural and the supernatural. It meant little else. To talk about a God who existed before all other life and was radically separate from all other substance was to demand some category over and above Nature. Spiritualists would not hear of it. The requirement did not fit their notions of science. It still baffled critics how a movement that could on occasion entertain a majestic vision of Nature, "where God's own finger has written in indelible lines," could betray that vision day after day in the unnatural setting of a medium's parlor.[34]

If the religious ideas expressed by many spiritualists tended to dissolve the personality of God, they had no similar effect on the concept of human individuality. Despite their belief in a divine principle that flowed through and connected all forms of nature, spiritualists maintained a firm insistence on the uniqueness of the individual soul before and after death. Many religions that contain elements of pantheism—for example, Hinduism and some forms of Christian mysticism—eventually devalue individual personality as this characteristic comes into conflict with their belief in the ultimate oneness of things. After death, if salvation is attained, the individual soul merges into cosmic oneness or is overwhelmed by a feeling of relatedness to the whole.

Certainly it was in this tradition that American Transcendentalists, for example, while they cherished variety and the individual differences found in Nature, also stressed the discontinuity between the impersonality of pure spiritual life and individual bodily existence. In contrast, the spirits who delivered messages to Judge Edmonds were certain about continued individuality: "You will never lose your identity. If God designed to absorb all souls into himself, there would be no necessity at first to give off from himself distinct identical germs, possessing all the characteristics of independence." [35] Epes Sargent, the spiritualist publicist, likewise distinguished his position from that of the Transcendentalist Emerson, who wrote on the occasion of his son's death the couplet: "The master, Death, with sovereign rite / Pours finite into infinite." In rebuttal, Sargent wrote, spiritualism taught "the imperishability of the individual and the continuation of the identical Ego." [36]

Most American religions in the early nineteenth century provided very concrete and detailed portraits of the afterlife.[37] Spiritualism outdid them all. Spirits retained the discrete characteristics of their earthly personalities. A possible contradiction arose here, for it was also taught that the longer a spirit had been dead the farther it progressed through the heavenly spheres until it finally lost all contact with earth.

Presumably individuality took on a different shape in those outer reaches. But spiritualists were not greatly interested in the remote spirit realms, their attention being focused on existence in the second and third spheres of the spirit world, where society resembled a utopian vision of earthly life. Astral bodies of the departed looked in these places very much like their earth bodies had looked except that physical disabilities had disappeared. Spirit babies grew up into spirit men and women just as they would have done had they lived. The spirit realms presented landscapes very similar to terrestrial ones. Not only could the distance of each spiritual sphere from the earth be calculated, but its scenery, social organization and government could be described down to the last detail. One spirit speaking from the third sphere detailed the environs there: "In the distance were seen numerous mountains, dipping their lofty ridges in the crescive splendor of a Celestial Sun, while the music of the waterfall was heard sweetly blending its voiceful eloquence with the harmonial carollings of paradisciacal songsters. The flowers wafted forth a fragrance belonging alone to Heaven, while the gorgeous-tinted butterfly flitted from one to the other, sipping the celestial sweetness which sparkled, like morning dews, on each perfumed petal." [38] The splendor promised in such messages contained the comforting assurance that the departing spirit launching itself, say, from Kansas, into the next world would be leaving behind a good bit that was drab but not all that was familiar.

The theological liberalism of spiritualism was most apparent in the attitude spiritualist publications adopted toward Christ. Christian spiritualists, of course, had to regard Jesus as in some sense divine—otherwise, there would be little point in holding to the label Christian—but even they tended to treat the divinity of Christ as little more than evidence for the divine side of all men. That view became after the Civil War a popular formula among Protestant theologians, who slowly abandoned a philosophy of Christianity preaching divine transcendence for one emphasizing divine immanence.

Non-Christian spiritualists took the humanizing of Christ much further. In their minds, he was merely a skilled medium who embodied in concrete form what men and women would someday all become through a process of ongoing evolution. He was, according to one spirit message, "a man designed for the elevation of his race in the promulgation of the truths which the darkness, bigotry, and narrow-mindedness of the world had obscured from man's understanding." [39] It was an important mission, but an explicitly human one.

Some spiritualist writers even questioned the propriety of holding Christ up before humankind as a moral model. While Christ had perfected his own spirituality, he could not show others what kind of perfection was appropriate for their own individualities. One's personal destiny was unique and had to be followed whatever the world thought. To urge everyone to be Christ-like was to hold to the theological idea that individual differences are of no ultimate importance. The social standings of those who took spiritualism's religious side most to heart ranged from the middle of the social scale downward. They did not have many devices, other than imaginative ones, with which to protect their individuality against the likelihood of increasing anonymity within an industrial society.

Most spiritualist writers had less interest in questioning the worthiness of Christ's life than in repudiating the Christian doctrine of atonement. The orthodox rendering of atonement, from the spiritualist perspective, flew in the face of common-sense moral principles and was "essentially unreasonable, mean, and unmanly." [40] Spiritualists took as an insult to morality the suggestion that a person could win salvation through someone else's effort or someone else's sacrifice. To insist further, as did most Christian denominations, on the limited nature of the sacrifice, which consigned many to hellfire or permanent extinction, just made matters worse.

Most spiritualist writers did not believe that people chose to sin and were for that reason accountable before God. God did not damn people because of human frailty, and no punishable blame attached to individuals because of inbred defects of character. On the other hand, spiritualist writers did feel that the responsibility for self-improvement rested squarely on the individual. Spiritualists drew on many of the teachings of the Universalist church and believed in salvation for everyone. Unlike the Universalists, however, they did not recognize Christ's role in human salvation. Nor did they, as did most Universalists, believe that God placed all individuals on an equal footing after they died. A belief in eternal progress underlay all the other common views found in spiritualist publications; and that implied, among other things, the spiritual progress of each individual soul after death in an unbroken, evolutionary fashion from the point it had reached in this life.

Spiritualists had a pluralist view of Heaven—there were heavens—and no idea of Hell. They derived most of their ideas about Heaven from Swedenborg, although Swedenborg did believe in Hell. The most spiritualists would concede was that the spirit domains closest to earth, where those who had made little moral advancement in this life would begin life in the next, were not very pleasant. The idea that unpleasant surroundings would not be especially conducive to further moral progress never occurred to them. They believed that every soul, no mat-

ter where it started out in the next life, would make inevitable
progress toward moral perfection at a pace appropriate to its
abilities.

Salvation, as spiritualists defined it, was not a static state of
being that one either achieved or did not. It was progression
through a series of heavenly spheres (seven was the most common number given in spirit messages) corresponding to higher
and higher states of moral perfection. Spiritualists disagreed
over many points of detail regarding this doctrine of everlasting
cosmic progress, but in general, it commanded more assent
among them than any other idea except that of spirit communication itself. Even those men and women whose belief in
the spirits amounted to no more than casual assent accepted the
logic of ongoing moral improvement. It was, after all, a notion
perfectly suited to American standards of fairness. In the afterlife no one got something for nothing—the higher rewards
required work and time—but the opportunities for advancement were theoretically unlimited. Individual endowments
were not all equal, but handicaps did not put people perma-
nently out of the race. The spiritualist spheres implied that
there were such things as rank and status in Heaven. But they
were not based upon money, and they were not permanent.
Given eternity, there was no barrier that individual human
beings could not surmount.

Spiritualist mediums and lecturers who categorically rejected
the doctrine of atonement and the Calvinist emphasis on predestination and original sin chose, they said, to stress the responsibility of the individual for his own moral development.
To their religious critics, these views sanctioned a moral holi-
day. An editorial in *Harper's Weekly* called on officials to close
down the spirit circles, which were placed in the same category
as "gambling dens and other places of ill-fame." Because the
"dangerous delusions" of spiritualism led to "moral abomina-
tions," many critics of spiritualism demanded the outlawing of
professional mediumship.[41] In their minds, the human vehicles
of spirit communication and the many people drawn into their
circle of influence were walking down a straight road toward
broken homes, drunkenness, and insanity.

Spiritualist publications responded in a mixed way to the charge of immorality. They naturally resented and rebutted the idea that spiritualist teachings sanctioned lewdness or crime. Spiritualism, according to the *Banner of Light*, "teaches love, charity, and good will to man and forgiveness of injuries." [42] The God of orthodoxy, that "devil creator, plaguer of the human race, framer and jailer of hell, and tormentor of the damned," was more properly blamed for the absence of a kindly spirit among people. According to William Denton, a spiritualist lecturer, the cause of morality was better served by a religion that opened human hearts to the "sunshine and the songs of birds, the sounds of purling brooks, the joy of the living word, ripening in God's smile." [43]

Spiritualists did not necessarily deny the many charges of immorality that were leveled in their direction.[44] However, they did not blame spiritualist teachings for the immorality. They blamed society's persecution of many spiritualists and the difficult economic circumstances in which they lived. Doubtless spiritualism appealed particularly to the social outcast, a theme I will develop further later on. Spiritualists liked to cite the case of Mary Magdalene. As history demonstrated, a sullied moral reputation did not preclude divine favors. After all, the argument ran, it was not the "fat and sleek priests" who could expect angel visits.[45]

Whatever spiritualists said, those of their critics who believed the movement was spreading immorality in America saw the problem as one of doctrine. Christian ministers felt that the disregard of conventional morality displayed by many promoters of spiritualism followed logically from their disregard of Hell and their emphasis on human sinlessness. A number of spiritualist writers, especially those influenced by Davis's "Harmonial Philosophy," simply refused to give a metaphysical standing to evil. In his book *Whatever Is, Is Right,* A. B. Child argued that nothing on earth, no force, no idea, no behavior could properly be called evil. "Every law of Nature," he argued, "is a law of God, every jot and tittle of which must be fulfilled. God being infinite, there can be no nature or law outside of infinitude.

God being good, all that is in God is good. So every deed of human life is good—not one is evil." [46]

Andrew Jackson Davis refused to label anything a "positive evil," holding that sin was "an atavism merely." "Evil is altogether an arbitrary term, which men apply to those inequalities and misdirections which they have themselves morally as well as intellectually outgrown, but which others far less developed may still continue to perpetuate." Good and evil carried meaning as "social distinctions" and in that sense could furnish useful standards by which to measure misconduct. But on a higher level, all things represented some aspect of God's universal self-expression and played a necessary role in the development of the world.[47]

Christian theologians had on occasion made similar arguments in praise of God's glory. Spiritualist philosophers, however, were interested in releasing man from the taint of any kind of sin, not just original, and as a consequence, from his dependence on divine grace. For any belief that individuals happened to hold, for any of their outrageous behavior, however much it went against conventional standards, they had the right to the stamp of divine approval. God was the author of it. People did not obey God's commandments or even ask what they were. They did what they pleased, pointed to the upward road on which they must surely be traveling, and invoked divine blessing.

One pamphleteer, for instance, in setting out the firm opposition of Seventh-Day Adventists to spiritualism, said of Robert Hare's conversion to Christianity by spirit voices: "The Doctor was a believer in Christ, not because he endorsed the Gospel of Christ, but because Christ endorsed him! Who would not be a Christian on such terms?" [48] Hare's conversion had in fact changed very little about his beliefs, except perhaps his views on an afterlife. As an old man he was susceptible to more consoling ideas about immortality, but not to alterations of his views concerning much else. He became a Christian only when the spirits tailored Christianity to suit his own settled and orderly view of the world.

The difference between a Christian moralist and most spiritualist moralists was fundamental. The latters' concept of inevitable individual advancement, at least in the forms most common in nineteenth-century spiritualist publications, reduced God's role to insignificance. Their secularization of ethics followed general intellectual trends of the early nineteenth century, but they turned away altogether from divine sanctions. Thomas Wentworth Higginson, whose Unitarian background prepared him to take spirtualism's heresies in stride, said with simple candor that people were not likely to change their ways merely because God was watching them. If, on the other hand, a person could be persuaded that a "sainted mother, his wife, or his friend who was dearest on earth" could see him, his attitude would be quite different.[49]

In his popular writings about the spirit manifestations, Epes Sargent maintained the same line of argument: "Let a man or child be thoroughly convinced that a deceased mother or father he reverently loves is living a more intense life than ever, and can read his every thought and scan his every act, and such a conviction must have a restraining influence upon him, when tempted to evil." [50] God, as fearsome judge, abdicated the role of public enforcer of morality to an assorted set of relatives and human dignitaries hovering about sixty miles out beyond the earth's atmosphere.

However unorthodox these views remained for many Protestants, they unquestionably had a wide appeal in nineteenth-century American society. In 1865, acting with Francis Ellingwood Abbot, Octavius Brooks Frothingham led a group of religious radicals out of the National Unitarian Conference to form the Free Religious Association. Their conviction that traditional Christianity was unprovable and hence irrelevant to the modern scientific world was precisely what spiritualist publications had been arguing for over a decade, and many spiritualists showed their interest in participating in this new association.

Both Frothingham and Ellingwood were uncomfortable with their new coreligionists. Abbot thought spiritualist demonstrations a crude approach to questions about future existence, and Frothingham felt that there were remnants of superstition behind spiritualism's scientific pretensions.[51] Be that as it may, spiritualists were "generally a good sort of people, since they were free thinking, liberal . . . and enemies of prejudice." [52] Robert Dale Owen served as a vice-president of the association. He shared with Abbot and Frothingham as well as his fellow spiritualists a rejection of creeds, an emphasis on man's moral and rational powers rather than on his sin, a stress on God's immanence in the world, and a separation of the meaning of Christ from his suffering on the cross.

Whether spiritualism ruined the "fair gardens" of orthodox Christianity quite so dramatically as Frothingham's good humor led him to estimate is doubtful. We are frustrated in our attempts to know with certainty how great a revolution spiritualism wrought within established religious orthodoxy, partly because we do not know how many people took interest in nineteenth-century spiritualism and partly because we cannot know how much attention believers in spirit communication paid to spiritualist publications. Certainly religious liberalism would have made its way in nineteenth-century America without the help of spiritualism, just as it would have made its way without the help of Charles Darwin. The theological revision that spiritualism drew from had its roots in the eighteenth century. Spiritualism rose after the decline of Calvinism was well along in America, and it contributed little to the intellectual sophistication of liberal theologies.

Nonetheless, Frothingham's estimate of the importance of spiritualism as a liberalizing force was not outrageously off the mark. It was a truly popular movement in nineteenth-century America, the influence of which was felt strongly for about twenty-five years. Spirtualism spread the mood and presuppositions of religious liberalism beyond the audiences reached by Universalists or the Harvard Divinity School.

It also took the message of liberalism down the social scale. Spiritualist mediums and lecturers were constantly on the move. The rappings began in a village, spread to small towns, and reached the largest audiences in the cities. Because of the opposition of most early spiritualist leaders to slavery, spiritualism did not travel well below the Mason-Dixon line. Otherwise, from 1850 to 1875, it encountered few demographic limitations. Even Henry Ward Beecher, who was as uneasy with much of spiritualism as was Abbot, Frothingham, or Theodore Parker, owed part of the enormous prestige he enjoyed to the efforts of spiritualist leaders.[53]

Lester Ward, one of the founders of American sociology, spent many hours as a young civil servant in Washington at spiritualist lectures and séances. Because of spiritualism, he said in 1870, the world was "in the very act of changing its faith." Spiritualism in his mind was the only religion that could satisfy a modern skeptical inquirer.[54] Ward's fascination with professional mediums eventually declined, although he retained his interest in the kinds of phenomena reported by spiritualists.

Like so many other Americans and Europeans in the late nineteenth century, Ward continued to attach importance to these matters because he found himself caught "between science and religion." [55] To the highly educated, and to many Americans of common sense, a biblical faith made little sense. They found no consolation in regular church attendance. Yet medical science had not yet made much headway against the omnipresence of death. The people who became interested in spiritualism were enthusiastic supporters of science, but they feared a science without direction and a world without meaning. They called spiritualism science, but it was also a surrogate religion. The spirit voices were all they had to keep them from capitulating to the logic of nihilism.

Of course spiritualism's attempt to present itself as a rational religion did not quite succeed. Spiritualism placed great weight upon rationality and observation, a fact that impressed many people who were trying to break America of some conservative habits of thought. However, while insisting that the extraordinary was ordinary and not at all mysterious, spiritualism also tried to stretch the human imagination beyond accepted common sense. Whatever its naturalistic framework, and despite its impatience with religious dogmatism, spiritualism surely provided comfort for its adherents analogous to that felt by believers in special providences.

The nineteenth-century American psychologist George Beard was very interested in spiritualism, not because he believed in it, but because he saw it as an odd and intriguing mixture of impulses. Spiritualism claimed to be positivistic, "an attempt to apply the inductive method to religion, to make faith scientific, to confirm the longings of the heart by the evidence of the senses." Beard regarded this goal as self-defeating, for as many other critics pointed out, "a religion proved, dies as a religion, and becomes a scientific fact." But Beard thought it unlikely spiritualism would prove its facts. In theory a religion of demonstration, it was in practice based on absolutely blind trust. "The Ultramontane Catholic" was "in his most credulous moments a wonder of scientific incredulity in comparison with the victim of dark séances, where a slight movement of the hand, or a well-directed kick, would reveal, even to a non-expert, the baldness, the grotesqueness, and vulgarity of the performance by which he is about to be entranced." [56]

The emotionalism that clouded the judgment of grief-stricken séance goers should not by itself gainsay the honest desire of many spiritualists to base religion on observable evidence. The degree of skepticism that a firmly committed spiritualist carried into a séance obviously varied. Some took incautious delight in the materialization of some loved one, while others coolly looked for marks of physical identification and weighed the genuineness of apparitions with greater detachment. But any such "proof," no matter how carefully it was weighed, simply could not establish the spiritualists' basic claim that the spirit of dead mortals communicated with the living. How was a poor sitter to distinguish the spirit of his deceased father from that of some lying angel or demon who had never lived on earth but who knew enough of what went on below to impersonate dead human beings?

Despite the enormous effort on the part of spiritualists to establish the identity of spirit voices with certainty, they were never completely able to get around the possibility suggested by some of their critics that someone out in space was putting them on. Extraterrestrial voices, even if their reality should be proved ten thousand times, could not of themselves establish that the dead live again. Spiritualists tried honestly and tire-lessly to cut through the dilemmas involved in trying to prove religion. They criticized both those who relied on past miracles to guarantee the validity of the Bible and those who attempted to base religious truths solely on individual intuition. In their minds, no religion that depended on the correctness of histori-cal statements about mysterious events in a foreign country in a remote period could claim real evidence, nor was intense feel-ing an adequate substitute for such evidence. Evidence had to be immediate, and it had, in part, to rest on something subject to empirical confirmation.

On the other hand, while the summoned spirits satisfied both these criteria, mediumistic trances were not the same as mys-tical illumination, and spirit messages did not relay reliable in-formation. Joel Tiffany, during the 1850s an editor of a spiritual-ist monthly, sided with those leaders in the movement who warned against an exclusive concern with summoning disem-bodied spirits. "As a means of becoming wise," he wrote, "it becomes necessary for us to seek by some means to come into interior communion with the Spirit-world and Divine Being, since we can not by outward means arrive absolutely at the truth." [57] For the most part, spiritualists defined science in a way that prevented much attention to an argument of this sort. Their publications simply piled up more and more outward evi-dence, and they hoped that this would stave off the hard ques-tions needed to be asked about what this material proved.

A chart of spiritualist influence upon American religious thought would show a sharply rising line in the early 1850s, a leveling off during the rest of the decade, and a decline during the Civil War years. After the Civil War, the chart would show a recovery fed by the wish of many people to communicate with those who had perished during the war. A veritable spiritualist mania swept the country in the form of a modified ouija board called a planchette. [58] The recovery lasted until the late 1870s.

After that, although spiritualism continued to attract what seems from our day an extraordinary amount of newspaper at-tention, especially in editorial statements, Christian churches grew much less concerned with its danger. Among liberal clergymen, spiritualism continued to find individual supporters. In the 1890s, Minot J. Savage, who preached to large Unitarian congregations in Boston and New York City, declared his belief in spirit communication. R. Heber Newton's career in the Episcopal church during the same decade read like an early version of the exploits of Bishop James Pike. His tentative belief in spirits was only one of the heterodox views he held that outraged the other clergy of his church.

In the early part of the twentieth century Douglas Clyde Macintosh of the Yale Divinity School explored spiritualist claims in hopes of finding support for his own efforts to make religion an empirical science.[59] Nonetheless, while the number of declared spiritualists did not necessarily decline in the late nineteenth century, their pretensions were taken less seriously. The movement by no means came to an end, but its novelty faded. By the end of the 1870s it was much less important as a widespread cultural phenomenon.

The declining significance of spiritualism to American religious thought can be traced to many factors. For one thing, the major Protestant churches themselves grew more liberal. They avoided the crassness associated with spiritualism by stressing again what had been the original point of liberalism: the belief that the divine voice spoke within every human heart.

For another thing, twenty years of activity had made it clear that spiritualism was not going to gain the scientific credentials it sought. Particularly in the 1870s, when materialization séances became immensely popular, almost every serious investigation uncovered a fresh scandal. The spiritualist press lost all credibility by defending the tricks of the Eddy brothers, J. V. Mansfield, and Henry Slade. In one well-publicized case in 1874, a newspaper reporter actually turned up the paid accomplice that Mr. and Mrs. Holmes of Philadelphia had used in pretending to materialize the spirit of "Katie King." The incident humiliated Robert Dale Owen, whose own favorable account of the Holmeses' séances, appeared in the *Atlantic Monthly* just as their duplicity was exposed.[60]

The climax of the scandals came with the confession of Margaret Fox. In 1888 she told a large audience in New York

City how she and her sisters had produced the raps by cracking their toe joints. The public was no longer interested in her mediumistic displays, but they were willing to pay one last time to find out how they had been gulled.[61]

Other incidents in the late 1870s worked to weaken the influence of spiritualism. The occult Theosophical Society that Madame Blavatsky had founded in 1875 drained away support. More important, the type of educated person who once willingly encouraged spiritualists now wrote them off as hopelessly credulous. While many of these people still called for an inquiry into puzzling phenomena that seemed to violate known scientific laws, they regretted the democracy of spiritualism. They thought that scientific investigation required an elite organization sponsored by recognized men of learning.

In the 1880s, William James talked some of his Harvard colleagues into founding the American Society for Psychical Research. Intended as a new field of scientific experimentation, psychical research was in fact a direct outgrowth of spiritualism.[62] But those who sponsored it believed that if the interests of nineteenth-century spiritualists were going to be carried into the twentieth century, the institutional forms of spirit investigation desperately needed recasting.

This of course was true. The general laxness of organizations promoting spiritualism compromised the movement from the outset. Spiritualism was helpless to police its frauds. Aside from the brief existence of the Society for the Diffusion of Spiritual Knowledge, the only attempt at national organization prior to the 1890s began in the last year of the Civil War. In August 1864, Chicago was the scene of a national spiritualist convention. The National Organization of Spiritualists, as it was called, met for the next several years. Reorganized in 1868 as the American Association of Spiritualists, the organization claimed an affiliation with eighty local churches.[63] The annual conventions did provoke lively debates.

In 1867 Andrew Jackson Davis and his supporters engaged in what finally amounted to a futile attempt to get spiritualists to renounce as fraudulent most of the strictly physical phenomena (i.e. table-lifting, levitating, materialized forms) produced by mediums. During the early 1870s, when Victoria Woodhull presided over the organization, the conventions were especially turbulent. However, almost a decade of national activity amounted to very little. The American Association of Spiritualists expired in 1873 without having in any way addressed the question of who was qualified to speak for spiritualism. A person became a spiritualist lecturer or medium merely by claiming to be one.

In the period after the Civil War, spiritualists did find ways other than national organizations to keep in touch. After 1865 the *Banner of Light* and the *Religio-Philosophical Journal* both exposed their readers to more or less the same religious teachings. Moreover, the various beliefs were reinforced in innumerable meetings—not only in the services of spiritualist churches but also in highly popular one-day excursions and picnics. Camp meetings also provided an important sense of coherence and cohesion. Over a period of weeks and months these meetings brought together a great many spiritualist lecturers and mediums. Some of the camp meetings became permanent sites of spiritualist activity. The most famous of these, the Cassadaga Free Lake Association, was founded in 1879.[64] By 1906, when it was renamed Lily Dale, this eighty-acre site in western New York had several hundred cottages, indoor and outdoor meeting places, a hotel, a store, a post office, and a library.

The National Spiritualist Association, the first permanent national organization, was not established until 1893, well after the period when spiritualism had attracted the most public attention. The NSA, with its headquarters in Washington, D.C., reflected no real enthusiasm for organization. One of its resolutions adopted in 1898 read: "Spiritualism, as a fact, does not depend on organized societies, ordained ministers, or concert of action by its adherents." [65]

The association was largely a response to legal persecution. Mediums, especially during the last few decades of the nineteenth century, were compelled to justify their work as a religious practice of a particular sect or labor under the legal restrictions that were placed on conjurers and fortune-tellers. The NSA, in a half-hearted way, encouraged the ordination of spiritualist lecturers and mediums. Morris Pratt, a wealthy Wisconsin spiritualist, even founded a school for mediums in Whitewater.[66]

Unfortunately, this semblance of a national organization did not solve any problems for spiritualists. Financial support was meager. The pattern of dependence upon private benefactors, which had started in the mid-nineteenth century, was never altered. Marcellus S. Ayer, a wholesale grocer, built a spiritualist church in Boston at a cost of $300,000; and in 1885, he presented it to the Spiritual Fraternal Society of Boston. This was the only spiritualist church structure of any size ever constructed in America. The generosity of spiritualists to their own cause was accurately measured by the support they gave to their fifty-year jubilee held in Rochester: it went $3,000 into debt.[67] At the turn of the century the vast majority of spiritualist church members (about 35,000) met in rented halls or private homes.[68] By 1907 the *Banner of Light* had folded, and the NSA had undergone its first schism, the Progressive Spiritual Church setting itself up as a rival national organization. In 1913 yet another group splintered off, the National Spiritual Alliance.[69] The spirit rappers never swerved more than slightly from their extreme congregational beginnings.

The independence of action that characterized spiritualists, while it originated in a firm belief in the inadequacies of existing human creeds, left spiritualism with few resources by which to sustain itself. Spiritualist religious beliefs satisfied many Americans because they provided definite answers to troubling questions about human destiny. At the same time, spiritualism did not ask very much. It promised "mansions of peace and delight" in the soul world even to those who did not believe in its doctrines.[70] Nothing better summed up one aspect of its appeal than the brief message from the spirit of one John Hubbard: "The yoke of spiritualism is easy and the burden is light, and ye who wear it may find peace in believing and joy in receiving, if ye will cease to do evil and learn to do well." [71]

In a "plain talk" to and about spiritualists, Dean Clark summed up the result of their trying to build a liberal religion among people who did not want to sacrifice anything to a church: "So soon as they become satisfied that there is no death, no eternal hell, no angry God to appease, or vindictive or seductive devil to escape from; so soon as their fears have been quieted . . . and they are required to make effort and use time and means to bring these facts and means before the world, their zeal falls below zero." [72] As we shall see, during its period of greatest influence, the organizational deficiencies of spiritualism weakened its efforts to reform the world even more than its efforts to change the world's religion.

3

The Rise and Fall of Spiritualist Reform

In 1859 Gerrit Smith once again campaigned, as he had done for many years past, on behalf of those politicians who called for the abolition of slavery. Because he believed in spirit communication, he was gratified to find that the spiritualists he met in his travels also shared his views on what was wrong with society. He wrote: "The Spiritualists I met in my tours through the State last fall, were nearly all reformers. . . . I have no doubt that, in proportion to their numbers, Spiritualists cast tenfold as many votes for the Abolition and Temperance tickets as did others." [1]

Their sympathies should not have surprised him. American spiritualist leaders had set out, as we have seen, to liberalize science and religion. Their rhetorical commitment to progressive change in the realm of ideas led naturally to a practical interest in various schemes of social improvement. It was a good thing for the movement that it did. Spiritualism's subsequent association with reform would serve to give it a lot of publicity it might not otherwise have enjoyed.

Before the Civil War, spiritualists gained their most influential defenders from men and women who managed to support the rappers with the same enthusiam they supported Fourierism, temperance, antislavery, health reform, and women's rights. Horace Greeley's *Tribune,* viewed by many as a radical newspaper, quite appropriately gave the Fox sisters their first big publicity break. Concurrently, almost all the prominent abolitionists fell under the spell of spiritualism. William Lloyd Garrison, Joshua Giddings, Benjamin Wade, Henry Wright, and Thomas Wentworth Higginson probably held more common ground on the subject of spirit rappings than on the tactics of combating slavery. Lydia Maria Child, Robert Dale Owen, Adin Ballou, Lorenzo Fowler, and John Edmonds were only some of the other public figures associated with various other causes who saw a clear relationship between spiritualism and the cause of "practical" reform.

According to most historical accounts, once the Civil War ended, American reformers found it far more difficult to keep alive a moral outrage against other social ills similar to that which had finally toppled slavery. Yet in spiritualist literature, this decline was not apparent, and the people who attended the many spiritualist conventions and camp meetings in the late 1860s and early 1870s seemed more willing than ever to declare "their enthusiasm on every question involving the welfare of mankind." Victoria Woodhull, whose radicalism did as much as anyone's to enliven debate on social questions during the inglorious years of Reconstruction, agreed totally with one speaker who called spiritualism "a grand revolutionary movement: a vast scheme for social, political and religious reconstruction; a new dispensation of divine truth and power, for the liberation, civilization and spiritualization of mankind." [2] Herself president of a national spiritualist association, she consistently took up the cause of society's underdogs,* and throughout the 1870s and 1880s, spiritualist editorials argued along with her for fairer treatment of American Indians, the abolition of capital punishment, prison reform, equality for women, higher wages for workers, and the right of labor to organize for cooperative goals. [4]

In nineteenth-century American fiction, the spiritualist me-

* Victoria Woodhull offended Karl Marx with the suggestion that the goals of the International Workingman's Association and the goals of spiritualism were the same. [3] She subsequently managed to offend almost everyone else, including fellow spiritualists, with her championing of free love.

diums who appeared as characters in novels were almost always portrayed as aiding and abetting some radical social cause. Orestes Brownson's *The Spirit Rapper* (1854), Bayard Taylor's *Hannah Thurston: A Story of American Life* (1863), John Hay's *The Breadwinners* (1884), and Henry James's *The Bostonians* (1886) provide the most important examples.[5] The writers who portrayed mediums in this way did not mean to flatter either radicalism or spiritualism, both of which were depicted as mindless and socially disruptive practices; they were simply reproducing what they saw. But spiritualists could at least be grateful, given all their declarations favoring a new era of social harmony, that the connection between rapping and reforming had not been missed. And, more important, that it would be taken seriously.

By establishing "a rational religion in the minds of men, founded upon the operation of Nature's laws," and by waging "an educational warfare upon Ignorance, Superstition and all forms of Supernaturalism," spiritualism, according to many of its leading proponents, automatically allied itself "with all genuine reforms looking to the betterment of social conditions of humanity." [6]

Rhetoric can of course be deceiving. So can a long list of specific individuals who devoted themselves with equal enthusiasm to spiritualism and to social reform. Harrison D. Barrett, who at the end of the century served both as president of the National Spiritualist Association and as editor of the *Banner of Light*, expressed some reservations about just how much spiritualism had contributed to the great cause of rejuvenating human society. "Spiritualism," he wrote, "has done many things for the world, but it has done them in spite of many of the Spiritualists, and not with and through their aid." [7] This was only a few years after he had delivered the following brave words to delegates at an annual NSA convention: "We shall work together for the purpose of showing the world that Spiritualism is the greatest reform movement that has ever blessed mankind." [8]

Many people, Barrett knew, flirted with spiritualism at one time or another for reasons that had nothing to do with the plight of the poor. The private messages of consolation received at small séances usually contained no mention of general humanitarian concerns. As critics of the movement had already noted, the average spirit who appeared at a séance more than likely proved to be much more adept at flinging around calla lillies than at throwing loaves of bread to starving families. [9]

Be that as it may, spiritualists who in the nineteenth century took the "philosophy" of their movement seriously did regard themselves as reformers. And many American reformers who had been fighting social injustice long before they attended a séance came to regard the rappers as brothers and sisters engaged in a common struggle. One cannot of course estimate how many believers in spirit communication paid attention to the reform issues discussed in spiritualist publications. And one cannot be sure that reformers who grew interested in the possibility of receiving spirit messages always saw a connection between the activity of making the world better and that of investigating mediums. Even if they said they did, one is left wondering whether spiritualist ideas had any significant impact on the reformers' attitude toward reform.

Despite these difficulties, the evidence does make it clear that the connection between spiritualists and certain kinds of reformers was not accidental. Spiritualism was born between two traditions of American reform: an antebellum push for the immediate purification of the nation's morals and a less hurried postwar drive that utilized Darwinian evolution as the key metaphor of social improvement.

In the early 1850s this midpoint position was nicely illustrated in the way announcements of the sudden outburst of spirit communications mixed together a dramatic view of a new age derived from popular millennial tracts with a more evolutionary and gradualist view of progress. Spiritualists eventually emphasized the latter more than the former, and the shift had important consequences for spiritualist reform endeavors. But there is no doubt that throughout the last half of the nineteenth century, spiritualist publications consistently recognized and lent whatever prestige they had to movements for change, and on that basis alone, spiritualists were within their rights in claiming a place within the shifting currents of American re-

form. In addition, because the currents of reform did not necessarily flow within the American mainstream, spiritualists and
reformers often shared a common pariah status that gave them a
strong sense of mission. They developed almost ritualized patterns of rhetoric to emphasize a common martyrdom that their
destinies forced upon them.

By the end of the nineteenth century, spiritualism had lost all
credibility as a reform movement. Those who continued to hold
a strong commitment to reform left the movement and spiritualist societies grew increasingly conservative.[10] The social indifference that would characterize twentieth-century spiritualist
churches was perhaps inevitable given the fact that nineteenth-
century spiritualist leaders never understood the many contradictions in their thinking about social change. While they carried over into the postwar era an aversion to forcing people to
be good, they ignored many of the supporting ideas that justified the anti-institutional and antipolitical spirit of antebellum
reform.

In the end, their very general philosophic ideas were not
adaptable to the type of pragmatic political and professional
reforms beginning around the turn of the century that would
guide the most creative thinking during the American Progressive Era. Nevertheless, the efforts of spiritualist reformers
should be chronicled. If their ideas about social betterment remained muddled during the nineteenth century, they were
doing no worse than many other reformers who have received
far more attention from historians. Their shortcomings should
not lead us to think that they did not accurately reflect some important attitudes within their culture.

We must begin our analysis with an examination of the goals
of antebellum reform, for that historical context also shaped the
attitudes of spiritualist leaders toward reform. William Lloyd
Garrison was one of the most influential and historically significant of these antebellum reformers; he would also, in time, take
an interest in spiritualism. An examination of his values, then,
may tell us something both about that larger historical context
and about spiritualism's place within it. Garrison was a universal reformer, a Christian nonresistant, and a militant abolition-

ist. Nothing was more important in the formation of his ideas than his upbringing in a strict traditional Christian pietism.[11] As a child he learned, and he subsequently never forgot, that sin was a damning thing. Because slavery was a sin and invited God's terrible judgment, Garrison learned to hate it. Because the Constitution and the Union compromised themselves in complicity with that sin, he came to hate them as well. Garrison's contemporaries called him a radical, and most historians have found the label appropriate.

In the 1830s Garrison's ideas rather quickly lost the basis they originally had had in Calvinist orthodoxy. He came under the influence of the Christian Perfectionism of John Humphrey Noyes and adopted the antinomian position that man's personal relationship to God transcended both church and biblical authority. His belief that people could accomplish a perfect and immediate break with sin increased his sense of urgency in calling for the emancipation of the slaves. At the same time, it drove him away from politics or any use of force as a means to accomplish his goal.[12]

The problem of evil, Garrison believed, resided in the human heart, not in the institutions that had molded the heart. Hence the tactics of Christian pacifism, which he adopted, began and ended with a self-righteous and unrelenting moral assault upon those who refused to follow divine truth. To most later reformers, and to most of his fellow abolitionists, Garrison's tactics seemed willfully unrealistic, but Garrison thought Perfectionism the most practical of goals. He perhaps never grew so hopeful as to expect Southern slaveholders to fall suddenly on their knees and renounce their sin. As a first step toward a moral suasion that would ultimately be effective upon the South, he did believe that Northerners must recognize their own culpability in maintaining ties to the South and with that recognition he hoped they would renounce them.

By 1850 Garrison's religious views differed in many particulars from spiritualist teachings. Nonetheless, the liberal orientation of Garrison's theology made him thoroughly sympathetic to the spirit of independent inquiry adopted by spiritualists. He was at one with them in regarding the true mission of religion as "practical reform"—a phrase absolutely central to the vocabulary of nineteenth-century reformers. On some specific points Garrison held ideas that were at least similar to positions being put forth in the spiritualist press. For example, the doctrine of eternal and inevitable moral progression sustained his own attitude toward Perfectionism. He approved of the spiritualists' emphasis upon the responsibility individuals bore for their own improvement, and both he and the rappers played down the need for reliance on scripture or church discipline.

Garrison found in the spiritualist camp a host of men and women who shared his aversion to the use of laws, institutions, and force as instruments to make people better. On this point, the pipeline from the spirit world in the 1850s carried a consistent message: "Compulsory measures are dangerous weapons." [13] According to the spiritualist medium Emma Hardinge, all reform programs, including spiritualism, had to focus on the improvement of individual character: "If this great movement should succeed in preparing the atom for a worthy and final aggregation into the mass of humanity, it will be found to have effected a far more valuable and efficient reform than any which attempts to deal with mankind by wholesale, and converts masses, whose atoms contain the seeds of corruption and decay." [14] Not all spiritualists were pacifists, but most spiritualist publications advocated nonviolence up until the very eve of the Civil War. Until Lincoln asked for a declaration of war, they supported a policy of letting the seceding states go in peace. [15]

The reluctance of spiritualist leaders to use force on the wrongdoer derived from a general Emersonian aversion to association and a belief that in the dawning new age all the old institutions were corrupt. "It is a great error," read an editorial in the *Banner of Light* three years before the Civil War, "and a popular one, that there is nothing like association to carry forward any reform, or to advance any measure that ends in the development of the soul." [16]

Some reformers who accepted spiritualism, just like some spiritualists who promoted reform, carried that idea further than others did. Garrison's tactical nonresistance was at odds with the ideas that led Gerrit Smith to organize the Liberty party or Adin Ballou to lead a communal experiment at Milford, Massachusetts. Yet the latter two found, as readily as Garrison had, something in spirtualist teachings to bolster their own particular ideal of free association. Aside from encouraging millennial expectations, the spirit messages approved the break many antebellum reformers had made with what they considered to be illegitimate church discipline. Through the spiritualist movement of the 1850s, a number of reformers continued a process, which they had begun long before, of self-purification through antiorthodox engagement. [17]

However, while spiritualist publications did successfully appeal to the sentiments of many people who wanted to purify and transform America, there were some problems. Spiritualism, reflecting transitions in thought during the period it first became important, suffered from certain doubts about just how rapidly the world might be changed. Compared with most of the other would-be regenerative movements that proliferated in the years before the Civil War, spiritualism was a latecomer. It emerged as a widespread public phenomenon well over two decades after Robert Owen founded New Harmony. It trailed by about as many years the first appearance of Garrison's *The Liberator*. As Whitney Cross argued some years ago, spiritualism appeared after the religious enthusiasm of the antebellum period had abandoned its original biblical outlook. [18] And the enthusiasm had cooled along the way.

The effects of late arrival were not all detrimental to the ardor for reform. In the early 1850s many of America's millennialist reformers saw the raps as signs of a prophecy heralding the beginnings of an age of perfect human brotherhood. By that time their reform expectations needed all the help they could get. And despite the many things spiritualists said denying special providence, they did not object to interpretations of the sudden plethora of spirit voices as examples of special providence. To them, and to many abolitionists, temperance crusaders, and utopian colonists, the séance manifestations had portentous significance for modern times. "Nothing," one spiritualist wrote, "can avert the universal hurricane of which the murky air has for sixty years (and now each day and hour more emphatically) gives note of unmistakable protent. And what better evidence can a loving man want to convince him of the infinitely wise goodness of the Divine Providence that the normal and most quiet introduction of these spiritual facts and processes as this juncture furnishes?" [19]

On the other hand, there was a tone in these statements that suggested less-than-fervent conviction. Spiritualists tried very hard to give a fresh face to the proposition that mankind was approaching a decisive point of transformation. But they did not succeed in making reform sound all that urgent. Their antidogmatic theology was in part to blame.

If the liberal outlook of spiritualism proved compatible with the tactics Garrison advocated to abolish slavery, it was not because the two movements shared the common ground of similar philosophies. In fact, it was just the opposite. Although the radical reformers of the antebellum period sought to move beyond biblical Christianity and Calvinism toward a rational and noncreedal religious position, this was not what brought out the uncompromising immediatism stressed in their demands, especially those of the Garrisonian abolitionists. These attitudes grew out of a very literal belief in Christian perfectionism, Christian millennialism, and a Christian concept of damnable sin. No spiritualist seemed to fear, as Garrison once did, that a society permitting slavery was in danger of going to Hell.

In the 1830s, as David B. Davis has demonstrated, the abolitionists' acceptance of the demand of immediate emancipation signified their own immediate spiritual transformation and purification. It was their badge of conversion. [20] By contrast in 1852 a spiritualist medium forwarded to William Lloyd Garrison a message counseling gradualism. It supposedly came from the spirit of Nathaniel P. Rogers, a man who in his earthly life had strongly advocated immediatism. "While I still loathe," the message read, "the hideous form of slavery, it appears to me now that that gradual emancipation, which must come through the operation of the love principle upon the hearts of all, is far better than to *force* the master—even by words—to relax his grasp upon the heart of his victim, by clutching his own throat; for while, in this case, I could rejoice in the escape of the slave, I should be compelled to weep for the transfer of the same condition to the master, who then becomes a *slave* to the power which *compels* him to release his slave." [21]

The spirit of Rogers argued for gradualism because it no longer believed in sin. As we have seen, the idea of human sinlessness, a belief distinguishable from Garrison's notion that some people might purify themselves by their actions, became very popular among spiritualists in the 1850s. Andrew Jackson Davis, who was as important as any of spiritualism's moral instructors, regarded both sin and evil as illusory.[22] Certainly in his mind personal sin did not form the root of social injustice. There were in this world, as in the next, people whose lives reflected greater and lesser degrees of moral advancement. But at any point in time the spiritual state of each person was in exactly the shape it should have been. No two people followed the same pattern of development.

Spiritualists envisioned a universe without an avenging God. There was nothing to avenge, for man had never fallen. In the history of the human race and in the lives of individuals, one could never speak of regression—only eternal moral advancement. In trying to work out the implications of a world in which nothing was out of harmony with what was intended, the spiritualist writer A. B. Child praised the person "who sees no evil" as the person who best aids the cause of progress." [23]

Nothing could have been further removed from the ideas that motivated the most militant abolitionists and temperance leaders. In stark contrast to them, influential spiritualists avoided making self-righteous proclamations that drew absolutely clear-cut distinctions between good and evil. Like many other antebellum reformers, they regarded individuals as the primary vehicle of their own moral advancement. Their particular attitude toward progress, however, led them to view human weakness without moral outrage.

The best result of this outlook was a tolerant compassion. Spiritualists were not at all certain that as a group they were more moral than other people. However, in losing a passion to hate the evil it seeks to eradicate, they also lost a good deal. What could lead to tolerance could also generate social indifference. It could also result in a body of teachings that was hopelessly ill equipped to challenge the abuses of a new industrial order that would become dominant in America during the late nineteenth century.

As we have seen, one of the chief attitudes that spiritualists inherited from the antebellum reformers was a strong belief in the sanctity of individual conscience. Not wishing to force rectitude on people, including those who had joined a spiritualist society, most spiritualists answered the problem of authority with a mild form of anarchism. Within their own circles, they rarely passed a resolution of any kind without adding that it was of course not binding on anyone who did not like it. While most paid their taxes and did not challenge the legitimacy of existing governments, their vision of what the social order might someday become included a community of freely associating individuals. The future order would grow from the steadily widening influence of small circles of congenial spirits who had been drawn together by the law of affinity. "We shall come together," went one message, "in obedience to the common law of social attraction; we shall blend by the power of a moral cohesion, and the more subtle chemistry of our spiritual life." [24]

Spiritualism's challenge to authority neglected some central attitudes that had informed antebellum reform, and the absence of these views from spiritualist rhetoric had important consequences. In the antebellum period the revolt of many radical reformers against traditional institutions began with the assertion that over the individual soul only God was sovereign. In the minds of these radicals, Christian pietism, sometimes mixed with Transcendentalism, produced the axiom that man's relation to God was a private, devotional matter open to no one else's scrutiny. This freedom from coercion was to apply to saints and sinners alike, but saints had a special obligation to stay clear of restraining forces that were not of their own making. Persons who had perfected their own faith and had ceased to commit offenses against God had an absolute duty to reject authority threatening to compromise their moral purity. The discipline imposed by governments, political parties, and churches were at best irrelevant, and at worst dangerous, to persons engaged in the enterprise of purifying their souls.

The spirit of come-outerism, one of the most striking manifestations of antebellum reform, strongly affected the spiritualist movement, but in a guise that was mostly devoid of religious fervor. In accepting the Perfectionist notion that people could avoid sin, spiritualists did so less out of a belief that God had led some men into the paths of righteousness (or would soon lead all men) than out of the sense that people worried too much about the supposed evil of human beings. An anti-institutionalism based on Christian Perfectionism could justify itself because of the present possibility of the individual approaching moral purity. Spiritualists who joined communitarian societies and some others in the movement who believed in the near arrival of a new moral world talked in such terms. Mostly, however, the consideration of relative degrees of righteousness was irrelevant to their suspicion of authority. It did not matter whether individuals were particularly good or even whether they yet had a very clear idea of what goodness was all about. To justify their belief that the highest form of government was interior, spiritualists simply pointed to the fact that people would improve if left to themselves. No one, therefore, not even a spiritualist, was surprised that spiritualism frequently became a refuge for unsavory characters who were looking for some kind of shadowy sanction to justify the deceits they habitually practiced.

The spiritualist protest against "all combinations, societies, churches, sects, associations, phalanxes, etc. which swamp individuality, and constrain the freedom of its expression" recalled some aspects of Enlightenment thought and veered into a strictly secular liberalism that did not always in the nineteenth century prove useful in promoting the specific reform goals spiritualists espoused.[25] Their weak associations, including those composed of people supposedly drawn together simply by the law of affinities, aspired neither to moral authority nor to political power. On the eve of the Civil War the following appeared in the *Banner of Light:* "No man is responsible for his neighbor; he is responsible, first and last, for himself; . . . Every person ought to resolve to stay at home with himself; what he has in surplus, he will give forth imperceptibly and naturally to those who happen to be in want; and he will impart it much more acceptably, and therefore effectively, by not interposing his own momentary feelings of pride, or his always ambitious will." [26] For a journal that taught that the natural goodness of people still had a long way to develop, it was a curious counsel of inactivism.

Spiritualist reform thought ran into even more difficulties after the Civil War. The great appeal after the Civil War of the concept of evolutionary, though not necessarily Darwinian, progression was in direct conflict with Christian millennialism, but it sat quite well with the gradualist side of spiritualist doctrine. Andrew Jackson Davis readily incorporated the phrase "survival of the fittest" into his vocabulary. [27] Because spiritualists regarded "the future as but a continuation of present individual life," they simply extended the time necessary to gain human perfection indefinitely. [28] But the effect was again to strip reform of any urgency. The secular aspects of spiritualism encouraged human beings to better their society, but gave them considerably more time than that allowed by the impatient Jehovah of earlier American Perfectionists. After the Civil War, spiritualists had to wonder whether their evolutionary doctrines could lead anywhere other than to the Social Darwinist conclusions of William Graham Sumner. There were aspects of spiritualist teaching that left in serious doubt whether the reformer, once he understood the natural laws of evolution, was left with a positive function to perform.

Spiritualist teachings about the inevitable moral progress of the human soul often rested on some doctrine of necessity. Andrew Jackson Davis quite explicitly rejected any notion of human free will. "But I tell you," he wrote, "that man *is not free,*—he is not free even to choose, except so far as his faculties are cultured to see, and his heart is intuitive to understand; but such culture and such intuition, for the most part, are effects of his inheritance, and of his surrounding circumstances." [29]

In making this argument, Davis intended to lessen the blame that attached to humans for making unavoidably wrong choices. Emphasizing guilt, Davis said, could never promote a sympathetic understanding between people or extend the spirit of charity in the world. However, for all the intended benevolence, Davis left unclear how his doctrine of necessity left room for humanly concocted schemes to make the world a better place, or for that matter how it meshed with the spiritualist belief in individual responsibility for self-improvement. If human intervention, no more than divine intervention, had much to do with the course of evolution, then could any endeavor speed up the process of human improvement? Apparently the spiritualist writer A. B. Child did not think so. At least he argued that no human action of any kind could make the soul better or worse.[30]

To be sure, not all spiritualists talked about necessity, and those who did were cosmic optimists. Davis rested content with the notion that "man is not the creator of the inexorable laws of his being" because he believed that those "inexorable laws" could only push the individual upward.[31] All the same, his belief cast into doubt the role of the reformer. How was such a doctrine to avoid a fatalistic sociology, one that urged people to get in tune with their destiny rather than trying to affect it? The logical conclusion of this particular line of spiritualist reasoning was that individuals should be left alone to develop according to inner laws. It did not lend obvious support to a reform mood—not in any case the one that began after the Civil War to suggest a greater role for the government in bringing about a better society. Davis's "inexorable laws" guaranteed progress, but they set clear limits on human control over that progress.

A balanced assessment of spiritualist reform activities during the final three decades of the nineteenth century is difficult to make. On the negative side, there are many points to enumerate. For all the reasons that have been mentioned, and despite their popular image as radicals, spiritualist leaders were guilty of talking more than they acted. Even in the area where for the longest time they made the strongest commitment—women's rights—their declarations made little impact on the general public. A number of feminists, including Susan B. Anthony, Elizabeth Cady Stanton, and Francis Willard, were interested in spiritualism. But they never publicly identified themselves with the movement or stressed a linkage between the two causes.[32] The only feminist who did was Victoria Woodhull, and she proved to be too much of an activist for most other spiritualist reformers.

While in the early 1870s she was elected president of a national spiritualist association three times—something that would certainly have been impossible in any other American religious organization in the 1870s—she received little support for her radicalism in the spiritualist press. Her presidency in fact precipitated so serious a rift in the spiritualist camp that it destroyed the only national organization spiritualists had formed up until then.

The suspicion with which spiritualist leaders continued to view coercive measures left them in something of a quandary about what stand to take on reform proposals requiring government intervention. The ideas of many spiritualists never broke out of laissez-faire formulations. Giles Stebbins, for example, had gone around the country in the period before the Civil War lecturing on behalf of spiritualism, abolition, and temperance. After the war he did not cease to lecture or to urge reform, but he could imagine no way to effect social improvement other than hard work and thrift on the part of individuals. The only demand he made of government was to keep trade free. While he could see much wrong with the world, the leadership of men like U. S. Grant, Andrew Carnegie, and Leland Stanford made him sanguine about the future. To Stebbins, they symbolized dynamic progress and the triumph of individual will over social inertia.[33]

On the one hand, the spiritualist press in the late nineteenth century never stopped urging a greater social justice for Indians, wage earners, and women. On the other, it rarely made legislative proposals, and it never backed political candidates. With respect to most specific reform proposals made in the late nineteenth century, it said next to nothing. These would include demands for government control over interstate commerce rates, for an income tax, and for antitrust legislation. The Lyceum schools that spiritualists promoted in their own societies were about as far as they ever got in making a concrete application of their reform ideas.

Andrew Jackson Davis and several other leading mediums made these schools a favorite project after the Civil War. Progressive in intent, they sought to avoid the "stuffing method" of other educational procedures. Spiritualist exponents of the Lyceums argued against the view of education as "principally the acquisition of knowledge" and "the learning of the thoughts of others," and worked for instruction based on the attitude that each person had his own spiritual potential which should be allowed to develop in its own way at its own pace. "Unlike St. Paul's plan, it seeks neither to conform nor to 'transform' the child, already claimed to be 'created in the image of God,' into the likeness of Christ, or any other being, but, on the contrary, to give the best possible unfoldment of *its* divine nature." [34]

The virtues the Lyceum method sought to bring out proved to be traditional ones—purity, chastity, temperance, honesty—but it tried to recognize the fixed natural limits in each person. Consistent with spiritualist ideas about reform, it sought not a forced conformity but the removal of artificial encumbrances to individual development. It sought to ensure human betterment by sharply restricting the areas in which one human being could legitimately interfere in the life of another. Unfortunately, America in the late nineteenth century proved to be a discouraging place for humanitarian reformers who counted on the natural emergence of a spirit of social harmony.

Spiritualists, in their role as reformers just as in the role of church builders, found it difficult in the late nineteenth century to interest those who came to them for their own personal problems in programs to help others. More than anything else, spiritualism carried a message of personal consolation. John Shoebridge Williams, an ex–civil engineer and road builder, took his troubles to his everlastingly understanding spirit voices for over fifteen years. "Is it not a consolation," he wrote, "for a man of my years and sensibilities, who has been as much misunderstood as I have been, to find he is better understood by spirits and angels than by men?" [35] People seeking personal reassurance were not, as it turned out, easily interested in social protest.

Emma Hardinge tried for years to raise among spiritualists enough money to build a home for "fallen women." It seemed to her the least one could expect from people who deplored the low legal status of women and who professed a brotherly identification with criminals and other outcast people. Hardinge, of course, never got close to her goal.[36] The ease with which spiritualists' hopes for general social betterment could be ignored even by those who faithfully read spiritualist publications bothered spiritualist leaders. But there was little to be done. For all too many of its adherents, the only interesting things about spiritualism were the manifestations.

Another hindrance to the effectiveness of spiritualist reform appeals lay in the very concrete references spiritualists made to the comforts of the next life. Spiritualism, despite the interest it generated in a life after death, was not necessarily otherworldly in its outlook. It too closely defined the spheres of the afterlife in terms of what went on here. The people who contacted the spirits of the dead were in no particular hurry to join them. Yet spiritualism did portray a heaven where the injustices of unequal earthly existence were corrected. There would be not only enough but plenty for all. Without question many of the people of low social status who joined spiritualist churches did so not because they expected advancement in their life on Earth but because they hoped for it after death.

Andrew Jackson Davis warned that an exclusive concern with the displays of mediums took people's eyes off this world. Like "effete forms of Christianity," spirit manifestations turned men and women dreamily toward a "far-off" land and discouraged work toward the elevation of human society.[37] J. H. Hyslop, whose contributions to spiritualism and psychical research will be discussed in a later chapter, was not altogether sure that Davis was right. At least he saw no harm in furnishing the poor with the knowledge that what could not be provided in this life would materialize in the next: "We who have our livings guaranteed and who have aristocratic society for our enjoyment may well be indifferent to the hope of a future existence. . . .

But 'the dull millions that toil foredone at the wheel of labor' and have no rest or culture . . . must always invite the sympathy of the humane; and when no physical help is possible, the hope of another life . . . may temper one's moralities to the harsh treatment of nature, and mollify the passionate cry of injustice." [38] Hyslop could hardly have explained more precisely, though unwittingly, why Marxists regarded religion as an opiate.

The fine line between gradual meliorism and social indifference was in post–Civil War America almost impossible to hold in view. Spiritualists were, in the end, like most other people in their less-than-total commitment to humanitarian causes. Nor were spiritualists alone among Americans in coming to understand practical reform as technological innovation rather than a greater social justice or a more moral community. Yet it was in failing to maintain a difference between themselves and other people that spiritualists missed their greatest opportunities. Too frequently spiritualists came to regard the mechanical inventions whispered into the ears of mediums as the highest expression of practical endeavor. J. M. Peebles, one of the better-known spiritualist lecturers, wrote, according to his biographer, "a sparkling pamphlet" entitled "The Practical of Spiritualism: a Biographical Sketch of Abraham James, and Historical Description of his Oil-Well Discoveries in Pleasantville, Pa., through Spirit Direction." It contained, in the biographer's assessment, "a happy blending of the spiritual with the practical, demonstrating that the spiritual philosophy is destined to open up the hidden wealth of earth in mines, oils, gases, plants, jewels, and be, in the hands of inventors and mechanics, the science and rule of new improvements in human industries." [39] Peebles's concern for human betterment was genuine, but his spirit was entrepreneurial.

The Oneida Community was one of the most long-lived of the nineteenth-century utopian ventures. Founded in the antebellum period by the ultraist Christian Perfectionist John Humphrey Noyes, Oneida thrived for two decades on a strong sense of religious mission. A more secular socialist justification of the communal venture did not overtake the enterprise until the 1870s. Following that change, Oneida, at least in its strictly communal aspects, began to flounder. Secularism, it might be noted, would have the same impact on many other nineteenth-century utopias.[40]

By the end of the 1870s the residents of Oneida had replaced the original government with a corporate charter. Another manifestation of the growing secularism at Oneida was the spreading interest in spiritualism among the members, a subject Noyes had originally dismissed as unworthy of interest.[41] Spiritualism was not the cause of the demise of Oneida, although it is true that when the spiritualists took over the management of Oneida's successful industries, they almost drove them into bankruptcy. Still, the conclusion that an interest in spiritualism fed on the discouragement of reformers does suggest itself. Perhaps it was appropriate that a movement dedicated to the demonstration of life after death should attach itself to a reform movement at the moment it showed signs of dying.

None of these harsh judgments can obliterate entirely the positive role spiritualism played in maintaining the interest of many Americans in reform. Given all the reasons why spiritualist leaders might have begun to ignore social questions (as they now do in the twentieth century), their loyalty to the idea of a better society in the nineteenth century deserves more than a small measure of admiration. However ineffectual their "practical" endeavors, the visions spiritualists entertained of a better and radically different social order did cast into doubt the legitimacy of existing social arrangements. Many spiritualists may have subscribed to the theory of evolutionary change and to the advice that "the happiness of man does not depend upon political changes, revolutions or any other social modifications." [42] But consistently or inconsistently they picked out elements in the social environment retarding the development of the soul and called for their elimination. Davis and others saved their philosophy from social fatalism by recognizing the impact of the social environment on individual growth. That fact encouraged some spiritualists to argue for collective action to change the environment, though of course they tried always to respect the principle of voluntarism.

Despite spiritualism's emphasis upon individual and voluntary action, a few post–Civil War reformers who argued for increased government regulation found spirit communication an exciting prospect. One of these reformers was Lester Ward. While working for the Treasury Department after the Civil War, he visited almost every medium who passed through Washington.[43] The spirit manifestations still seemed novel to him. If real (and he was never convinced that they were), they signified a breakthrough in human knowledge that would have repercussions in every corner of social life.

Interest both in spiritualism and in a "dynamic sociology" also manifested itself in the coterie of Boston reformers who gathered around B. O. Flower's *Arena* magazine in the 1890s.[44] Flower, Hamlin Garland, Minot J. Savage, and Margaret Déland all became convinced of the spiritual origin of the psychic phenomena they so avidly investigated. Garland followed mediums around for the rest of his life and wrote far more about them than about the "main-traveled roads" with which he is more closely identified.[45] These Bostonians contributed articles on reform to *Arena* and articles on spirit communication to the lesser-known *Psychical Review.* Frequently they combined the two subjects. Spiritualism struck them as a perfectly natural ally in their efforts to awaken Americans to the ruinous effects of unregulated industrial development.

Though spiritualist reformers made many mistakes, they did not regard poverty as a blessing and test of human fortitude. "Brutalizing toil," one spiritualist wrote, "leaves no opportunity for soul-development, but instead dwarfs and cripples the spiritual in man." [46] Although most spiritualist teachings emphasized that "the discipline of personal character is the first and constant duty of every reformer," spiritualists showed surprisingly little interest in late-nineteenth-century campaigns to make society better by improving its leadership.[47]

Spiritualist spokesmen remained indifferent to Civil Service legislation. Their dogged championship of the outcasts of society made issues that excited "Mugwump" Republicans seem irrelevant to them. The reform issues to which they addressed themselves concerned social equalization. That was natural.

Like the people whose cause they sought to defend, spiritualists were not quite respectable. They certainly wanted respectability, and they frequently laid a claim to it. However, while they had important defenders, they could not prevent society from labeling them eccentric, which hurt their pride but made them better reformers. Thomas Wentworth Higginson surely had them in mind when he wrote: "This tendency of every reform to surround itself with a fringe of the unreasonable and half-cracked is really to its credit. . . . Without a little crack somewhere, a man could hardly do his duty to the times." [48]

Higginson's point suggests a different perspective on this whole subject. The common bond that turned spiritualists into reformers and reformers into spiritualists, both before and after the Civil War, appeared in many cases to be a shared sense of martyrdom. A belief in the otherwordly origin of spirit voices and the defense of an unpopular reform had one thing in common in the nineteenth century: they were both likely to get people into trouble with their neighbors. Suffering for one's ideas created a sense of community among apostates and gave importance to the thing being done. Spiritualist "outsiders" often pursued with great relish reform activities that led to increasingly severe feelings of estrangement from normative society. They certainly mentioned estrangement in their publications over and over again. Spiritualists did not find the labels "free lover" and "labor radical" any more damning than the epithets "fraud" and "fool," to which they had grown accustomed. In a similar way, the additional respectability an abolitionist or a communal socialist lost in courting mediums was marginal.

The self-portrayals of three reformers who became spiritualists may convey something more specific about the point suggested here. The careers of these three men began in the antebellum period, but the tendencies of each to emphasize self-sacrifice and to boast of social ostracism were also common in spiritualist reformers after the Civil War. Eventually, of course, spiritualist reform rhetoric lacked the intensity to promote any real enthusiasm for martyrdom. At that point, some time between 1880 and 1900, spiritualist churches began to discourage proselytizing.

Warren Chase wrote two autobiographies, one entitled *The Life-Line of the Lone One* and the other, less plaintively, *Forty Years on the Spiritual Rostrum.*[49] Together they comprised Chase's plea for the pity of posterity and a defense of his bravery in the face of relentless persecution. Born an illegitimate child, before reaching the age of five he was left "fatherless, motherless, penniless, friendless, worthless, useless." Things did not get better fast. The town of his birth, finding itself with a foundling charge, sold him out to a farmer who was, according to Chase, "one of the most cruel and cold-hearted masters." He later fell into a family of Universalists who treated him better and exposed him to about as much theology as he was ever to master. Yet, according to Chase's account, throughout his childhood he led a rootless life that left him always without a home.

Having no settled convictions, he was as a young man susceptible to a number of new movements. Well before the Fox sisters publicized the spirit rappings, he had looked into phrenology and mesmerism. He read Swedenborg and LaRoy Sunderland and wrote for *The Univercoelum,* the first journal associated with the teachings of Andrew Jackson Davis. He even tried his hand at organizing a Fourierist phalanx, which soon collapsed, much to the relief of his wife.[50]

For a time, none of Chase's activities adversely affected what in the late 1840s was becoming a normal political career. A Democrat, he was in 1847 elected to the Wisconsin Constitutional Convention, where he fought against capital punishment, legal discrimination against women, land monopoly, soft money, and all laws for the collection of debt. However, after one elected term in Wisconsin's first state senate, he had no further success in politics. He blamed his subsequent defeats on the unpopularity of his ideas. At home he was getting little support, for his wife expected him to be like other men and invent schemes to get rich. Chase's autobiographies depict that nagging woman as one of the great trials of his unsuccessful political years and as a major source of his increasing sense of isolation. In the interest of spiritual betterment he quite suddenly announced to her one day his intention to end marital "carnal relations"—a step he recounted in his autobiography in the same sentence as his decision to follow a new dietary reform.[51]

Chase understood that the pattern of his adult life was leading the society around him to regard him as peculiar. Such estrangement, he claimed, was the burden of any reformer who chose to make an example of his life. Chase's political disappointment preceded by only a few years the rise of spiritualism, a cause whose truth he immediately recognized. In directing his future reform energies through that movement, Chase found justification for a life that even his wife had written off as a failure.

From the early spirit messages he received, "he discovered the cause of his abandoning every field of labor where worldly honor and distinction was before him, and success almost certain, and the reason why he had let every opportunity to acquire wealth escape him, even when he knew it was within his reach by honorable means. Now he saw why he *must* be poor and full of human love." In this case, the desire for consolation and the desire to reform went hand in glove. Taught that his mission was to preach the true gospel of the new age, Chase was not embarrassed to compare himself to Christ. In 1851, "boldly, fearlessly, he took his staff and travelled on, lecturing . . . picking up here and there a few dimes, about equal to his expenses in amount, as the voluntary contributions of hearers or friends." Unquestionably Chase regarded the abuse that he received in preaching the message of spiritualism as a sort of crucifixion. For the "lone one," it became his most important source of self-esteem.[52]

In John Murray Spear we encounter an even more extreme case of a man whose spiritualism encouraged a social isolation and a peculiar set of ideas concerning reform. Spear was born in Boston in 1804. His parents named their son after the founder of the American branch of the Universalist church, John Murray. Losing his father while a child, Spear was reared under difficult economic circumstances by his widowed mother and paternal grandparents. As an adolescent he worked in a cotton factory and got only a rudimentary education. Despite that handicap, by 1830 he had become a Universalist minister with a church in

Barnstable, Massachusetts, and was happily married to a woman socially above him. Nothing at that point in his life hinted at the utopian questing that marked his later career.[53]

Spear's first break with respectability came with abolitionism. By the late 1830s he had become a man very much like Garrison, one who could not await "the moving of the custom-bound, popularity-seeking, fold enchained souls." His abolitionist views moved well ahead of those of his congregation, and by the late 1840s he had lost his church at Barnstable and later ones at New Bedford and Weymouth. He had even less luck persuading the general public to accept his views than he had had with his congregations. Among other things, in 1844 Spear was severely beaten by a crowd of men who objected to his speech on behalf of abolition. One year later he decided, despite the need to support a growing number of children, to devote himself full time to the cause of reform.

Even more than abolitionism, he became identified with the crusade to better the condition of prison inmates. Spear's visits to prisoners turned him into a critic of the justice his society meted out. They also encouraged him to identify himself with the social outcast. As a reformer he gained a reputation for working alone. In explaining his reason for refusing official appointments he said: "Should I become the agent of the State, visit prisons and courts under its direction, then I fear that demands would be made upon me for aid. I should lose all my moral power, and become impotent for good." [54]

Before 1851 and his conversion to spiritualism, Spear's reform activities had forced him into unpleasant public confrontations, but they had also received support. After the spirit voices revealed to him his mission as a spirit medium and healer, the support dwindled. He found himself more often than before a target of both scorn and ridicule. Spear's guardian spirits were not shy about delivering messages. Nor was Spear hesitant, in contrast to most other spiritualists, in treating his messages from such men as Daniel Webster, Thomas Jefferson, and Benjamin Franklin as detailed guides to specific action. In 1853, according to one biographical source, Spear's hand was involuntarily moved to write "a document announcing to himself and the world the hitherto unhinted facts, that an association had been formed in the spirit world for the purpose of accomplishing on this earth certain specified beneficent ends." The instructions of this "Association of Beneficents" ultimately filled thousands of pages.[55] While the shift in Spear's career left him with few followers, the course of his life, which for over a decade had been shifting away from conventional ideas of success, had never in his mind been clearer.

The rest of Spear's career reads like burlesque. The spirits dictated that he abandon his wife for the companionship of a female amanuensis. In the mid-1850s he founded the Harmonia Community near the Kiantone Creek in western New York. The colonists were to renounce property, live in octagonal houses, drink water from springs certified as magic by Spear's spirit controls, and look for buried treasure. Just before that enterprise got off to an unpromising start, Spear conducted the experiment that would become, among all his attempts to demonstrate the practicality of spiritualism, the most publicized.

Prompted by a group in the spirit world that styled itself the "Association of Electric-Izers," Spear set out to astound America by constructing a spirit-designed perpetual motion machine. It aroused no end of curiosity, especially when one of Spear's female disciples consented to serve as the "Mary of the New Dispensation" and in ways not clearly specified contrived to impart life to Spear's contraption. There was disagreement as to how well the machine worked. One spiritualist went to the site of the construction at Lynn, Massachusetts, and left saying that it couldn't so much as turn a coffee mill.[56] While Spear insisted that it had moved out of its own self-generated power, even he expressed disappointment that the new life force had at most kept the machine going for only a few seconds.

Spear did not have ample opportunity to improve the construction. A mob of residents in Randolph, New York, a place to which the "New Motive Power" was removed, judged Spear's whole enterprise to be blasphemous. "Under the cover of night," they descended on his storage shed and "tore out the heart of the mechanism, trampled [it] beneath their feet, and scattered it to the four winds." [57] This was the second time in

Spear's life when violent mobs tried to dissuade him from speaking what he thought of as the truth.

Like Chase, Spear came to measure the success of his life by the extent of hostile criticism heaped upon him. According to an admiring biographer, he was forced to become "an annunciator of unpopular causes." The spirits intended that the newborn truths be wrapped in the "swaddling clothes of misconception and odium" and that Spear bear popular censure.[58] The significance of his activities cannot be judged by their concrete results, for there were none. Garrison had been tarred and feathered. Birney had watched his printing press be thrown in the river. Lovejoy was murdered. Like them, Spear wrote, it was the example of faithfulness to a cause that counted. In due time, as other men advanced in wisdom and knowledge, the sacrifice would be justly appreciated and wisely honored.[59]

Spear's life provides an example of the almost pathological extremes to which the spiritualist and reformer might go in welcoming public abuse. In Adin Ballou, the isolation imposed upon the reformer and that imposed upon the spiritualist reinforced one another in a more constructive way. Ballou had been one of the first promoters of Spear's mediumship, although he became Spear's critic during the latter's attempts to set in motion the "New Motive Power." [60] Ballou never placed such absolute reliance as Spear did on spirit messages. He also objected to what he regarded as Spear's expectation of "some wonderful and unparalleled event to be brought about mainly by spirits for the regeneration and harmonization of the world." [61] That belief, according to Ballou, discouraged efforts by humans to improve themselves through their own efforts. It also placed too much emphasis on the possibility of a sudden change taking place within the immediate future. Hope for a New Dispensation and belief in Perfectionism were the two attitudes that influenced Ballou's own reform efforts. His less-extreme conclusions, however, made him appear to his contemporaries a saner man than Spear.

Born in 1803, Ballou had a happy childhood, social alienation not setting in until he was a young man. In his autobiography, he carefully recorded the steps in the development of that alien-

ation.[62] First, he broke with his family's religious teaching and
was excluded from his parents' church on charges delivered by
his own father. The new faith that he embraced and for which
he suffered such severe estrangement was Universalism. Within
this new denomination he quickly set himself at odds to the
majority. He sided with a schismatic minority group, the so-
called Restorationists. They rejected the dominant Universalist
view, taught by Adin's kinsman Hosea Ballou, that after death
the souls of all people knew the same condition of universal salvation. While agreeing that God ultimately saved everyone, the
Restorationists maintained that there was a finite period of suffering for those who had not perfected their faith in this life.
For taking the minority position, Ballou, who had become a
Universalist minister, was expelled from his pulpit in Milford,
Massachusetts. As he told the story, his beliefs brought upon
him "coldness, detraction, harsh accusation, invective, denunciation." [63]

During the 1830s, Ballou remained associated with the Resto-
rationist Society and first ventured into reform activity. He espoused the goals of temperance in 1832 and quickly moved into
a support of abolitionism. In doing so, he underwent "a new
baptism of vituperation and reproach." "I knew," he wrote,
"what it was aforesaid to be scorned and hated on account of
theological and ecclesiastical offences, but now I must endure
ill-will and denunciation as a moral reformer, seeking only the
personal good of my assailants." [64]

Influenced by the ideas of Christian Perfectionism, he found
the number of people with whom he could share his religious
views growing smaller and smaller. In 1838 a split among the
Restorationists in effect left Ballou unattached to any church. In
1841 he said of himself and a small remnant that had been
saved: "We were 'a peculiar people' in the professing Christian
world. . . . We had gathered a new species of grape from the
primitive Christian vintage, and had extracted therefrom a sam-
ple of the 'new wine' of the Kingdom of God. But where were
the bottles to hold and preserve it?" [65]

In answer to his question, Ballou decided to fashion his own
container. In 1841, he founded the Hopedale Community, by all

measures one of the most successful of the antebellum utopian ventures.* Ballou conceived it as an experiment in noncoercive living. He sought a middle ground between human government (arrangement) and anarchy (spontaneity). On the other hand, Ballou's early and strong interest in spiritualism was natural enough. (He wrote one of the first histories of the movement).[66] Spiritualism's rejection of force, its notion of a natural affinity among people of like conscience, the ideal of a harmonial society freed of coercion—all these Ballou believed in the 1850s would be exemplified some day at Hopedale.

Compared to the abuse heaped upon the explicitly spiritualist communities founded in the 1850s, Hopedale enjoyed surprisingly untroubled relations with the surrounding population. Ballou may have endorsed abolitionism and the Fox sisters, but he at least kept Hopedale untainted by the charge of free love. Spear was less careful in that respect with his settlement at Kiantone and suffered accordingly. The settlers at the spiritualist-oriented New Jerusalem Community at Mountain Cove, Virginia, also offended American sexual mores.[67] Nevertheless, while Ballou had better luck than the people at Kiantone and Mountain Cove, all the antebellum utopian ventures encountered some hostility. In some cases, communitarians may have perceived more hostility than there actually was, but they did not lack for opponents. John Orvis and John Allen, two members of Brook Farm who later became spiritualists, went on a lecture tour in 1847, not long after a fire destroyed the new phalanstery at Brook Farm. Speaking in western New York towns on behalf of the American Union of Associations, they found audiences unresponsive. "The very name of Association," they concluded, "is odious with the public, and the unfortunate people who went into those movements . . . have been ridiculed till . . . they have slunk away from the sight and knowledge of their neighbors."[68]

* The list of communitarian leaders who would in the 1850s welcome spiritualism included Ballou as well as Robert Owen, Robert Dale Owen, Josiah Warren, Thomas Lake Harris, Mary Gove Nichols, and Stephen Pearl Andrews. Of course, spiritualism was not a formative influence on what most of them thought about communes. Hopedale, for example, was founded before the rappings began.

When Ballou wrote his autobiography, some years after the demise of Hopedale, he had, he said, gotten beyond the stage where he expected his enterprises to win general public approval. In his preface and in his conclusion he asked posterity to judge him according to his intentions rather than his achievements. "I gave up expecting to accomplish much for the reformation of my fellowmen in my natural lifetime and was led to devote more and more of my energies and pecuniary means to the benefit of my successors."

Neither spiritualist beliefs nor the example of Hopedale carried Americans as far toward a better society as Ballou had originally imagined they might. The failure mattered less than something else that had explained his attraction to spiritualism in the first place. The persistence that spiritualist leaders consistently demonstrated in trying to gain recognition for an unpopular idea sat well with Ballou's own strongest belief: "What is right and good is always best, regardless of circumstances or consequences, both to him who acts and to all beside." [69]

The point of this description of these three lives is to suggest that spiritualism offered a psychological boost to at least some American reformers. In the nineteenth century, spiritualism did not in any significant instance account for the zeal that had first gripped a reformer, but it frequently did help to sustain this enthusiasm. To individuals who felt themselves isolated from the mainstream of social thought, it offered what amounted to religious sanction. The lack of that sanction within established Christianity had driven many of these individuals out of their churches in the two decades preceding the rise of spiritualism. Sometimes, as in Spear's case, it led to increasing isolation and sponsorship of causes where it would become extremely difficult to distinguish a call for reform from social irresponsibility. But it also enabled a man whose life had been punctuated by a series of ruptures to keep his mental equilibrium. From all indications, Chase, Spear, and Ballou ended their lives in contentment.

Undoubtedly a series of commitments to unpopular causes can provoke outrageous behavior. Nineteenth-century contemporaries charged spiritualism with encouraging a socially useless deviancy. Those who felt an affinity with it were already, it was claimed, leading dangerously unbalanced lives. Consorting with mediums only compounded the problems of those in an unhealthy state of social dislocation. Obviously in many cases these charges were nonsense and said more about those who made them than about those against whom they were directed. Just as obviously they were sometimes accurate.

While spiritualism did not bear the chief responsibility for the temporary insanity that overtook, for example, Robert Dale Owen late in life, a period of deep humiliation and bewilderment resulting directly from his obsessive defense of spiritualism preceded Owen's derangement. [70] Others who found themselves outcasts upon coming out with articles expressing a belief in spirit communication spent the remainder of their lives consumed with the search to find new evidence to demonstrate the correctness of their original position. They became oblivious to what even their friends recognized as patent fraud. [71] In these cases (and the same sort of obsessiveness could and did overtake other reformers), the original moral point of fighting for something one believed to be true simply became irrelevant.

The constant repetition of the theme of martyrdom in the literature of spiritualist reform does suggest a kind of paranoia. But it also suggests something much more obvious and much easier to describe. Even if they exaggerated the extent of the persecution, many spiritualists *did* suffer, and they were persecuted not for their behavior (though admittedly that could be part of it) but for what they believed in. The gentle Judge Edmonds was driven off the bench by his conversion to spiritualism. The *New York Times* argued that his addiction to spiritualism "must render the operation of his intellect utterly unreliable and destroy all confidence in the continued justice and correctness of his judicial actions." [72] His fate foreshadowed that of Henry Kiddle, the highly respected superintendent of New York City's schools. He lost his job at the end of the 1870s after he published a volume of spirit messages. The martyr's posture that he then adopted ("Let us be brave knowing we are doing God's will and a Crown awaits" [73]) was, given his beliefs, a reasonable reaction.

In the late nineteenth century, persons who spent their time chasing after spirits could be judged legally insane. Radical reformers faced even stronger forms of social ostracism. These facts, more than the content of any one spirit message, go further to explain the sympathy expressed in various spiritualist gatherings for the slain Paris communards, the betrayed American Indians, or the imprisoned Eugene Debs.[74] What spiritualists throughout the nineteenth century thought they shared with abolitionists, temperance leaders, feminists, and trade unionists was the frustration of selling what appeared to them to be obvious truths to a very stubborn world. And in many cases reformers thought likewise. The interaction betokened no class consciousness, only the belief that if American conservatism was to be vanquished, attacks would have to come from every direction.

In its effort to exert a formative influence on American reform endeavors, spiritualism of course failed. Its individualism and its dislike of collective action, derived as they were from Jacksonian America, were outmoded strategies long before the end of the nineteenth century. It was the sad fate of the movement to come too late to embody in a clear way the most radical aspects of the Perfectionist spirit of antebellum reform. Its evolutionism, which dampened expectations of a quick approach to the millennium, was not intended to suggest William Graham Sumner. But spiritualist writing on the subject of reform fell a lot closer to Social Darwinism than to some of the more professional ideas about social and economic planning that emerged toward the end of the century.

In the 1880s and 1890s the democratic individualism to which the National Spiritualist Association remained loyal could find no better evils to combat than efforts by states to license doctors and enforce compulsory vaccination.[75] Spiritualists remained innocent of the social sciences. There is something to be said for that, although they had no alternative tools to understand a complex, industrial society.

The rise of the expert, the bureaucrat, and the social engineer left the spiritualist stranded in the past. They had nothing to say to the more innovative thinkers who tried to shape a better

America during the Progressive Era. In earlier decades spiritualism had appealed most strongly to those reformers whose lifestyle was something other than respectable. During the twentieth century, exponents of a counterculture would again view it as a useful aid to revolution. But at the turn of the century, the movement that had sold itself as a new science, a new religion, and a new wave of reform was looking distinctly unmodern.

4

The Medium and Her Message: A Case of Female Professionalism

Up to this point our inquiry into nineteenth-century American spiritualism has focused on the attitudes and beliefs that shaped the movement. Not every reader will approve of this emphasis because it leaves so much unexplained about the social, economic, and psychological factors that lay behind the widespread interest in spiritualism. In truth, we know very little about these things. And unfortunately the things we do know suggest only general interpretations that are not very helpful.

For example, while many people unquestionably went to séances out of grief (they still do), that fact explains next to nothing about the nineteenth-century controversy over spirit communication. And although social and economic change characterized the decade in which the Fox rappings first aroused public interest, it characterized all the other decades of the nineteenth-century as well. Americans, both when they turned their attention toward spiritualism and later when they ignored it, had plenty of anxieties relating to their social status and to their economic situation.[1] But the anxieties that led Cornelius Vanderbilt to summon mediums were different from those that drove an Ohio farmer named Jonathan Koons to build himself a spirit room.[2]

The difficulties in trying to understand what one chooses to regard as an odd belief by reference to social disruption are endless. As has been indicated, perhaps the most perplexing problem in coming to a sociological explanation of the mass interest in spirtualism is related to the fact that so many in the society, facing the same anxieties, did *not* succumb to the arguments of spiritualism, and in fact strongly opposed them. As a group, spiritualism's opponents may well have felt the stress of social change even more than the spiritualists.

One small truism seems beyond doubt and was recognized even by those who regarded an addiction to séances as pathological. Spiritualism helped the people who believed in it to function. It helped them adjust to personal tragedy. It allowed them to adopt a stance of scientific skepticism while retaining faith in an ultimate purpose to life. It justified their alienation from the social establishment; or, just the opposite, it gave them a sense of moving up the ladder of wisdom and influence.

Participation in séances satisfied a great variety of unarticulated but deeply felt psychological needs. Of course the benefits spiritualist belief provided were often short-lived. Moreover, whatever the benefits, a conversion to spiritualism often cost the individual some things as well: friends, spouses, even jobs. Worse, they frequently courted illusions that, when exploded, left the lives of those who had been affected in shambles.

One group of people who throw a lot of light on the positive and negative aspects of spiritualist practices have not yet received sufficient attention. An analysis of professional mediums may in some way compensate for our lack of attention to the dimensions of spiritualist behavior that lay under the expressed systems of belief. Because this occupation was primarily identified with women (in fact most observers associated the whole of the spiritualist movement with women even though many of the publicists were men), mediums make a doubly rich area of investigation. Through their lives we may study the uses to which those individuals who suffered social dislocation because of their profession *and* their sex put spirit communication.

In his journal Emerson included the spiritualist medium among the new professions that had emerged in America in the 1850s. It was not a happy admission for him, for he thought the sudden and rapid proliferation of men and women who claimed access to scientific evidence of an afterlife, which they would share with others (for a fee), to be anything but a sign of a spiritual awakening in the United States.[3] His listing of the medium along with the daguerreotypist, the railroad man, and the landscape gardener represented his troubled concession to the realities of a country that already had more than its share of hucksters and humbugs. The leveling ethos of Jacksonian America encouraged all, even the "unlearned," to aspire to professional status. None pressed the claim more vociferously than those who presumed to act as channels of communication with the spirit world. Once the Fox sisters had demonstrated that people would pay money to witness spirit manifestations, mediums appeared in almost every city and town in the country.

Not all of them demanded remuneration (most of them would take it), and those who did, even in the age of the common man, encountered many difficulties in carving out their claim to professionalism. Mediums, first of all, faced the difficult task of establishing a reputation for honesty. After that, an inevitable ambiguity clouded the issue of whether they were selling a skill acquired by their own efforts or were tastelessly exploiting a divine gift. If what mediums did required no education and no planned effort, then what right did they have to ask for a professional fee? In fact, was it not a denigration of their spiritual gift to set a price on it?

Believers in the reality of spirit communication advanced various and conflicting answers to these questions.[4] Most of the leading spokesmen of the spiritualist movement, however, eventually joined in a defense of the professional nature of mediumship. Whatever the source of inspiration, they said, mediums had expenses, their work was tiring, and they performed a service that not everyone could render. One medium who originally had worked for free changed her mind and said to her critics: "If my mediumistic gift is the one most in requisition, it is no less worthy of being exchanged for bread than any other." [5] Thus in the last half of the nineteenth century the most successful mediums advertised in the press, hung out shingles, and roamed all over the country to earn a living because, in their minds, they gave something beneficial to their "clients."

Professional jealousy ran high, and mediums were never successful in building organizations to protect professional standards and interests. However, the Mediums Mutual Aid Association, which was founded in Boston in 1860, and a few similar short-lived groups did what they could "to secure favorable conditions for the development and instruction of those who use mediumistic powers professionally as a business or means of support." [6]

The identification of mediumship with women occurred even though many of the practitioners of the medium's art were men. One census of spirit mediums carried out in 1859 showed a fairly even balance between the sexes—121 women as against 110 men. [7] The men even accounted for some of the most famous nineteenth-century spirit communicators. For example, no female medium in Victorian America ever quite captured the attention accorded over many years to Daniel Dunglas Home. Home's admirers in a dozen countries claimed that he not only put his sitters in contact with the dead, but also levitated his own body and floated horizontally above their heads. In his most celebrated exhibition he reportedly floated out of a window seventy feet above a London street and came in through another window seven and a half feet away. [8]

Despite Home, however, and despite other men allegedly adept at invoking spirits, the popular impression that mediumship was female persisted. Newspapers hostile to the vogue of spiritualism characterized male mediums as "addle-headed feminine men." [9] For according to unfriendly sources, mediumship represented above all else the corruption of femininity. A medium was, so her enemies saw her, a person whose generalized female traits had developed in perverse and bizarre ways. Spiritualists themselves, while they rejected the notion that mediumship involved any corruption of womanly qualities, at least agreed with critics that mediumship was an occupation especially suited for women. In any case, it was one of the few career opportunities open to women in the nineteenth century. The females who took advantage of it did nothing to discourage the notion that successful mediumship grew from the cultivation of specific traits that in the nineteenth century defined femininity. [10]

A search through nineteenth-century spiritualist literature readily reveals those traits. Phrenological studies, which figured in many essays about mediumistic powers, reported the same thing. Mediums were weak in what were considered to be the masculine qualities of will and reason and strong in what were considered to be the female qualities of intuition and nervousness. They were impressionable (i.e., responsive to outside influence) and extremely sensitive. Above all, they were passive. After all, it was queried, what spirit could manifest anything through a medium whose own personality was strongly assertive? The success of spirit communication depended on the ability of mediums to give up their own identity to become the instruments of others. [11]

Self-sacrifice and passiveness were among the things, in the nineteenth-century understanding, that made for the moral superiority of women over men. These were the qualities women used in the home to promote domestic felicity. [12] The uses to which female mediums put those same qualities in areas outside the home appeared dangerously inappropriate, even rebellious, to many people. But if putting nineteenth-century female traits to professional uses was rebellious, the conservative aspects of the rebellion, at least in the case of mediumship, need to be kept in mind. [13]

Female mediums did not reject the Victorian concept of womanhood in its entirety. Having no alternative models, they accepted sickness, suffering, and self-sacrifice as part of the natural lot of women. In fact those ills served to justify the importance of their profession. A belief in their martyrdom served them in much the same ways it had served the reformers discussed in the previous chapter. Their everlasting willingness to give of themselves for the spiritual benefit of others—even to the point of their own physical impairment—made mediumship in their eyes a dignified calling. The medium could not boast of a college degree to justify her professional status. A long illness preceding and accompanying the career of a successful medium served as a common substitute.

The female medium's acceptance of the categorization of the skills of her job as feminine was not merely a ploy contrived to gain a place in a man's world, which she was determined to have anyway. She took her womanhood seriously, and her concept of femininity affected her professional behavior in a variety of ways. For one thing, she was extremely reluctant to accept personal responsibility for her vocational choice. She blamed her course of action on the spirits that controlled her. The story is the same in all autobiographies of female mediums. They were, they reported, frightened by their powers and reluctant to develop and demonstrate them. However, the spirit controls insisted and forced them to comply.

Emma Hardinge, for example, came from England to America as a young person, and after failing as an actress, she became one of the most successful public mediums of the nineteenth century. She first learned of her professional destiny at a spirit circle; horrified, she rushed out of the room and in her haste took a tumble down the stairs.[14] Miss Ellen D. Starkweather, when initially confronted with the news that she was to become a medium, also tried a dash from the room. She luckily was saved from a similar fall down the stairs when a table mysteriously slid across the room to block her exit and seal her fate.[15] The most famous of the nineteenth-century mediums, Mrs. Leonora E. Piper, "cried all night after the discovery of her gift." Left to herself she would not have pursued it because "it meant giving up much of her home life and being separated from her young children." [16]

Female mediums almost always went on the stage as "trance" mediums. In this respect they differed significantly from their male counterparts. Male mediums had their own rationalizations for taking up work in so highly controversial a field as mediumship, but once set upon their course, they at least did not have to overcome additional scruples about the appropriateness of their sex appearing before a public audience. In contrast, the female medium who gave public performances stood in defiance of St. Paul's admonition against women preaching in public—an admonition that in the nineteenth century was still heeded by most American churches.

Speaking in trance was good theater. It was also a way to blunt the defiance. The words of the female medium, delivered while she was in a deep state of somnambulism, were supposedly not her own but those of her spirit control. In the campaign to make the truths of spiritualism known to the world, female mediums left what was termed "normal speaking" to the men. [17] In contrast to men, they generally mounted the public stage as passively as possible. Even in private sittings, female mediums usually worked in a deep trance.

In view of the deference many female mediums paid to social conventions, one must of course ask why they bothered with a professional role at all. The deference was certainly not sufficient to placate critics. In many instances mediums faced the scorn of family members and friends, most of whom disapproved generally of women who worked, and especially of women who worked in so public and controversial an enterprise. The use of the trance and the shifting of the blame to spirit controls did not make the work more palatable to those who thought that either trickery or the Devil was behind spiritualist performances.

If the money had been better, the motives of the female medium would pose less of a problem. Wealth overcame in the nineteenth century as many principles as it does in our own, and it provided compensation for the friends one lost in the process of acquiring it. Yet mediumship, contrary to the charges frequently made by the enemies of spiritualism, was usually not a way to get rich. Sometimes a wealthy benefactor would act as a patron of mediums. For example, Horace Day used some of the profits from the manufacture of rubber products to house Kate Fox in comfortable circumstances in New York City. In the mid-1850s he paid her a $1,200 annual salary to give free sittings for all interested investigators. Cornelius Vanderbilt, Charles Partridge, Henry Seybert, Henry J. Newton, and David Underhill were others who at one time or another rendered financial aid to various mediums. Luther Marsh, an aging New

York attorney, went so far as to turn over his handsome private residence to Madame Diss Debar, one of the most notorious charlatans of the 1880s. [18]

A few American mediums managed to move in European aristocratic circles, for spiritualism became an entertainment demanded by the crowned heads of England and the Continent. D. D. Home, surely the most successful in this respect, levitated tables for Napoleon III, Tsar Alexander II, and Queen Sophia of Holland. He also married a Russian noble lady, whose estate unfortunately did not pass to him after her death, and almost succeeded in getting a seventy-five-year-old English widow worth 140,000 pounds to adopt him as her son and legal heir. [19]

Normal earnings, however, for both male and female mediums were modest. In the last half of the nineteenth century, the average medium—and the available evidence indicates that the sex of the medium was not important with respect to fees—got five dollars for an evening's work away from home. Private sittings in their own home brought in a dollar an hour. [20] Income was irregular because mediums normally could not depend on a regular clientele—at least for extended periods of time in any one place.

When a medium traveled, the financial returns were no more dependable. While public lectures and demonstrations brought in as much as a dollar a head, the spiritualist who conducted them had to cover expenses. Warren Chase, whose career as a public spiritualist lecturer spanned forty years, reported a typical year's earnings as $425, a sum derived from 121 lectures. He paid for his own travel arrangements and a good share of the cost of food and lodging. [21]

In their letters to the spiritualist press, female mediums complained bitterly of low compensation. [22] Of course, such complaints are no indication that mediums could have done better in any other line of work. On the other hand, enough of them ended their careers as paupers to make one wonder whether expected monetary returns were the primary inducement to become a professional medium. The work involved real hardships. While the self-conscious frauds who entered the field cared nothing about social ostracism, many others who believed in the worth and dignity of what they were doing felt a great loss when they were repudiated by neighbors and family. Yet they persisted in their calling, some for amazingly long periods of time.

Personal conviction drove mediums on in their calling. And so did the attention they received. The women who gravitated toward mediumship had rarely received public attention, first, because they were women, and second, because they came from a level on the social scale where the men they knew reflected little glory on them. The vicarious sense of fame that came from being wives of respected husbands was by and large unknown to them. Some had lost their fathers early in life or had not been doted on in childhood. Many had had unfortunate experiences with male suitors and husbands. There was no consistent marital pattern among mediums: some were married, some had been divorced and remarried, and some remained single. But almost all who began their careers as adults had felt neglected and useless before undertaking professional life.

The most successful mediums in the nineteenth century derived enormous satisfaction from public acclaim. In their autobiographies they made no effort to conceal that fact.[23] Acclaim made up for any public abuse, which was itself better than no notice at all. Even imagined applause can bring genuine pleasure. Confined to a sickbed during her last years, Cora Maynard recalled her days of glory when as a young girl she had been Mrs. Lincoln's favorite medium. However flawed her memory of specific events, her professional life had most certainly brought her into contact with important Washington officials, including the president. While Lincoln had not issued the Emancipation Proclamation at the command of her spirits, her conviction that he had goes a long way toward accounting for her behavior. In her memory, she, "an unlettered girl," had been led "to become the honored guest of the Ruler of our Great Nation, during the most memorable events in its histories."

Those present at her séances, when her spirits had counseled on important affairs of state, "had lost sight of the timid girl in the majesty of the utterance, the strength and force of the language, and the importance of that which was conveyed, and seemed to realize that some masculine spirit force was giving speech to almost divine commands." [24] Perhaps from a logical point of view, Mrs. Maynard had no reason to take personal pride in what her spirit controls accomplished through her when she was unconscious. A considerable ambiguity attached to the question of just what personal credit mediums could claim for their work. But it did not detract from the immediate satisfaction they felt in knowing that they had impressed an audience.

Mrs. Maynard's seizure by a "masculine spirit force" suggests that part of the satisfaction felt by female mediums derived from their assumption during the trance state of an otherwise forbidden male social role. Time and again under the influence of their spirit controls, they turned into swearing sailors, strong Indian braves, or oversexed male suitors. In one trance, a female medium "was hunting and calling her dog, and loading her gun, and taking her swig of whiskey, all of which were done to perfection." While the same medium in other trances danced, pantomimed, and did embroidery, the specifically masculine behavior became too regular a feature of séances to lack significance. G. Stanley Hall later observed with reference to mediums: "Such tender and delicate girls often feel themselves possessed by some rugged, potent and often uncouth male spirit, and delight to swagger in diction and manner." He could cite many examples. One of his patients, "a medium in the bud," had retreated into "the world of imagination." Her mediumship, which Hall regarded as a sign of sickness, developed to save "her sense of the value of her personality by evolving an inner world that more than made up for all that she missed from the outer reality." [25]

The best of the female mediums displayed an impressive talent for acting. A staggering variety of spirit characters performed through them. At one typical "materializing séance" in the 1880s, thirty-one spirits paraded out of the medium's cabinet. Captain Hodges, a "firm erect military man," was followed by Alice, "a tall queenly soprano." Further along came Helen, who sang "Sweet Beulahland," Little Wolf, "a perfect Indian brave," and Mrs. McCarthy, an Irish lady whose vocabulary amused without offending genteel taste.[26] Allowing for the deliberate fraud in many of these performances (the incidence of fraud was especially high among materializing mediums), one may still suggest that in the personalities of the spirits trance mediums found outlets for unexpressed and inexpressible desires. If a spirit control kept throwing the medium's wedding ring away, the medium could with all sincerity disclaim responsibility.[27]

The possession trance has served similar functions in cultures very different from nineteenth-century America. For example, Judith Gussler, in a study of the Nguni in South Africa, has argued that trance behavior in that society provided compensation for its hardest-pressed members, most notably the women and children.[28] As has been noted in studies of hypnotized subjects, the trance personality showed none of the signs of subservience of the normal personality and was universally acclaimed as evincing more brilliance than the normal personality.[29] Moreover, according to Lenora Greenbaum, in an analysis of various cultures of Sub-Saharan Africa, possession trance was more common in rigid societies where simple decision making was fraught with danger from internal and external social controls.[30]

While in comparison to traditional African societies nineteenth-century American society was flexible rather than rigid, women enjoyed the advantages of its egalitarian and democratic features far less than men.[31] The trance condition relieved individual women of personal responsibility for decisions by temporarily changing their identity into that of a spirit. At least one American medium tried (unsuccessfully) to plead irresponsibility as a legal defense against charges of fraud.[32] The medium and the petitioner seeking the medium's services could, under the cover of the séance, solve problems in making crucial life decisions without personally challenging the established order of society.

This worked especially well in divorce cases. Nineteenth-century spirits freely issued sanctions to American wives to divorce their husbands. One famous case involved Andrew Jackson Davis. When strapped for funds to publish his first book, he applied to Mrs. Silone Dodge, a wealthy admirer of his. Mrs. Dodge, who was twenty years older than Davis, supplied the money and much more. She shared Davis's bed, and after a few months, upon the advice of spirits, she divorced her husband to marry him. Of course, the sanction could be extended to both sexes. Much later, after Mrs. Dodge had died and Davis had been remarried for many years, he cited spiritual authority in the casting off of his second wife.[33]

The envy of male and more powerful social roles discernible in the utterances and behavior of female mediums assumed some interesting variations. For one thing, female mediums took obvious joy in conquering male adversaries. Emma Hardinge and her equally famous rival Cora Richmond both wrote autobiographies that recorded scores of such triumphs. In one of Hardinge's first public lectures at Rondout, New York, she encountered an entire audience of "rough-looking" men who refused to take their hats off. Coming to scoff, they stayed to cheer. She remembered those hats when later in her career she overwhelmed a similar audience in Glasgow, Scotland. The baring of heads was, just as it had been earlier, the signal of her victory.[34]

Unlike Hardinge, Richmond never subdued a band of armed robbers in Nevada, but she had the satisfaction of reducing Issiah Rynders to tears. Rynders was a Tammany Hall ruffian whom the New York machine used to disrupt one of William Lloyd Garrison's rallies. But on another occasion the spirit voices of Richmond were more than a match for Rynders, and at the end of her address, which he had come to heckle, he cried with conviction.[35]

Both Hardinge and Richmond were "trance lecturers" and followed a similar routine in their public performances. They invited the audience to choose a jury from among themselves that would in turn select a topic of discourse for the medium. Announcing the subject to the medium, the audience then gave her a few moments to enter a trance. Once in a trance, she would proceed to talk, usually for longer than an hour. The address constituted the test of her powers. The subjects were almost always chosen by all-male juries, and usually concerned "manly" scientific questions; the topic would therefore presumably be something that the uneducated medium could not tackle unless the spirits came to her aid. As even hostile newspaper accounts admitted, the discourses, whatever their deficiencies in scientific accuracy, usually at the very least left the audience with a healthy respect for the extemporaneous speaking abilities of the medium.

Hardinge (and her spirits) surely knew less Hebrew than a Canadian rabbi who tried to challenge her explication of a Jewish text, but the majority of those present took her side.[36] According to Cora Richmond, Lincoln and the Joint Congressional Committee on Reconstruction sought her advice because she could answer "questions that involved a practical knowledge of finance, history, political economy, jurisprudence, and the science of government." [37] Her memory of events is more important here than the actual facts. Just as Cora Maynard had, Richmond recalled her days in Washington as a period when she had met men on their own turf and bested them all. For her, those occasions were the best times in the life of a medium.

When Hardinge, Richmond and other mediums were not out subduing hostile male audiences, they were busy conquering communities where male spiritualist lecturers had previously met with dismal failure. Hardinge journeyed to Indian Valley, Nevada, to help out a local male spiritualist preacher who just happened to be a cripple. Whereas he had never been able to draw much of an audience on the arid western deserts, her own Fourth of July address made believers of everyone. Of the crowd's reaction to her speech, she wrote: "The cheers grew into shouts; the clapping of hands into perfect leaps and yells of applause; and at the end of about an hour's address . . . I was literally pelted with flowers. The women kissed my dress, and held up their dear little children for me to kiss also, whilst the men almost wrung my arm out, and my hand off, with grips and shaking." [38]

Not all the adulation that mediums received from males in their audience proved equally welcome. Hardinge was thoroughly indignant over the attention of one young man who wrote love letters to her and followed her (in his "astral body") everywhere she spoke. She finally had the satisfaction of seeing him confined to an insane asylum.[39] But an admiring note from afar could be flattering so long as it did not threaten the medium's professional independence. Richmond could not resist recording the text of one such letter: "To possess such a lovely, fairy mortal—for her intellect and genius—I would have given a kingdom, or braved a world of dangers." [40] She did not in this case even bother to remind her readers that the "intellect and genius" ascribed to the medium belonged rather to the spirits.

Aside from the acclaim that went with it, the professional life of public mediums gave many women an opportunity for travel and sexual adventure far beyond the lot of the average American woman, the travel being easier to document than the sex. Mediums of both sexes were an itinerant bunch; the many advertisements that spiritualist speakers placed in the *Banner of Light* and other spiritualist publications provide abundant testimony to their continuous movement. While some women restricted the engagements they would accept to specific localities, most of them thought little of long absences from home on trips covering many miles.

K. Graves traveled through the subzero weather of the Midwest, constantly losing her health and having to stay in the homes of strangers in order to carry out her professional duties. Miss Jennie Leys, operating along the Pacific Coast, regularly trekked from San Francisco down through San Jose, Stockton, Santa Barbara, and Los Angeles to San Bernadino. Many advertised a route in advance and offered to accept engagements along the way. Mrs. Laura Gordon, for example, announced that she would start west on April 1 to "receive calls to lecture during the month of April on the route from Boston to Quincy, Ill., via Buffalo, Cleveland and Chicago." Laura Cuppy and Lizzie Doten turned up everywhere. Perhaps none outdid Mrs. C. M. Stowe, a "devoted wife and mother," who "traveled unaccompanied, by steamboat, railroad and stage, day and night, and the latter over roads that would appall many a man who has never traveled over these mountains." In an average five-week trip, she covered eight hundred miles, entering towns she had never seen, hiring her own hall, doing her own advertising, and entertaining her own audience.[41]

In any line of work traveling is not always viewed as an advantage by the person forced on the road. Many mediums kept on the move, not because they cared for a life of wandering, but because their displays bore only limited repetition in any one locale. Complaining endlessly about the hardships of travel and the lack of hospitality they encountered en route, many of them defined themselves as ministers of the spiritualist religion and urged the movement to follow the example of other churches and support them in fixed parishes.[42] Since spiritualist believers in the nineteenth century who cared to form churches at all generally lacked or refused to contribute the funds to provide long-range and regular support to a permanent minister, constant travel presented itself to most public mediums as one of the necessities of the job.

On the other hand, there are many examples of female lecturers who traveled by choice and rejected offers of permanent settlement. When she married, Emma Hardinge briefly advertised herself as a healing medium with the specific intention of setting up an office in Boston. But she soon grew restless and resumed her lecture tours. Cora Richmond did accept a permanent position that a spiritualist congregation in Chicago offered to her—but only on the condition that she could take long leaves of absence to continue her routine of travels to England, across America, and to Australia.

In addition to the gratification of seeing the world, travel provided mediums, just as it did other Americans in the nineteenth century, with an opportunity to walk away from personal problems. Husbands and domestic life often. Unhappy love affairs occasionally. Routine always. In the act of escape mediums proved something to society. They were tough, albeit gentle. They were resourceful, albeit mild. And they had a service to offer that was too important to be confined within narrow geographic boundaries.[43]

The efforts of feminist leaders after the American Civil War to liberate women from "the narrow limits of the domestic circle" received strong vocal support at nearly every spiritualist convention held in the latter part of the century. Women's rights was, in fact, the most popular cause of the spirits. Of course mediums had a vested interest in battling the opponents of feminism, those who charged that women, once removed from the constant surveillance of their male spouses, would fall victim to every sensual temptation lying in their paths. "In every work and reform," they declared, "whose united object it is to correct the evils existing in society . . . should woman be allowed to labor by the side of man. God created her on an equality with him, and endowed her with the same glorious rights and privileges, the same capabilities and powers, to advance His Infinite Kingdom." [44]

The working of some of the resolutions adopted by spiritualists left their intent not entirely clear. For example, in saying that "a female whose talents are valuable to the public . . . should not be tongue-tied and pen-tied by the ceremony of marriage," were spiritualists joining Victoria Woodhull in attacking the institution of marriage? [45] Or were they, in milder tones, only suggesting the compatibility of marriage with a career other than household management? Most spiritualist publications supported the latter interpretation and defended "the exclusive conjugal love between one man and one women." [46] But both points of view had their supporters among spiritualists, and those who declared themselves in favor of both marriage and female professionalism had to then deal with all the evidence linking mediumship to divorce and infidelity.

In his novel *The Bostonians,* Henry James linked feminism to spiritualism and damned them both. It was a common attitude. Spiritualism, it was charged time and again, promoted immorality by tolerating, even encouraging, divorce and remarriage. Critics did not usually bother to make precise distinctions. By approving of women who operated independently of men, spiritualism was in their minds ipso facto a free love movement. The *Los Angeles Times* complained of a woman who, after hearing several spiritualist lectures, divorced her husband to run "around the country playing doctor." In prompting five or six other ladies in the area to do the same thing, her example, in

the opinion of the *Times,* posed a serious threat to sexual morality in southern California.[47]

In the early years of the spiritualist movement, Dr. Benjamin
Hatch, the first husband of Cora Richmond, published a sensational pamphlet that described mediumistic practices as
"shameless goings on that vie with the secret Saturnalia of the
Romans." Divorced by his wife, who then went on to become
Cora Daniels and Cora Tappan before assuming her final matri-
monial surname, the aggrieved Hatch charged that of three
hundred married mediums he had surveyed in the northern
states, half had dissolved their conjugal relations. A large proportion of the remainder had abandoned the bed of their
partners to cohabit "with their 'affinities' by the mutual consent
of their husband or wife."

Apparently the problem went beyond spiritualism's tolerance
of women who entered public life, because male mediums were
as guilty as female mediums of forming these "promiscuous"
marriages. Thus, Hatch's sinners included John Murray Spear,
the Universalist clergyman and reformer who had turned spiritualist. He had, according to Hatch, forsaken his wife to travel
with his paramour, who "last Fall, bore to him what they call a
spiritual baby." Other examples are S. C. Hewitt, who left his
invalid wife in a water cure to go off lecturing with his "spiritual affinity," and Warren Chase, who harbored a wife "in
every Spiritualist port." [48] But male promiscuity was nothing
new, so what most bothered critics of feminism and spiritualism was the encouragement they saw both movements giving to
women's desertion of the home and family.

Many spiritualist spokesmen, as already noted, admitted to
the accuracy of some of the reports of sexual misbehavior. La-
mentably, they said, the discordant relations reported among
spiritualist mediums had a basis in fact. "We are compelled,"
one disgruntled source wrote, "to admit that more than half of
our traveling media, speakers and prominent spiritualists, are
guilty of immoral and licentious practices, that have justly provoked the abhorrence of all right thinking people." [49] Purity
was the one trait of Victorian womanhood that did not seem at
all necessary to the practice of good mediumship. On their part,

spiritualists argued that actual promiscuity should not be confused with the advocacy of promiscuity, nor should their approval of certain divorces be understood as a blanket approval of free love. Editorials in the *Banner of Light* blamed low wages for whatever deficiencies could be charged against the morality of mediums. When mediims were paid better, the *Banner of Light* argued, mediums, especially female mediums, would no longer have to seek favors from people of questionable character.[50]

While it is hard to fault the logic of the editorialists writing for the *Banner of Light,* their arguments remind us that the professional life of a medium was not all bliss. There was a vast difference between feminist leaders, spiritualist or otherwise, who spoke against marriage as a form of slavery, and underpaid female mediums who in their travels spent the night with any man who would buy them food and drink. In part the problem goes back to the underlying assumptions about the nature of a medium's professional skills. It was difficult at best to maintain professional status on traits universally recognized as qualities of physical and intellectual weakness, even if they did imply moral superiority. Female mediums risked the real possibility of actually being taken for what they described themselves to be— passive agents controlled by outside intelligences. In their professional roles, by their own repeated admissions, they were simply "obedient instruments" or "humble followers."

Such self-definitions, as we have seen, elevated the medium's sense of self-importance. At the same time they undermined it, reducing the importance of the medium in the eyes of her audience. Séance goers often treated a private medium, because of her passiveness, as an unimportant intermediary, to be praised if things went well, but only for her strange gifts rather than for her trained skills. A good sitting might save the medium a scolding, but not necessarily the humiliation of being bound, gagged, and searched to insure proper "test conditions." In tracing the sad fate of one medium who wound up in an insane asylum, the *Banner of Light* blamed her unhappy end on the selfishness of those "who sought her to learn of the future, to obtain advice in business and to hear from spirit friends." They treated her as a mere employee. According to their friends, mediums needed both respect and protection. Yet, in view of existing sexual stereotypes, they sometimes forfeited a claim to the former in asking for the latter. Many never received much of either.[51]

The public trance lecturer enjoyed higher professional status and escaped some of the pettier trials of the private "test" medium. So long as she confined her activities to speaking and did not try to lift tables or materialize grandmothers, her audience had no occasion to strip and search her. But the trance speaker, perhaps to a greater degree than other types of mediums, viewed herself as "a negative passive instrument." She worried about falling under the influence of "inharmonious, impure" spirits and of the unwholesome thoughts of people in her audience.[52]

Mediums of all types emphasized the danger of their calling in hopes that the hazards would increase its prestige. Thus, they reported without embarrassment an instance when a crew of spirit pirates took over the "organism" of the medium and almost strangled her.[53] In another case reported in spiritualist literature, two leading trance speakers viciously tore at each other only to find, after being forcibly parted and restored to consciousness, that their spirit controls were bitter enemies.[54]

Unfortunately, critics of professional mediums saw no heroism in the "particular susceptibility to surrounding influences" that they manifested.[55] On this point, opponents of spiritualism made clear why they regarded mediumship as a corruption of womanhood. Reverend William H. Ferris, a harsh critic of the movement, quoted the following doctor's description of the traits of a medium: "I never knew a vigorous and strong-minded person who was a medium. I do not believe that such a one can ever become one. It requires a person of light complexion, one in a negative passive condition, of a nervous temperament with cold hands, of a mild, impressible, and gentle disposition. Hence girls and females make the best mediums." [56] Ferris recognized what he considered to be the traits of womanhood, but failed to see how they could be transformed into professional virtues. As far as he was concerned, these traits were good reasons why women should stay home and perfect the arts of domestic science. Whenever they voluntarily relinquished whatever will, reason, and self-assertion they had in the first place, and did so in an unprotected environment, they were asking for trouble.

Female mediums accepted their frailty as readily as they had their passivity. Their accounts agreed with the one cited by Ferris: vigorous and healthy people did not become mediums. To convey their messages, spirits needed a person of a "nervous temperament." Cold hands and a pallid skin, accompanied by a long record of illness and physical suffering, were the best possible signs of budding mediumship. Mrs. Marietta Munson, born with a "peculiarly delicate" constitution, developed her mediumistic powers after a severe attack of lung fever. Another talented medium, Mrs. J. S. Adams, suffered from a "general weakness of her whole physical being," and was often confined to her bed in the throes of constant pain "almost beyond endurance." Two other mediums, who were sisters, were "very slight frail persons, suffering under the most pitiable conditions of ill-health." Mollie Fancher, the "Brooklyn Enigma," became clairvoyant after landing on her head in a fall from a horse. A series of incredibly painful illnesses ensued. "Confined to her bed, subject to tortures, from the contemplation of which the mind will naturally recoil," she made her living promoting articles for invalids manufactured by the George F. Sargent Company. "We have no faith," read an article in the *Banner of Light*, "that the 'nature of things' permits high mediumship unaccompanied by intense suffering." "Every pain we suffer," one spiritualist postulated, "helps unfold our medium powers . . . all suffering is friction to the material covering of the soul, that makes the gem within shine brighter." [57]

Female mediums tried in the only ways open to them to reconcile conflicting impulses. In becoming professional, they did not want to cease being feminine. Cora Richmond's repeated emphasis on her own "etherial, virgin beauty" and "her gentle and mild saintliness" testified to her desire to retain her feminine virtues despite her entrance into a man's world. But her own early career gave eloquent testimony to the difficulties of

combining the qualities of femininity (she was described by admirers as a "frail bark") with professional independence.[58]

Dr. Hatch, her first husband, had lived off her earnings. His
bitter narrative of the marriage, which he published in the same
pamphlet containing his exposé of the sexual lives of mediums,
was extremely flattering to himself. According to his account,
when he discovered Cora, she was an indigent teenaged girl
with an undeniable gift, but with no sense of how to use it to
elevate herself. Having married her, Hatch began, with "untir-
ing toil," to take his wife on the lecture circuit. He attended to
all the business details, did all the promotion, and finally managed to lay some money aside above expenses. Hatch admitted
that he kept firm control over the profits, but he was, he said,
extremely generous in the outlays for his wife. "My rule was to
anticipate her wants as far as possible, and thus supply them
before requested to do so." Meanwhile, while Hatch was doing
all this hard work, Cora lay around lazily with not even the
need to prepare speeches between her appearances.[59]

Understandably, Cora Richmond recalled this epoch in her
life differently. In her version of the story, which was supported
by the evidence gathered in a subsequent investigation by several prominent spiritualist gentlemen, she accused Hatch of
seeking an unfair advantage from her immaturity. Lying to her
about his social position and financial status, he gave up his
own dentistry practice after the wedding. His income thereafter
came strictly from what she earned. As sole manager of the fi-
nances, he was stingy with both her and her mother. He let her
wear her few decent clothes only during performances. Moreover, Hatch boasted to his new wife of his infidelity to his old
one and made sexual demands upon her that Cora claimed
damaged her "health and delicacy." He forced on her the company of a woman of "abandoned character," whose miniature
he kept, and gave her the distinct feeling that it was not "safe to
cohabit with him."[60]

Undoubtedly neither husband nor wife gave an entirely accurate account of the marriage. Only shortly before the divorce,
one spiritualist leader had seen nothing wrong in the conduct of
Dr. Hatch. In fact, he had viewed Hatch's masculine qualities

and Cora's feminine ones as perfect complements: "His strong will and determined purpose and powers of mind, acting with her passive and feminine mildness, are doubtlessly well-calculated to bring out and present her medium excellences in a way to affect the greatest amount of good for the people." [61] However, given the wide range of possibilities, in the nineteenth century, for males to abuse their female partners, one's instinctive sympathy lies with the young Mrs. Hatch. Her husband's outraged reaction to her charges against him further testifies to the superior role accorded husbands in nineteenth-century America. "No right minded woman," he wrote, "would ever leave her husband on such a basis, were the complaint true." [62]

Cora Richmond left her husband and learned enough from this first experience of matrimony to retain control of her subsequent earnings through a succession of husbands. Not every female medium who traveled with a male manager was callously exploited. Some, like Mrs. Semantha Mettler, supported the family when their husband's business ended in bankruptcy. [63] She was one of many women who used her mediumship to push into the male-dominated vocation of healing.

Emma Hardinge married after her career had been successfully established (there apparently had been an earlier brief marriage before she came to America), and at that point in her life she was happy enough to turn over the promotional and financial details of her tours to her husband. She remained the star of the show, and her willingness to surrender the management of the practical matters of life served her no better or worse than it did leisured ladies in any time and place. Men could be useful protectors as well as business partners. In addition to her husband, Hardinge had the comfort of Arrowhead, an Indian spirit who stood over her in times of danger brandishing a war hatchet. [64]

The dangers of exploitation may have been greatest when the medium was young, for many female mediums made their professional debut when their fathers started dragging them around the countryside. Cora Richmond's father, not Benjamin Hatch, first put her on a public platform. Laura Ellis's father advertised her presentations of spirit wonders when she was thirteen. Bound and gagged before audiences along the East Coast, she somehow managed to get spirits to play musical instruments that had been laid beside her in a darkened room.[65] The older sister of the Fox girls started them on a public career when they were barely adolescents.

These children in all likelihood did not feel abused. They enjoyed the attention they got, and were happy when the spirits ordered them to quit school. As in the case of adult women, mediumship provided the child with a way to act out subconscious needs. Child mediums, prior to taking up their public role, had often been lonely individuals given to daydreaming and autistic behavior.[66] Looking back upon her earliest recollections, Hardinge remembered that "I was never young, joyous or happy, like other children; my delight was to steal away alone and to seek the solitude of woods and fields, but above all to wander in churchyards, cathedral cloisters, and old monastic ruins." She too, in "these immature years," liked "to be laid on a bed of sickness." There she could "pass away in dreams . . . and go off to the unknown and fascinating fairy land." [67] Occasionally a father would become obsessed with the spirits and would turn the whole family's attention totally away from other things. In instances such as this, the obsession sometimes destroyed the family fortune.[68] More often, however, the child medium became a modest and welcome source of supplemental family income. The only question was whether the young medium thereafter ever achieved a healthy psychological independence both from the flattering encouragement of her manager and from the expectations of her audience.

Potentially the most crippling damage accompanying the practice of mediumship was not exploitation but serious self-deception. Of course, as has already been suggested, a fantasy that was taken seriously by the medium had its uses and comforts. Mediums who in trance acted out forbidden desires or expressed repressed aspects of their personality were often making the only approach to reality their society and culture allowed them. Much evidence suggests that mediumship got many women up from their sickbeds. Whatever the throat and chest afflictions, the lung hemorrhages, and the rheumatic aches, mediums traveled long distances with little rest and somehow felt a renewed burst of health when they mounted the speaker's platform. Miss A. W. Sprague lay utterly prostrate in a darkened sickroom for two years. Medical doctors ministered to her in vain. Then, from spirits speaking through her sister, she learned that she was to become a great medium. She recovered sufficiently to begin a career as a trance speaker, and as her career advanced, her health improved.[69] As we all know, Mary Baker Eddy's miraculous regaining of her health was not a unique story in the nineteenth century. What we may not yet realize is the extent to which such recoveries were commonplace.

On the other hand, self-delusion put as many people into sickbeds as on their feet. Unless we assume that mediumistic phenomena were genuine (i.e., produced with the aid of spirits) or, alternatively, that they were all the contrivances of conscious fraud, then we must suppose that honest mediums on some psychic level were kidding themselves. And if something damaged the medium's image of herself and forced her to recognize herself as an imposter, the result could be tragic. It was safer to be a fraud from the beginning.

Biographies of spiritualist mediums contain many puzzles that defy explanation. One particular pattern, however, does seem to fit many of their lives. They associated their first awareness of spirit company with the early years of lonely childhoods and dated their actual mediumship from adolescence. In other words, a belief in their spiritual powers began with childhood reveries and received reinforcement in a period of life when they desperately wanted to impress adults. They did believe in the specialness of their gift even if later they also came to believe that the gift needed the gilding of trickery to render it truly impressive. Mediumship was a competitive business. Practitioners all too commonly found that a reliance on one dishonest prop forced them to keep seeking for others.[70] After all, the medium who failed to produce spirits on any given occasion and made excuses about bad conditions lost her reputation and her audience. As professionals, they had a mystique of infallibility to concern themselves with. Seeing themselves as behaving like a lawyer who defended a guilty client or a doctor who did not recognize the disease, they proceeded to do their best in unfavorable circumstances. Average séance goers had no knowledge of professional secrets; this ignorance coupled with their predisposition to accept any sign that a spirit relative was near made it easy to cheat. And what was a poor medium to do when her overeager clients claimed to see more spirits than she herself believed to be present in the room? Mediums faced as many moral dilemmas from too much success as from too little.

When by degrees conscious deception became the normal practice of the medium rather than the exception, she was eventually forced to wonder whether she had ever been anything other than a willful deceiver. The reckoning could be a hard one. When in 1888 Margaret Fox tried to reclaim her dignity by publicly confessing to her fraudulent methods, she had long before turned to the comfort of drink. Her almost instant retraction of that confession raises the suspicion that she never knew exactly what she was up to. Willful deceit may or may not explain the first raps that Kate and Margaret Fox heard in the cottage of their parents in Hydesville. It may or may not explain their first successes in New York City and their ability to attract the attention of the educated and the well-born. But in the long run, it certainly explains their wrecked lives. At the time of their deaths even spiritualists refused to honor them: in 1892 a general appeal to spiritualists to contribute money for an ailing Margaret Fox netted $86.80. [71]

In their pursuit of self-respect, mediums got very little support from the society around them. Increasingly during the nineteenth century they found themselves the objects of legal restrictions. As early as 1865, Charles Colchester, one of the several mediums reputed to have conducted séances for Lincoln, was arrested in Buffalo for failing to purchase a license as a juggler. Although Colchester defended himself by citing his right to pursue whatever religion he chose, a jury found him guilty and fined him $40 plus $743 in court costs. [72] Legislative bodies on occasion levied heavy fines on the activities of mediums or banned them altogether. The raising of state medical standards put spiritualist healers out of business. In the 1890s the city of Philadelphia made a wholesale roundup of spiritualist mediums, mostly women, and jailed them for violating a city ordinance against fortune-telling.[73]

The egos of professional mediums took a beating from psychologists as well as lawyers. To George Beard, an important neurologist who wrote a book about American nervousness, mediumship was a disabling malady. Writing in the *North American Review* in 1879, he said: "Trance is a very frequently occurring functional disease of the nervous system, in which cerebral activity is concentrated in some limited region of the brain, the activity of the rest of the brain being for the time suspended." [74] Particularly in the last quarter of the nineteenth century, with the emergence of a psychology of the unconscious, mediumship became the subject of lively commentary in the journals of abnormal psychology. Psychologists pored over the life histories of mediums for information about hysterical behavior. The medium, as will be discussed later, became a key figure in the development of the concepts of split and multiple personality.

There is no question that the behavior of mediums sometimes gave occasion for serious alarm. For every one who found new strength and happiness in her work, others by their own accounts regularly succumbed to hysterical sobbing fits and convulsions. At the end of a séance many a medium had almost no pulse and remained rigid and cold for hours, or in extreme cases for weeks.[75] Even Emma Hardinge—comparatively speaking, a rock of stability among mediums—did some peculiar things. The "snapping doctor" of St. Louis, a man celebrated for the "unwashed filth" on his hair and body, once kept her rolling on the dirt floor of his office for over two hours, at one moment worshiping the sun, at the next rattling and hissing like a snake.[76]

Still, the historian may wonder whether much of this behavior would have suggested the need for medical treatment if certain elements in the culture had not seen it as socially disruptive. Rachel Baker was a trance speaker who was cured of her disease. According to William Hammond, a nineteenth-century

American neurologist who told her tale, she had drawn large crowds to her performances. And though Hammond was intent on linking mediumship to mental derangement, he admitted that her "discourses were highly respectable in point of style and arrangement, and were interspersed with Scripture quotations." Rachel's parents, who were unhappy at having an odd daughter, sought out the doctors who "restored her health." Rachel Baker lost her faculty of trance preaching and never regained it.[77] Undoubtedly a happy ending for the parents and for Hammond, but nothing in the story indicated that the girl was any happier for her cure. As a matter of fact, it never occurred to Hammond to ask.

If belief in one's own spiritualist powers was a malady, a lot of nineteenth-century American women suffered from it. And if a conviction that spirit phenomena were real constituted a dangerous delusion, many of America's most talented women were led astray by it throughout their adult lives. Whatever the clinical conclusion, mediumship and a belief in spirit voices had their uses for those who accepted them.[78] They offered relief from boredom, routine, and responsibility. They provided consolation in the face of family deaths, marital abuse, and loneliness. And of course in many cases they also helped to launch successful professional careers.

Amanda Jones, for instance, used her mediumship, which was discovered during several periods of protracted illness, to further her other careers as a poet and an inventor. Believing her actions to be governed by spiritual guardians, she shared credit with her spirits in securing patents for an oil burner and a vacuum process for preserving food. The spirits gave her less useful advice about business practices, for her enterprises usually failed financially. But her autobiography, written with the strong encouragement of William James, indicates that she had lived a satisfying life. She died, unmarried and self-supporting, at the age of seventy-nine.[79]

Mediums bore the double stigma of doing something most women did not do in the service of a cause many people laughed at. Yet they persisted, many of them for decades. As one writer noted, mediumship was an occupation not often pursued by women who enjoyed physical well-being, economic security, a happy family and social life, and sexual fulfillment. But for other women, further down the social and educational scale, mediumship, whatever the seamy sides of its practice, offered the possibility of transforming a miserable life into one that brought happiness for oneself and not infrequently for others.[80] The frail sensitiveness that characterized nineteenth-century womanhood was put to worse uses. To be sure, a medium's career could also end in unfortunate ways. But if we can cite examples of mediums who in the last half of the nineteenth century led degenerate and unhappy lives, we should understand that the profession was not the most important cause of the degeneracy or the unhappiness.

II
Psychical Research

5

Psychical Research as Psychology— From William James to James Hyslop

In 1897 the family of John Armstrong Chanler had him declared insane and committed to the Bloomingdale Asylum at White Plains, New York. The great-grandson of John Jacob Astor, Chanler had B.A. and M.A. degrees from Columbia University, belonged to the New York State bar, and was a member of sixteen clubs in New York City. Had he not taken up automatic writing and communicating with his "X-faculty" while in a "Napoleonic trance," his life might have gone forward in a more unruffled way.

As it was, Chanler had to escape from Bloomingdale, assume a false name, establish his sanity in Virginia, and spend twenty years recovering control of his estate in New York. His tale, as recounted in *Four Years Behind the Bars of Bloomingdale,* attracted the attention of prominent American psychologists, psychical researchers, and spiritualists.[1] Each of them might argue, as did those who knew him, that Chanler was "mentally peculiar."[2] But that phrase seemed to cover more than one possibility. A mental peculiarity might render persons stark raving mad. Or it might put them in contact with God, the spirit world, and the highest sources of human genius. Even more interestingly, it might do all of these things at once. The idea that certain types of madness had something in common with divine illumination received a great deal of attention in America around the turn of the century.

Spiritualism, even before one part of the impulse merged into psychical research,* played a significant, though usually unwitting, role in the development of American psychology. Its earliest critics had suggested that spiritualist phenomena had their origin in the involuntary nervous and muscular activity associated with mesmeric trances, or as the newer phrase termed it, hypnotic states. Samuel W. Johnson wrote in 1858: "The whole history of a spirit circle is a capital illustration of the hypnotic condition, of the ease with which many people may spontaneously assume it, and of the effect of sympathy in propagating it." [3] Johnson and others cited with particular frequency Michael Faraday's demonstration in the 1850s that the unwilled muscle action of sitters around a table, not spirits, accounted for the table's movement. This view was entirely compatible with the then-existing medical understanding of the brain and nervous system.

In the middle of the nineteenth century American psychiatry (which owed some unacknowledged debts to phrenology) understood mental events (the mind) as functions of physical changes in the body. Hence mental disorders or insanity had, it was thought, to result from an organic breakdown of the brain or some part of the nervous system A lesion, the concept normally used to visualize that breakdown, might stem from hereditary degeneracy or physical trauma or simply the dangerous habit of masturbation. Curiously, while nineteenth-century neurologists frequently traced insanity to an activity that seemed more mental than physical, such as frequent attendance at the theater, they saw nothing important in mental states other than how they might physically impair "a highly impassionable and irritable nervous organization." [4]

Their cures were therefore not in the least concerned with what was on a patient's "mind." While ideas might lead to excessive stimulation that caused organic damage, they could not

* For the purposes of this study, psychical research means the systematic inquiry into whether human minds receive information in ways that bypass the normal channels of sensory communication, or interact with matter in ways not yet comprehensible to physical science.

repair the damage once it had been done. Neurologists relied on physical agents, most commonly quinine tonics, bed rest, and rich diets, to restore the vigor of the nervous system.

These assumptions led to one of two conclusions about mediumship. The first, that the medium was a fraud, had from the physiological standpoint the advantage of dismissing any question of disease. The question then resolved itself into one that related to medicine only in a peripheral way. That is, it was asked, why did so many mediums choose to become social malingerers. Neurologists posed the same query about their female patients who suffered from hysteria. Granted, they said, the actions of women who feigned hysteria or trance possession often stemmed from something more complicated than deliberate lying. The patients really did suffer. Nonetheless the distinctions that might be made between various kinds of pretenders raised moral issues, not physiological or medical ones.

William B. Carpenter, the eminent nineteenth-century English physiologist, regarded the widespread interest in spiritualism as an "epidemic delusion" not unlike earlier withcraft crazes. States of the brain, he explained, expressed themselves unconsciously and involuntarily in muscular action, and that fact accounted in his mind for most cases of alleged divination or thought-reading. Mediums, he wrote, whether or not they worked for fees, were simply in the habit of dissembling:

> It is perfectly well known to those who have had adequate opportunities of observation, that there is a class of persons (especially, I am sorry to have to say, of the female sex) who have an extraordinary proclivity to deceit, even from a very early period of life; and who enjoy nothing better than 'taking-in' older and wiser people, even when doing so brings no special advantage to themselves. Every Medical practitioner of large experience has met with cases in which young ladies have imposed in this way, by feigning disease, not only upon their families, but upon their previous doctors; the supposed patients sometimes undergoing very severe treatment for its cure.[5]

In Carpenter's opinion, those cures produced no medical effect. They proved their worth, however, if they scared a woman, whether a medium, hysteric, or both, back into a proper sense of social obligation.

The second conclusion derivable from the assumptions of nineteenth-century psychiatry did regard mediumship as a serious medical problem. George Beard, an important American neurologist, saw such intimate connections between spiritualism and abnormal behavior that he wrote: "Spiritism is, indeed, a precious mine of psychology, the veins of which grow wider and richer the longer we work them." The mediumistic trance, he believed, was an extreme expression of the "involuntary life" that destroyed normal mental operation. Rather than dismiss it as an example of malingering, Beard defined trance as "a very frequently occurring functional disease of the nervous system, in which the cerebral activity is concentrated in some limited region of the brain, the activity of the rest of the brain being for a time suspended." [6]

While some historians have argued that Beard broke away from many of the physicalist assumptions of nineteenth-century neurology, nothing in his statements on mediumship differed substantially from those of earlier nineteenth-century medical people who had linked spiritualism to insanity.[7] They had commonly blamed the hallucinatory delusions of spiritualism on an excessive excitement of weak nervous systems. In 1869, G. W. Sampson, the president of Columbian College in Washington, D.C., warned that experiments in spirit communication overstrained the nervous system. Nerves, he wrote, were similar to muscles. He likened séance attendance to attempts "to gratify my curiosity or my vanity" by raising a heavy weight and "disabling myself for life." [8]

The characterizations of mediums as persons suffering from "defective physical organization" apparently crested in the 1870s. William Hammond, a "professor of disease of the mind and nervous system" in the Medical Department of the University of the City of New York, drew an analogy between mediums and historic saints "who were the victims of some severe disorder of the nervous system, by which they were rendered peculiarly susceptible to hallucinations." Fortunately there were things to be done for such dispositions. The "persistent administration of iron and strychnine" was a useful remedy, as was the routine provided "within the domain of home management." [9]

Frederic R. Marvin, a "professor of psychological medicine and medical jurisprudence" in the New York Free Medical College for Women, made perhaps the most extensive delineation of the pathology and treatment of what he called "mediomania." [10] It was most common, he thought, in young women whose "process of menstruation is interfered with." The disturbance of the cycle resulted in an abnormally organized brain. He was not entirely consistent on this point, because mediomania also appeared to be a subcategory of uteromania—a type of insanity caused by an improperly angled womb. "Tilt the organ a little forward . . . ," he wrote, "and immediately the patient . . . embraces some strange and ultra ism—Mormonism, Mesmerism, Fourierism, Socialism, oftener Spiritualism. She becomes possessed by the idea that she has some startling mission in the world. She forsakes her home, her children, and her duty, to mount the rostrum and proclaim the peculiar virtues of free love, elective affinity, or the reincarnation of souls." Marvin worried about spiritualism's effects on sensitive nervous systems because, more than other religions he knew about, it operated upon the human organism to convert oxygen into carbonic acid. Apparently none of these conditions was hopeless because Marvin prescribed all sorts of treatment. Most were quite conventional: proper doses of strychnine and quinine, moral habits, plenty of sleep, a diet of meat. In perhaps his only unusual prescription, he recommended that the symptom of constipation, which frequently complicated the miseries of mediomaniacs, be relieved by "an excellent enema of asafoetida and turpentine." [11]

However, if nineteenth-century neurologists reduced spiritualism and mediumistic trances to an organic nervous disorder, other people, including those of paramount concern in this chapter, seized upon the same and related phenomena to argue something quite different. Psychical research, as it developed into a field of study in England and then America, concerned itself first and foremost with the investigation of alleged "supernormal" powers of the human mind. In so doing, however, it became part of a new thrust in psychology that resisted turning every discussion of conscious and unconscious mental states back toward the physical condition of the person being examined. Antireductionist and antimaterialistic, the early psychical researchers contributed to some important theories about an unconscious or subconscious mind that began to circulate widely in England and America beginning in the 1890s. In the period immediately preceding the general introduction of Freudian concepts, psychical research bore a close relationship to that branch of psychology which was attempting to define a category of mental illness "that was not objectively physical and could not be seen under a microscope." [12] That alliance, in the United States in any case, quickly miscarried. For a time, however, the cooperation of psychical researchers, who interested themselves in the "supernormal," and psychotherapists, who interested themselves in the "abnormal," promised to produce some enormously useful results. Moreover, it left some important intellectual residues, especially in Jungian analysis, which have not disappeared.

The founders of psychical research were English, and by and large had been educated at Cambridge. [13] Learned men and women with broad academic and practical interests, many were also moderately wealthy. That last fact was important. Edmund Gurney and Frederic Myers, both Cambridge graduates, were enabled by their independent incomes to devote themselves completely to the new enterprise. The Society for Psychical Research (SPR), which was organized in London in 1882, would never have gotten off the ground had it had to depend solely on small private donations. Certainly the extensive research and publication carried out under its auspices over a twenty-year period would have been unthinkable.

Aside from Gurney and Myers, its most active original sponsors included Sir William Barrett, professor of physics at the Royal College of Science, Henry Sidgwick, professor of moral philosophy at Cambridge, his wife, Eleanor, principal of Newnham College, and her brother Arthur Balfour, a future prime minister. Membership in the new society was not in the least academically or politically embarrassing. William Gladstone called psychical research "the most important work, which is being done in the world. By far the most important." [14] Sprinkled among the council members and honorary members of the society were eight Fellows of the Royal Society—Alfred Russel Wallace, Couch Adams, Lord Rayleigh, Oliver Lodge, A. Macalister, J. Venn, Balfour Stewart, and J. J. Thompson; two bishops; and such celebrated literary men as Alfred Tennyson, William Ruskin, and Charles Lutwidge Dodgson (Lewis Carroll). At the outset and in subsequent years, membership in the SPR placed one in distinguished company. [15]

In its basic goals, the SPR set out to accomplish what nineteenth-century spiritualists had long advocated: the systematic investigation of a whole range of phenomena associated with mediumistic displays. Some of its leading organizers—Alfred Russel Wallace and W. Stainton Moses, for example—were already committed to the position that spirit communication did in fact occur, and they vociferously advocated their cause. However, most of the officers of the SPR, whatever their initial biases, either for or against, agreed to begin their work on a platform of skepticism.

Accepting nothing a priori, these founders set up six working committees to investigate facts that, though repeatedly reported, had yet to be verified in a way that satisfied scientists. True, they were not the first to attempt a scientific explanation of such matters: a committee of the London Dialectical Society had attempted to do so in 1871, and had confessed its inability to explain certain phenomena it had investigated; [16] also in the 1870s, William Crookes, one of England's foremost scientists, had endorsed Miss Florence Cook of Hackney as a genuine medium who produced materialized spirits. [17] But Myers, Gurney, and the Sidgwicks proposed not to offer past studies, however respectable, as evidence. The working committees began from scratch, analyzing reports not only of spirit communication but also of a wider range of reported facts that, if true, suggested avenues of human communication and powers of human awareness completely transcending what seemed possible within existing categories of scientific understanding.

One committee, which apparently never did very much, took a fresh look at Reichenbach's Od force. More active committees delved into the possibility of thought transference, including the possibility that the souls of the dying telepathically communicated their ghostly apparitions to loved ones many miles away, and the likelihood of clairvoyant perception. In work that proved particularly suggestive to psychologists, psychical researchers studied the apparent relationship between the various reputed instances of "supernormal" perception and altered states of consciousness. Spontaneous mediumistic trances, artificially induced hypnotic states, and nonvoluntary hysterical disassociation—all of which psychical researchers took seriously—furnished evidence of a hidden life about which scientists knew nothing.

During the 1880s the officers of the SPR aggressively established a reputation for hardheadedness, never hesitating to expose fraudulent mediums. In one of its most famous and controversial early inquiries, Richard Hodgson, an energetic young Australian who met Sidgwick while studying at Cambridge, went all the way to India to study Madame Blavatsky. He eventually branded the miracles that her followers attributed to her, including the messages from her Tibetan masters, as fakes, and rather inexpert ones at that. Good empire man that he was, Hodgson went so far as to suggest that she was a Russian agent trying through the Theosophical Movement to undermine British authority in India.[18] While the early psychical researchers published what they considered solid evidence of telepathy and ghostly apparitions, they were apparently too cautious for those who made spiritualism a religion.[19] The latter made a general exit from the society in 1886.

While the first psychical researchers were honest, serious, hard-working, and intelligent, they were not quite neutral. Despite their skeptical attitude toward reports of the "supernormal," Sidgwick and those who carried out psychical investigations with him at Cambridge had some definite ideas about the direction in which they wanted to move science. In 1888 in his presidential address to the SPR, Sidgwick said of the founders:

> When we took up seriously the obscure and perplexing investigation which we call Psychical Research . . . we believed unreservedly in the methods of modern science, and were prepared to accept submissively her reasoned conclusions, when sustained by the agreement of experts; but we were not prepared to bow with equal docility to the mere prejudices of scientific men. And it appeared to us that there was an important body of evidence—tending prima facie to establish the independence of soul or spirit—which modern science had simply left to one side with ignorant contempt; and that in so leaving it she had been untrue to her professed method, and had arrived prematurely at her negative conclusions.[20]

As Frank Turner and Alan Gauld have shown, those who played the most significant role in launching the SPR had gone through a religious crisis in earlier life.[21] Reared by evangelical parents who placed religion at the center of things, they had been thrown badly off balance when their subsequent education brought their faith in conflict with their reason. While never again content to rest within the intellectual boundaries of a formal Christianity, they worried constantly, as they readily admitted, about what they regarded as the excessively materialistic biases of nineteenth-century science. They found the implications of the metaphysics of materialism morally abhorrent. If the belief prevailed that the mind or the soul had no independent existence apart from the body, they could not imagine how their society could avoid falling into a drift of purposelessness and despair. Psychical research, therefore, was not for them a casual investigation. Experimentation, they hoped, by validating the reality of any of a number of things—whether it was spirits, ghosts, telepathy, or hypnotic clairvoyance—would undermine the philosophical position of a Thomas Henry Huxley or a Henry Maudsley. More was at stake than the recognition by science of a few new facts.

Fortunately for psychical research, the mind-body problem was returning at the end of the nineteenth century to its accustomed state of confusion. Despite the acquiescence of nineteenth-century physiology and psychiatry to the view that mental phenomena occasionally accompanied but never determined the movements and interactions of the material world, a minority and contrary view was growing more important.

In 1868 the German philosopher, Eduard von Hartmann, had in *The Philosophy of the Unconscious* suggested what was to become by the end of the century one of the most widely discussed theories in psychology. He posited a realm of unconscious ideation (not merely involuntary neural operations) that had profound effects upon conscious behavior. Undoubtedly the source of abnormal and pathological behavior, this realm was also, von Hartmann argued, the source of human genius and possibly of a cosmic awareness that was totally independent of bodily conduits of information.

Of more immediate importance than the publication by von Hartmann of his new theory were the clinical experiments of Jean Charcot and Pierre Janet in France, whose work was contemporaneous with the founding of psychical research in England. Janet's ideas, which began to be published in the 1880s, exerted a major influence on psychotherapy in England and America. Working with hysterical women, he established to his own satisfaction a category of mental abnormality that resulted from a purely mental disassociation, having no apparent origin in physiological abnormalities in the patient. In some cases Janet achieved a successful integration of such personalities through hypnotism and mental suggestion. Though the old school of neurology equated hypnotic cures with the healing practices of Mary Baker Eddy, psychical researchers were among those who welcomed Janet's work. He returned the favor by joining the SPR. His work with hysterical women had inevitably involved him in case studies of mediums and alleged clairvoyants. Much like George Beard, he regarded the reports of the SPR as a rich mine of information for the practicing psychotherapist. [22]

Appropriately enough, the first man to forward the cause of psychical research in the United States was William James. His position on the Harvard faculty enabled him to gather together a list of sponsors and members of the American Society for Psychical Research as distinguished as that of the English society. Organized in 1885, the ASPR elected Simon Newcomb, the astronomer who headed the Naval Almanac Office, as president. Among the original vice-presidents were George S. Fullerton, a professor of philosophy at the University of Pennsylvania, Edward Pickering, head of the Harvard College Observatory, and Henry Bowditch, a professor in the Harvard Medical School. Josiah Royce, Andrew Dickson White, Henry Holt, Charles Eliot Norton, Francis Parkman, Charles Sanders Peirce, and Theodore Roosevelt were members or associate members. Psychologists and psychotherapists were well represented among the supporters. G. Stanley Hall, then at Johns Hopkins, served along with James as one of the society's vice-presidents. Joseph Jastrow, Morton Prince, and James Jackson Putnam contributed their names as sponsors and followed the publications of psychical research even after their attitude toward the field became largely critical. [23]

Unfortunately for James, the American sponsors of psychical research did not include anyone as self-sacrificing as Gurney, Myers, or Sidgwick. No one in America, not even James, was prepared to make psychical research a full-time vocation. Moreover, as the few publications of the American society during the 1880s made clear, many of the American founders of psychical research entertained greater skepticism about the reality of "supernormal" mental faculties than their English counterparts. They were not predisposed to believe.

In his inaugural address before the society, President Newcomb expressed his own doubts. Rather than viewing the work of the society as the scientific corroboration of anything so out of the ordinary as telepathy or spirit communication, he seemed to look upon the society to verify once and for all known physical laws. [24] And indeed, with the exception of one important experiment that James conducted, most of the experiments carried out by the original American society produced negative results with respect to establishing any supernormal categories of mind. Charles Sanders Peirce used the pages of the *Proceedings of the ASPR* to issue a scathing critique of the work of Gurney and Myers. The two Englishmen had consumed a staggering number of hours gathering evidence tending to substantiate reports concerning apparitions of dying people. Peirce wanted nothing to do with either their method or their conclusions. In fact, his argument, if taken seriously, brought into question whether psychical research was anything more than a waste of time.[25]

Since James was too busy to handle the work of the American society single-handedly, the British society in 1887 shipped over Richard Hodgson, the Australian who had investigated Madame Blavatsky, to act as its secretary. Two years later, the ASPR, owing to a lack of funds, was absorbed by the British society. Hodgson did stay on to manage the American branch, a post he retained until his sudden death on a New York handball court in 1905.[26]

James regretted the fact that his Harvard colleagues and Cambridge friends had not shown greater support for the original ASPR. But he also believed that the biased training of nineteenth-century scientists would be very hard to overcome. C. S. Peirce, in his hostility toward the works of Gurney and Myers, had demonstrated not much more scientific dispassion, James thought, than Peirce's own father, who in 1857, as part of a Harvard team of inquiry, had issued a report rejecting the validity of spiritualist claims in America. Peirce had argued that before facts as troublesome as ghostly apparitions could be taken seriously, they would require more than the reports Gurney and Myers had collected of individual cases. Since so much of the framework of physical science would be worthless if something as odd as telepathy or spirit communication should prove to be true, skeptics in general demanded, at the very least, "a single fact that can be demonstrated regularly in a laboratory." [27]

Instead they got an endless stream of articles about experiments, which were in no literal way repeatable, and were asked to bow before their collective weight. Obviously, with the important exception of some psychologists who were trying to think their way to a new position, most American scientists found the claims of psychical research easy to ignore. Even if some of the facts under investigation proved true, they did not seem usable.

James, of course, was an eloquent critic of what Thomas Kuhn would later call "normal science." [28] He found completely unjustified an attitude that systematically ignored those facts that could not conveniently be pigeonholed within the existing theoretical structure of nature. The neatness of science, which in James's mind unfairly required special tests of those facts threatening to spoil that neatness, acted as a severe obstacle to progress. "Science," he wrote, "has come to be identified with a certain fixed general belief, the belief that the deeper order of Nature is mechanical exclusively, and that non-mechanical categories are irrational ways of conceiving and explaining such a thing as human life." In his day, James argued, science had ceased to be open-minded investigation. It stood for a "certain set of results that one should pin one's faith upon and hug forever." [29]

Even worse, from James's point of view, science ran the risk of dehumanizing itself by chasing after the standards of an impersonal, and hence false, objectivity. There were personal dimensions of experience, James argued, that were true even if evidence of that truth could not easily be shared. For example, it might be that only people who believed in ghosts could see ghosts. Such a proposition obviously complicated the problem of verification, but James did not see how truth could be served by ducking issues. Fortunately or unfortunately, an important part of what people chose to call reality arose from innate personal preferences. Such biases, James thought, frustrated careful open-minded investigation not because they were there but because scientists by and large refused to recognize what powerful shaping forces they were. In the folly of believing they were free of biases, they reduced their chances of ever outgrowing their biases. [30] James was therefore less annoyed with people who had no inclination to study telepathy (temperament was a forgivable matter) than with those who militantly dismissed psychical research in the name of their self-assured objectivity. Their negative attitude toward the work of the SPR was "the verdict of pure insanity, of gratuitous preference for error, of superstitition without an excuse." [31]

To be sure, James's willingness to confront the evidence of

"ghosts and all" without "the irreversibly negative bias of the rigorously scientific mind" complimented his own temperamental preference to believe in a pluralistic universe.[32] Nonetheless, James considered the biases of the psychical researcher less damaging to open-mindedness than those of the average physical scientist. At least the psychical researcher was willing to take his own experience and that of others seriously. It just would not do, James thought, to call someone who was or felt something foreign to general experience a victim of delusion. While he himself never shared his father's certainty that God existed, he never doubted that the collective testimony of those who claimed to see God pointed to a realm of consciousness that any philosopher or scientist had to take seriously.[33]

The irony of James's philosophy was that his interest in bizarre or supernormal experience, as reflected not only in the papers he contributed to psychical research but also in the more famous *Varieties of Religious Experience,* arose from a preference for a metaphysical position that his own experience never quite confirmed. A philosopher who stressed the importance of the non-normal and the unexpected, James had to take his best examples from the lives of others.

The few times when James did encounter in his personal life something that smacked of the supernormal, he attached great importance to it. For example, in the fall of 1885, on the recommendation of his mother-in-law, James attended a séance conducted by a Boston medium, Mrs. Leonora Piper, who had only recently, during the course of an illness, become aware of her powers. "My impression after this first visit," James wrote, "was, that Mrs. P. was either possessed of supernormal powers, or knew the members of my wife's family by sight and had by some lucky coincidence become acquainted with such a multitude of their domestic circumstances as to produce the startling impression which she did. My later knowledge of her sittings and personal acquaintance with her has led me absolutely to reject the latter explanation, and to believe that she has supernormal powers." [34]

Later James referred to Mrs. Piper as his "white crow." [35] She was his experience of that something that flew in the face of every scientific generalization he knew about. Once one has seen a white crow, James would say, it does no good to ignore the fact or to accept the assurances of others that one is mistaken. In fact, given the rarity of white crows, one risks a great deal by turning one's back on them. For James, commonplace things as well as odd things could point the way to knowledge. If he worried about the latter a good bit more than the former, it was because humankind was so much more inclined to neglect the clues that they gave for advancing human knowledge.

As it turned out, Mrs. Piper proved to be the white crow of a good many other people besides James. The SPR in effect hired her as a permanent object of research and placed her under the charge of Hodgson.[36] For £200 a year she turned away from her professional career as a trance medium and put herself at the disposal of science. From the perspective of Myers and Sidgwick in England, as well as James in America, she seemed the perfect vehicle for testing the many psychological puzzles associated with mediumship. There was no hint of fraud. Hodgson, when he started to arrange the literally thousands of sittings that she gave under the sponsorship of the SPR, had had her followed by a detective who reported that she was most certainly not part of any spy network through which mediums reputedly got information about prospective sitters. In any case, people who sat with her often came to her in disguise and always used false names. With few exceptions they agreed with Charles Eliot Norton, who after two sittings with Mrs. Piper in 1894 had said that "there was no question as to Mrs. Piper's good faith." [37]

None of the physical manifestations that had generated so much obvious fraud in the spiritualist camp—table-tilting, slate writing, materializations—formed part of Mrs. Piper's repertoire. The sole manifestations of her mediumship were the messages she delivered after she had fallen into a trance. In an early phase of her mediumship, a spirit who called himself Dr. Phinuit claimed to speak through her. Later the messages were formed by automatic writing ostensibly controlled by a number of different spirits. The genuineness of Mrs. Piper's trance was relatively easy to verify and provoked little controversy among those who observed her. The controversy began when people tried to say what caused her trance and what lay behind the messages.

Mrs. Piper became a cause célèbre among psychical researchers in America and England. From the late 1880s well into the first decade of the new century, she became the SPR's most utilized testing ground. For many leading psychical researchers, Myers and Oliver Lodge certainly, she made the belief in spirit communication an intellectually respectable position. Despite the hesitation of some members, those who feared being associated with the more popular versions of spiritualism, the SPR became less hesitant to investigate mediums than it had been during its first few years of existence. Aside from reports favorable to Mrs. Piper, the SPR printed articles seeming to support the authenticity of the spirit controls of Mrs. Gladys Leonard, Rosina Thompson, Mrs. A. W. Verrall, and Eusapia Palladino.[38] Mrs. Piper's séances in due time put an end to the skepticism of some who had hitherto solidly opposed the hypothesis of spirit communication. Richard Hodgson, who studied Mrs. Piper more closely than he had any other person, succumbed so completely that James feared he had "got into a sort of obsession about Mrs. Piper."[39]

Had spiritualism been the only hypothesis advanced to explain Mrs. Piper, psychical research would have immediately degenerated into something a lot less interesting than it was. There were, however, other possibilities that helped to keep the work of the SPR broadly based. Following the lead of what psychical researchers regarded as good experimental evidence of thought transference, many members of the SPR interpreted the messages of Mrs. Piper and other trance mediums by reference to telepathy rather than to spirits. At one time Mrs. Piper herself expressed a preference for the telepathic hypothesis.[40] The information that she conveyed to her sitters, it was argued, though most certainly unknown to her in her normal state of mind, came to her through some sort of unconscious process of mind reading. James never quite decided whether spirits, telepathy, or something else accounted for the startling powers of insight that appeared to be a gift of certain individuals. He was sure, however, and his opinion was widely shared by other members of the SPR, that an answer would come from the new experimental work being done on those areas of the mind that lay outside normal consciousness.

In the 1890s Frederic Myers did more than anyone else to tie psychical research to the developing interest in submerged and unknown areas of consciousness, or as some psychologists preferred to say, the unconscious. The elaboration of his theory of the subliminal self, which first appeared as a series of articles in the *Proceedings of the SPR,* made Myers a major influence among those psychologists trying to understand mind as something a lot more independent of physical changes in the body than previous physiological theories had suggested.[41] In setting out his theory, Myers wrote: "I suggest, then, that the stream of consciousness in which we habitually live is not the only consciousness which exists in connection with our organism. Our habitual or empirical consciousness may consist of a mere selection from a multitude of thoughts and sensations, of which some at least are equally conscious with those that we empirically know. I accord no primacy to my ordinary waking self, except that among my potential selves this one has shown itself the fittest to meet the needs of common life." [42] The subliminal self was all those streams of consciousness, taken together, that did not form part of one's habitual consciousness. However hidden, it was as fully aware of itself (hence conscious) as that self controlling most of our normal waking behavior.

Some of Janet's ideas had been incorporated into Myers's theory, for Myers knew Janet's work very well. The Frenchman had suggested that independent centers of personality existed outside the area of normal consciousness, and that in certain circumstances those disassociated states of consciousness could seize the individual and disrupt normal behavior. However, between Myers's line of speculation and that of Janet there lay an important difference. Janet associated the condition of disassociation with mental sickness, especially hysteria. Chiding those who tried to explain genius or supernormal psychic illumination by reference to his conception of the subconscious, Janet insisted that he used the word in an altogether prosaic sense.

"The poor patients whom I studied," he said, "had no genius; the phenomena which had become subconscious with them were very simple phenomena such as among other men are a part of their personal consciousness and excite no wonder. They had lost the power to will and the knowledge of self. They had a disease of the personality, nothing more." [43]

Myers did not deny the possibility of a pathological condition arising from the subliminal self, but he was far more interested in the subliminal self as a source of genius and religious inspiration. The later Freudian concept that made the unconscious the receptacle of forgotten and repressed ideas bore little relation to Myers's ideas. The subliminal self was an independent center of mental life that opened human beings outward to worlds beyond themselves. It was that part of us that best fitted the needs of the "uncommon life." A "rubbish heap as well as a treasure house," it contained "degenerations and insanities as well as the beginning of a higher development." [44] Myers's most obvious predecessor was von Hartmann, and his most obvious successor was Carl Jung.

Myers's theory stimulated James because it pointed to an intriguing ambiguity in the common use of the world abnormal. That ambiguity formed an important opening theme in his Gifford lectures on religious experience. [45] If persons behaved oddly, they might be better off or they might be worse off than the rest of us. Or, what was more likely, they might be a little of both. James identified Myers's great contribution (he called the subliminal-self theory "a rather momentous event in the history of our Science") [46] as the coordination of a "lot of scattered phenomena" into a system "so that no one can now touch one part of the fabric without finding the rest entangled with it."

The previously unrelated phenomena that James had in mind included "unconscious cerebration, dreams, hypnotism, hysteria, inspirations of genius, the willing game, planchette, crystal-gazing, hallucinatory voices, apparitions of the dying, medium trances, demonical possession, clairvoyance, thought transference—even ghosts." In James's mind much work remained to be done on the theory. In reviewing Myers's *Human Personality and Its Survival of Bodily Death*, James wrote: "The 'scientific' critic can only say it is a pity that so vast and vaguely defined a hypothesis should be reared upon a set of facts so few and so imperfectly ascertained." [47] But many levels of James's thought suggested parallels with Myers's view of subliminal consciousness. James agreed with Myers that "each of us is in reality an abiding psychical entity far more extensive than he knows—an individuality which can never express itself completely through any corporeal manifestation." [48] In 1909, the last year of his life, James still considered human beings far more than the sum of their physical parts. He wrote:

> Out of my experience, such as it is (and it is limited enough), one fixed conclusion dogmatically emerges, and that is this, that we with our lives are like islands in the sea, or like trees in the forest. The maple and the pine may whisper to each other with their leaves, and Conanicut and Newport hear each other's foghorns. But the trees also commingle their roots in the darkness underground, and the islands also hang together through the ocean's bottom. Just so there is a continuum of cosmic consciousness, against which our individuality builds but accidental fences, and into which our several minds plunge as into a mother sea or reservoir. [49]

In this same year James congratulated Freud for his successful lectures at Clark University and made his famous remark consigning the future of psychology to the work of the Viennese scientist. But, as he made clear in private, Freud was too narrow for his taste. Freud's focus on repressed sexuality as the cause of dreams and neurotic behavior struck James as a less useful "principle of unity" than Myers's more encompassing elaboration of the hidden life of human beings. [50]

James was scarcely alone in admiring Myers's work. While Pierre Janet took a different view of the disassociated personalities that Myers bundled up together in his concept of the subliminal self, he regarded the nonclinical observations that Myers and other psychical researchers made as a solid contribution to science. As noted before, he regarded the phenomena of trance mediumship and the automatic behavior accompanying it as having great utility as tools by which psychologists might learn more about abnormal mental behavior. Alfred Binet, a French psychologist who followed Janet's lead in treating mental disassociation as a real, not a feigned, condition, also cited Myers's work for the light it shed on "detached, unconscious personality." Believing that there was "no essential difference between the experiments which I have described upon hysterical patients and the more spontaneous experiments that the spiritists practice upon themselves," Binet found the reports printed by the SPR about Mrs. Piper and others extremely suggestive in clarifying how autosuggestion might produce the "division of consciousness" characteristic of hysterical patients.[51] Myers's belief that Mrs. Piper's "disassociation" resulted from real spirit controls did not in Binet's mind destroy the value of his descriptions of her behavior. In combating the idea that trance and hypnotic states were imaginary things not to be taken any more seriously than other imaginary things, Binet and Myers shared quite a lot.

In the United States, a number of important American psychologists in the 1890s agreed with Boris Sidis that Myers's work, and also Gurney's, had done much to illuminate the obscure phenomena of subconscious life. Sidis, who had studied with James at Harvard, was an influential psychopathologist who worked from 1896 to 1901 at the Pathological Institute of the New York State Hospitals. In an important book on suggestion published in 1898, he quoted at length from the publications of the SPR and described how useful automatic writing and planchette had been in his clinical work. Like hypnotism, they were effective means to put the "primary personality" in "direct intercourse with the risen lower subwaking self." [52]

To be sure, the attitudes of most American psychologists and psychopathologists who became interested in psychical research were much closer to Janet's and Binet's than to James's or Myers's. That is, they were not inclined to make a metaphysical argument out of the existence of non-normal areas of consciousness. Joseph Jastrow, a psychologist who was to spend most of his academic career at the University of Wisconsin, judged the interests of those who pursued psychical research with the hope of finding "personal significance of immediate events" as "hokum." [53] (Jastrow also found "ill-advised" Hamlet's remark to Horatio about there being more things in heaven and earth than are dreamt of in our philosophies.) Nonetheless he followed the work of the society quite closely and wrote: "The study of the subconscious or the subliminal consciousness, of multiple personality, of mental automatisms, of involuntary actions, of induced visualizations, of sporadic hallucinations, may be cited as further illustrations of topics interesting to the 'psychical researcher' for their bearings upon the apparent transcendence of the normal, and to the psychologist for illustrations of important groups of mental processes and relations." [54]

G. Stanley Hall expressed a similar attitude toward psychical research. An original sponsor and vice-president of the ASPR, he said with respect to spiritualist phenomena that "most physiologists and psychologists are now convinced that here is one of the most interesting fields for scientific investigation." [55] While calling for a serious study of the field, Hall made it clear from the beginning that the value of psychical research did not lie for him in the discoveries he might make in the fields of telepathy or spirit communication. Rather, he looked to it to show "the utter inadequacy of current psychology in dealing with the unconscious." Once "the intricacy and complexity of the subliminal psychic processes" is understood, people, Hall argued, would stop regarding "every eruption from the unconscious . . . as of ghostly origin." [56]

Hall's hostility toward those who labeled "supernormal" what was merely "abnormal" perhaps reflected his own anger at himself for some of his earlier "boyish credulity." As a youth he had accepted the truth of spiritualist claims, and at one point in his student life he had, in company with Simon Newcomb, visited every professional medium in Philadelphia. Long after that, he confessed, he continued to have "a strange combination of aversion from and attraction to all the works and ways of believers." "The attraction," he wrote, "is entirely due to the conviction that there is something here of great moment that psychology has not yet fathomed, and the revulsion is toward the recrudescence in this cult of a savage superstition which belongs more to the troglodyte age than to our own." [57]

The *American Journal of Psychology,* which Hall edited, reviewed most books on psychical research with a shake of the head, expressing amazement that intelligent people could push such interesting observations about behavior toward such bizarre conclusions. Hall, however, admired some of the work in the field. Théodore Flournoy, the Swiss psychologist who was a correspondent of James, wrote a fascinating account of his experiences with Hélène Smith, a beautiful and healthy young spiritualist medium. The book *From India to the Planet Mars* unraveled the complex components of her messages, including those supposedly delivered in the Martian language, and managed to relate them all back to childhood memories.[58] To Hall, such a detailed tracing of the way subliminal fantasies were used to escape imaginatively from an unhappy life was the best product of psychical research.

Flournoy's thesis appeared in Hall's own later work and in an interesting book by one of his students.[59] Amy Tanner, who studied with Hall at Clark, wrote *Studies in Spiritism* in an effort to find some middle ground between those psychologists and biologists who argued with respect to subconscious ideas that there was "nothing here but neural action without consciousness" and those who posited "the subconscious . . . as our avenue of communication with God." "An appreciation of the wonderful complexity and delicacy of our psychical processes," Tanner wrote, "as well as the neural ones underlying them, is the most important net gain resulting from all these studies in Psychical Research." [60]

Morton Prince furnishes yet another important example of an American psychologist who at the turn of the century saw a relationship between the best work in psychical research and his own field of abnormal psychology. Prince, a close friend of Richard Hodgson, generously credited the pioneers of psychical research with their part in the revolt against strictly physiological definitions of mental illness. Prince was trained in neurology and diseases of the nervous system, so his part in the revolt was important. He gave Gurney equal credit with Janet in "demonstrating that the mind can be so disassociated as to exhibit two or more foci of activity—one of which the personal consciousness is unaware." [61]

To their everlasting credit, Prince argued, psychical researchers were among the first of a very narrow circle of people in America and England to recognize the importance of the subconscious as a clinical concept. Aside from his work as editor of *The Journal of Abnormal Psychology*, Prince's most important contribution to psychopathology was his study of Miss Beauchamp. Praised at the time as a valuable examination of a case of multiple personality, this study compared the abruptly changing faces of Miss Beauchamp to the changing personalities of the trance medium. In fact, one of the alter egos of Miss Beauchamp engaged in automatic writing and fancied herself in contact with the spirit world. While Prince disagreed with Hodgson, who accepted some types of secondary personality as real spirit entities, Prince could not understand how anyone engaged in psychopathological work could ignore automatic writing, crystal gazing, and a whole range of "seemingly 'occult' phenomena." Not only interesting in themselves, they also furnished modes "of investigating the nature and potentialities of processes outside of awareness." [62]

Therefore, while the ASPR had not become the booming enterprise in America James hoped it would, psychical research in the 1890s had not been brushed aside, either. Through the new psychology, it touched on a matter that would in a short time gain revolutionary significance. Respected academic psychologists paid attention to it and even dealt with it in university courses. Edward Scripture at Yale and Edward Titchener at Cornell viewed the field with contempt, but they had no sympathy with any psychological perspective that played around with anything so abstract as an unconscious mind. James at Harvard, Hall at Clark, and Edmund Delabarre at Brown included material on psychical research in their lectures. No doubt the most enthusiastic classroom teacher of psychical research was Harlow Gale of the psychological laboratory at the University of Minnesota. "Though I appreciate in the highest degree," he wrote, "and after four years' experience of the Psychological Laboratories of Leipzig and Berlin, the great work which experimental Psychology is consciously or unconsciously doing in freeing Psychology from Metaphysics and raising it to a worthy place among the Sciences, yet I deliberately believe that for immediate practical returns in education, the SPR has more to offer than all the Psychological Laboratories." [63]

The academic ties psychical research had to psychology were reinforced in popular writings about the unconscious. In books that were still absolutely innocent of Freudian concepts, various authors praised psychical research as providing "the necessary corrective for the materialistic conclusions toward which the investigations of the psychopathologists tend." [64] Typical of the popularizers was Thomas Jay Hudson. His first book *The Law of Psychic Phenomena,* published in 1893, was a hodgepodge of ideas from Janet, Myers, and his own imagination. It sold over one hundred thousand copies and was probably not a bad index of what sorts of ideas the new psychology of the unconscious suggested to the average American.

In brief, Hudson posited the existence in every human being of "two minds, each endowed with separate and distinct entities and powers." The objective mind, which in Hudson's terminology formed the rough equivalent of normal consciousness, was the one most used by people of healthy mental disposition. The subjective mind, in contrast, was the source of the extraordinary powers of spiritualist mediums and clairvoyants. Unfortunately, reliance on it drove people insane. That puzzled Hudson, and he tried to rescue from his bewilderment a logical proof of immortality. Since no faculty, emotion, or organism of the human mind lacked a functional purpose, he said, and since the subjective mind had no functional purpose in this life, God must have created it for use in another life. Human immortality, he concluded, "is as scientifically correct as it would be to predicate the capacity to navigate the air of an animal with wings." [65]

Just after the turn of the century James Hervey Hyslop emerged as the dominant figure in American psychical research. He was in some ways a man ideally suited to continue the work that James had begun in making psychical research a respectable branch of academic psychology. His intellectual development and his temperament were not unlike those of some of the founders of psychical research in England. Born on a farm in Ohio in 1854, Hyslop grew up in the Associate Presbyterian church, a "small but very orthodox and conservative denomination" that remained apart from the United Presbyterian church because of the latter's growing liberalism. He attended church services of that denomination until it died out in 1874.

Religious controversy was about the only thing that relieved the monotony of farm work. By his own estimate, Hyslop resembled his father. They shared an "intellectual and reflective temperament" that was ill-suited to the task of making money out of a farm. His disposition, however, was "firmer and more obstinate" than his father's—a quality that in later life did not always serve him well.[66]

"Until I was fifteen or sixteen years of age," he recalled, "our first Sunday task, whether we went to church or not, was to commit to memory a part or the whole of a psalm, House's Version, and to read some of the Bible. . . . The observance of Sunday, or Sabbath, which father always called it, . . . was very strict. We had preaching about half the time. There were also two sermons a day, lasting from ten or eleven in the morning until three in the afternoon." As might be expected, human depravity and the threat of damnation were the doctrines of his boyhood church he came most to resent. He faced death everywhere in his youth (he lost his mother, a brother, and a sister), yet religion made death a "frightful thing" to him.

However, at seventeen or eighteen he was still firm in his faith. To help keep him that way, his father decided not to send him to the University of Michigan. Instead, Hyslop went to West Geneva College, a Presbyterian institution in Northwood, Ohio, where, Hyslop recalled, "the chief object . . . was to give an education that would preserve the young man's religious convictions."

Nonetheless, religious skepticism began to set in. He left West Geneva College after two years and finished college at Wooster University. While the latter was also a Presbyterian school, it allowed Hyslop a freer hand in pursuing science. Accepting a teaching position after graduation, he found that he no longer knew what to teach about religion. At a precise moment, the memory of which stayed with him always, he decided to renounce the convictions of his father. "Well," he said, "I cannot believe it. I shall give up and take the consequences. I shall surrender every position in life and all my friends, rather than give up my conscience in this matter. I will take whatever consequences come." After that decision, he wrote, "I walked the floor crying like a child and perspiring like a horse for an hour and a half, but with a sense of relief that I cannot describe."

Hyslop's break with Christianity did not mean a turn to atheism. While he accepted the consequences of "the rationalistic point of view," religion, he said, had "a new and profounder interest for me." At that juncture in his life he traveled to Germany and attended Wundt's lectures at the University of Leipzig (a course of action that "nearly broke my father's heart"). In Germany he met his future wife (there were "no excitingly romantic incidents in my love affairs") and returned to a year's job at Lake Forest University and then a seven-month appointment at Smith College as H. N. Gardiner's assistant in psychology and ethics. He finished a Ph.D. under G. Stanley Hall at Johns Hopkins in 1887. Two years later he accepted a position in Columbia's Department of Psychology and Philosophy and rose during the next decade to the rank of professor.

At the same time as he was pursuing the steps of normal academic advancement, Hyslop became deeply interested in psychical research. An 1886 article in *The Nation* entitled "Telepathy Again" got him started. As had others before him, he hoped to find in psychical research something that satisfied both his religious and his scientific interests. A short time later Hyslop met Richard Hodgson in New York City and had some sittings with Mrs. Piper. He was impressed, and after a long investigation finally capitulated as totally as Hodgson had to the spiritualist interpretation of her powers.

In Hyslop's mind, neither telepathy nor any other plausible theory could explain the extraordinary "hits" that Piper's messages contained about his family life. Interestingly, Hyslop describes his decision to accept the spirit hypothesis in much the same dramatic language as that he used when he deserted the religion of his father. "I shall never forget," he wrote, "the incident that was the turning point in my convictions." In 1900, after giving a speech on psychical research, he again referred to a decisive moment in life with a reference to "burning his bridges." Yet another dramatic turn was to occur to change drastically once again the nature of his professional commitments.

In late 1900, his wife died. Then in 1901, his own health failed. "I had broken down," he wrote, "with nervous prostration and tuberculosis, with stomach complications." [67] James expressed alarm. On December 26, 1901, he wrote to Flournoy: "Poor Hyslop's work on Mrs. Piper, combined with the loss of his wife, so weakened him that the microbes of tuberculosis found him an easy prey. He is now in the country taking an open air cure in an almost arctic cold and leading otherwise the life of a vegetable. . . . He is a very manly fellow, who has had a very hard life, and I am afraid that this is the end of him for worldly purposes." [68] For Hyslop's critics, nothing in his later activities would prove James wrong. Though Hyslop regained his health, he resigned his position at Columbia and devoted the rest of his life to psychical research. He was the first American scholar to make this a full-time career.

Before Hodgson's sudden death on December 20, 1905, Hyslop had approached the former to suggest the possibility of merging a proposed organization of his own, the American Institute of Scientific Research, with the American branch of the SPR. Since 1900 he had toyed with the idea of reestablishing an independent organization for American psychical research. His problem, aside from personal crises, had been funding. The Carnegie Institution rebuffed him, and private money was difficult to obtain. Although Hyslop and Hodgson were unable to get together, Hyslop finally raised $25,000 himself, and after Hodgson's death, talked the SPR into an amicable dissolution of its American branch. The American Society for Psychical Research, which was technically Section B of the American Institute for Scientific Research, began publishing its journals and proceedings in 1907. [69]

Hyslop's original plans for the American Institute for Scientific Research were designed to take advantage of the sympathetic attention already accorded to psychical research by certain psychologists. The proposed Section A was to devote itself to psychopathology and abnormal psychology while Section B carried out related but quite separate work in "Supernormal Psychology." As Hyslop explained the scheme, Section A would investigate "such cases as functional mental disease, and all psychological disturbances due even to organic troubles; functional insanity and hallucinations; amnesia or loss of memory, especially of that type often taken for serious insanity, but curable by other than ordinary methods; secondary personality or unconscious mental action simulative of other agencies than the normal consciousness; functional melancholia and vicarious or sympathetic mental aberrations; neurasthenia and psychasthenia; hysteria and hystero-epilepsy; obsessions; fixed ideas or monomanias; phobias; delusions, alcoholism, and all functional troubles that may ultimately be made to yield to the various forms of suggestion." To deal with this rather staggering range of mental disorders, Hyslop imagined a "clinic and hospital of the Salpetriere, Nancy or Berillon type."

By contrast, Section B would consider cases of "alleged telepathy, alleged clairvoyance, alleged mediumship, and all claims to the supernormal acquisition of knowledge, as well as the alleged production of physical effects without contact." In Hyslop's mind the work of the two sections was to be complementary "because the abnormal is sometimes the medium through which supernormal facts find their way." "It is therefore important," he concluded, "that we articulate the results of investigations in both fields of mental phenomena while we keep the actual work of inquiry in each case independent." [70]

Although Hyslop appointed Dr. Titus Bull to head Section A, it never existed anywhere but on paper. It retained its titular status until 1922, but Hyslop in effect had to combine supernormal and abnormal psychology in the publications he issued through Section B. In spite of that disappointment he took active steps to reach an academic audience in America and Europe. Many distinguished scholars endorsed the work of the new organization. Hyslop collected and printed letters from, among others, Max Dessoir of the University of Berlin, H. N. Gardiner of Smith College, James Mark Baldwin of Johns Hopkins, E. H. Lindley of Indiana University, Nicholas Murray Butler of Columbia, and Charles Richet of the Physiological Institute of Paris.[71] All the psychologists and psychotherapists already mentioned in this chapter (except for Freud, who was yet to emerge in the English-speaking world as a major figure) added their tributes. Of course many of the academic endorsers attached greater importance to the projected work in abnormal psychology than to the work in supernormal psychology that most interested Hyslop. However, most of them acknowledged possible connections between the two areas of investigation and in addition seemed willing to judge the work of Section B on its own merits.

The cooperative scientific venture envisioned in Hyslop's original plan and endorsed by those letters did not work out very well. In large measure Hyslop had only himself to blame. He found it almost impossible to cooperate with people who could not be made to share his point of view. Hyslop ran Section B like a dictator, saying quite correctly that any democratically organized society devoted to psychical research would immediately forfeit a claim to scientific respectability. He faced the constant threat that his funds would be cut off because much of the financial support of the ASPR came from people who could be classed as spiritualists of the most credulous kind. It was one thing to protect the work of Section B from people who could not set "prejudice and emotion aside,"[72] but it was quite another to look upon the rest of the scientific world with open suspicion.

I. K. Funk, of the Funk and Wagnalls publishing house, was a spiritualist. He also very much wished to see Section B establish a reputation for solid scientific work. In a letter of June, 1906, he criticized Hyslop for not being more open to input from other scientists. Discussing the case of one "prominent" professor with whom he had spoken, Funk wrote: "He was deeply interested in such a movement, but unfortunately has a deeply seated feeling against yourself. He asks why men like Professor James, who did not hesitate to identify himself with the old society, do not lend their names to this one. Then he asks also why, after twenty-odd years of work in this country, no men better known for psychology and scientific work than Dr. Savage and Dr. Newton, can be found for your Board. He says your circular indicates it is a 'hyslop affair' throughout, and that no man with a reputation for science would risk it in a movement of this kind unless there is a strong board behind it." [73]

The "prominent" professor's objection, as related through Funk, had substance. Hyslop did not want a board of directors containing stronger voices than his own. Section B, he feared, might be pushed in a direction he did not wish it to go. For example, in a letter to Weston D. Bayley in 1912, Hyslop wondered whether it would be worth asking Professor Angell of Chicago and Professor Jastrow to sit on the board "merely to give respectability to the work." He decided against the idea because of the "power of mischief" that Jastrow and Angell could exercise. "You will remember," he said to Bayley, "how it was with Gardiner and Newbold; they wanted to dictate what should be published, without furnishing anything to be published, and that meant we couldn't publish anything." [74] He wrote again to Bayley: "How would it do to ask a lot of college and university men to go on an Advisory Council and Corresponding Membership. We could then use their names for the publications we send them and they would have no power to do mischief in our work." [75] Hyslop apparently never understood, or cared, how little chance there was for scientific cooperation when endorsements were sought on such terms. Under his direction the ASPR remained for all practical purposes a one-man operation.

His critics believed (and they were not entirely wrong) that Hyslop unfairly skewed the work of Section B to promote his personal belief in spiritualism—a belief that, not incidentally, predated the founding of the second ASPR. However meticulous his research—and Hyslop did seem tireless in his examination of detail—his conclusions had a way of coming back to the same point. A dreadful editor of his own writing, he never learned to distinguish between elaboration and repetition. "Propagandist" is not quite a fair word, but Hyslop's popular books on the subject of spiritualism did nothing to enhance his reputation as a scientist.[76] To be sure, Hyslop was not attracted to either popular spiritualism or spiritualist religion. "I do not care a penny," he wrote, "what the other life is like, nor for the pleasure of communicating with friends there."[77] He emphasized the spiritualist hypothesis because he believed it to be the best evidence that he had to counter scientific materialism. Nonetheless, his persistent defense of the theory began to look unbalanced.

Hyslop bore a particular animus against the idea that telepathy might better explain Mrs. Piper's supernormal awareness than spirit communication. Oblivious to the skepticism with which most psychologists viewed either theory, Hyslop made arguments out of what appeared to be the most tenuous logic. If Mrs. Piper's "hits" stemmed from something more than coincidence or a generous interpretation of the messages, then using telepathy as an explanation for them, as Hyslop argued, did seem to credit the medium with rather implausible powers of "cosmic thought reading."

Hyslop's frequent attempts to make a case for spiritualism out of the unlikeliness of telepathy, however, convinced few scientists. In fact it neatly played into the hands of those who doubted all reported cases of the supernormal. If implausibility was enough of a basis to reject a hypothesis, then scientists had no trouble getting rid of Hyslop's spiritualism. In fact, in many minds the vocation of promoting Mrs. Piper did to Hyslop what Morton Prince judged it had done to Hodgson: "It wrecked Dick Hodgson who had one of the most beautiful minds I ever knew. When once Dick . . . had accepted the concept of spiritualism all his critical faculty was lost; his sense of perspective and proportion went with it . . . he found it easy to explain all phenomena through spiritualism, and to the spiritualist concept everything was adjusted."[78]

Although Hyslop made genuine attempts to relate psychological theories about the unconscious, including Freud's when it came along, to the phenomena studied by psychical research, his ideas never led anywhere. Rather than establishing connections between abnormal and supernormal psychology, Hyslop at times seemed more intent on proving the absence of any connection. At the very least, as he wrote to George Dorr, he saw it as vitally important to separate truly supernormal mental capacities from any association with insanity.[79]

On this and related issues, Hyslop confessed genuine perplexity. The supernormal, he thought, often appeared within the framework of the abnormal. For example, a spirit control could be "superposed" on an unconscious secondary personality or "interwoven with it." [80] But spirits and secondary personalities were distinguishable, and Hyslop made it a primary aim of psychical research to learn how to see the difference. The interesting possibility that madness and divine inspiration were very close to being the same thing offended Hyslop's sense of classification. Hence he objected to Myers's theory of the subliminal self because in his understanding it assigned "to the same genus phenomena so diverse as organic reflexes, unconscious mental action and supernormal revelation." [81]

Hyslop never quite settled his two minds about the usefulness of abnormal psychology to psychical research. Certainly, he felt, no one could establish genuine mediumship without first exhausting every possibility that the alleged medium was a victim of a personality disorder.[82] On the other hand, abnormal psychology might tempt an investigator to discount evidence of the supernormal and prematurely adopt a theory of hysterical seizure to explain the facts.[83] With respect to the Doris Fischer case of multiple personality, which Walter Franklin Prince examined for the ASPR, Hyslop argued that a confusing variety of disassociated secondary personalities obscured the evidence of an incipient mediumship and even prevented its development.[84] Hyslop was never sure why "hysteria and its various complications" seemed to be either "the necessary precondition of the supernormal in any form or a frequent concomitant of it." Whatever the reason, it was too bad. Hysteria in Hyslop's mind most certainly hindered communication with the other side.[85]

Despite the confusion between disassociated secondary personalities and genuine spirit voices, Hyslop had no doubt that supernormal powers "have an extraneous origin that is wholly distinct from the origin of the ordinarily subconscious facts." [86]

To clarify the problem, Hyslop finally hypothesized that two distinct areas of mind lay outside of normal consciousness—the supracolliminal, which was above normal consciousness, and the subliminal, which was below it. The behavior that was stirred from the two areas might in some cases look the same, but the difference between behavior stemming from one as opposed to the other was profound.[87]

Hyslop's shortcomings are worth emphasizing because psychical researchers, much in the manner of nineteenth-century spiritualists, have too often blamed everything but their own actions for their failure to win scientific acceptance. To be fair to Hyslop, one must concede that his plans would have run into difficulty no matter what he did. A number of factors having nothing to do with Hyslop's behavior and attitudes hindered the efforts to institutionalize relations between abnormal and supernormal psychology. For one thing, Freud's influence, which began to be felt in the United States following his lectures at Clark in 1909, hurt Hyslop's cause. In his substitution of free association for the tools of hypnotism, automatic writing, and crystal gazing, Freud eliminated a whole category of things that had previously been of joint interest to psychical researchers and psychotherapists. Psychoanalysis changed the whole clinical approach to purported cases of multiple personality. Perhaps more important, Freudian ideas acted as an additional hindrance in the way of the notion that individuals might through their subconscious mind reach out beyond themselves into realms of transcendent knowledge. The Freudian unconscious contained only the stuff of instinctual drives, forgotten experience, and repressed desire. Popular accounts described it as "dishonest and cunning." In contrast to the "idealistic and romantic" ideas of Myers, the early Freudian school in America emphasized the unconscious as the repository "of the moral and aesthetic excreta of the idea life." [88] Psychical researchers suddenly fell under the scrutiny of psychoanalysts who wanted to know what childhood event had led to their odd interests.

Actually, though his support came too late to benefit Hyslop, Freud regarded psychical research with some seriousness. True, in his first published remarks about telepathy, which came in

any case after Hyslop's death, he expressed reservations about
discussing a subject so susceptible to popular misinterpretation.
He feared that if the facts of telepathy proved indisputable, the
absence of an acceptable theory to explain them would open the
floodgates of occultist fantasies. In that case, he wrote, "we may
anticipate a dreadful collapse of critical thought and of mechanistic science." [89]

Nonetheless, Freud was a corresponding member of the SPR.
In the early 1930s, when he published the *New Introductory Lectures on Psychoanalysis,* he no longer worried about the dangers
of subjects it investigated. "It seems to me," he said, "that one
is displaying no great trust in science if one cannot rely on it to
accept and deal with any occult hypothesis that may turn out to
be correct." He was confident that thought transference, should
it prove factual, would be explicable as a physical process that
would "favor the extension of the scientific (or, as opponents
would say, mechanistic) way of thinking onto the elusive world
of the mind." [90] Freud had no use for the category "supernormal." But he shared James's interest in stray facts. On one occasion, he even remarked that if he had his life to live again he
would devote it to psychical research. [91]

In the new century many of the American psychologists who
had taken some interest in psychical research found an association with the ASPR more trouble than it was worth. Less obstinate leadership from Hyslop could not have changed that
fact. The American psychologists who tried to make respectable
the idea of an unconscious mind had enough problems without
carrying the additional burden of seeming to support theories
linked in the popular mind to spiritualism. At the turn of the
century most psychologists viewed the physical processes that
explained consciousness and linked it to motor responses as the
only legitimate concerns of scientific psychology. Most of them
refused to believe that mental states, taken by themselves,
caused illness. The innovators in abnormal psychology who
suggested otherwise risked certain dangers in associating with
people interested in the supernormal. Joseph Jastrow indicated
what those were in writing: "The problems of psychical research engaged my active interest from the beginnings of that

movement, which in the closing decades of the nineteenth century was so prominent that in many circles a psychologist
meant a 'spook hunter.' " [92]

Hugo Münsterberg was especially hard on those of his colleagues who treated psychical matters with anything less than
contempt. James brought Münsterberg to Harvard in 1892 to
direct the university's laboratory of experimental psychology.
Most of his assumptions pointed in the direction of the behaviorist school founded by John Broadus Watson in 1912. The new
theories of unconscious mental life offended him. Prince and
Jastrow raised his ire because they had "developed theoretical
ideas of the subconscious which seem to the public not unfavorable to spiritualist claims." That, of course, had not been
their intention, but Münsterberg saw no essential difference between what they said and what Myers had said. "It is not the
least merit of the scientific physiological explanation," he
wrote, "that it obstructs the path of such pseudophilosophy." [93]
Anything not scientific by his definition was of necessity mys-
tical. He recognized only the two categories.

The habit of lumping together things meant to be distinct was
not confined to Münsterberg. During World War I, Knight Dunlap, a professor of psychology at Johns Hopkins, warned against
what he considered an alarming outburst of romanticism in his
discipline. Noting that booksellers shelved Freud's books on the
unconscious with books on spiritualism and religious mysticism, Dunlap wrote: "The fact that patrons who look over the
stock of one of these subjects are apt to be interested in the
others, has its foundations in the real unity of the three, which
runs through their diversities. And all three involve an assault
on the very life of the biological sciences; an assault which scientific psychology alone is capable of warding off." [94] Psychologists who took Freud more seriously than St. John of the Cross,
or at least could distinguish between them, naturally deplored
the waywardness of booksellers who shelved psychological
studies of the unconscious in the occult section. But they grew
cautious about doing anything that seemed to make it a plausible practice.

In his presidential address to the SPR, Frederic Myers had

said: "Our duty is not the founding of a new sect, nor even the establishment of a new science, but is rather the expansion of Science herself until she can satisfy those questions which the human heart will rightly ask." [95] Hyslop, who revived the work of psychical research in the United States, died in 1920, leaving the ties between his interests and those of leading American psychologists in a less promising state than he had found them. For his successors it was too bad. He willed to them an organization that was little more than a sect. It now talked about itself as a separate scientific concern in ways that would surely have bothered Myers. Moreover, getting the relevance of its work recognized by other scientific fields proved to be a more difficult task than James, for all his understanding of the problem, would ever have imagined.

6

Interim: The ASPR and Margery

Both the first American spiritualists and their successors, the psychical researchers, had encouraged independent scientists to conduct their own investigations of spiritual or psychical phenomena. However, in the period before World War I, the few university studies that were undertaken all turned up negative results. For example, Henry Seybert, a wealthy Philadelphian, left $60,000 to the University of Pennsylvania at his death in 1883. The gift, which was to endow a chair in philosophy, was contingent upon the university's appointing a commission to investigate modern spiritualism.

A committee of distinguished gentlemen was duly named and a study undertaken. Though at the outset of the work some on the committee had been inclined to accept spiritualist claims, the *Preliminary Report* of the committee (as it turned out, the only report from the committee), which was published in 1887, contained little more than a discussion of fraudulent mediumistic practices.[1] A later university study, this time emanating from Stanford, did more direct damage to Hyslop's attempts to interest the academic world in work of the ASPR. Leland Stanford's brother left a bequest sufficient to make psychical research a permanent branch of university study. John Coover of Stanford's Psychology Department spent part of that money conducting a lengthy and, for the time, sophisticated statistical test of the hypothesis of thought transference. He published his findings in 1917, stating that as far as he was concerned, they provided no evidence of supernormal cognition of any kind.[2] Although Coover continued to be interested in psychical research, the university subsequently spent Thomas Stanford's money with as little attention as possible to the specific terms of the gift.

Given his original aims, Hyslop accomplished relatively little as head of the ASPR. Coover's work at Stanford indicated the difficulties involved in establishing psychical research as a field of university study. Nevertheless, Hyslop did make psychical research a much better defined and controllable enterprise than nineteenth-century spiritualism had been. In his quest for academic standing, he and the later psychical researchers who followed his lead tried to avoid the religious and reform controversies that had helped produce the public visibility of spiritualism. For that reason, the cultural impact of psychical research upon America in the twentieth century sometimes seems less dramatic than that of spiritualism in the nineteenth. Psychical researchers set out to circumscribe the diffuse spiritualist impulse by confining investigations of the supernormal to a few reliable scientific organizations. In contrast to nineteenth-century spiritualism, which produced a bewildering array of leading figures, American psychical research has until recently been dominated by a handful of individuals. The historical investigation of psychical research necessarily centers on their labors.

On the other hand, though the audience for most journals of psychical research was intentionally less broad than it had been for spiritualist publications, the subject did receive substantial popular attention. In the category of marginal scientific "facts," only the post–World War II reports of flying saucers seemed as plausible to the general public as reports about extrasensory perception. The issues raised by psychical researchers related to a wide range of questions that people in many fields were beginning to ask about scientific work, especially in the aftermath of the twentieth-century revolution in physics.

Psychical researchers continued the spiritualists' attempt to accommodate science and religion, but in the context of a society that had grown far more professional and specialized. Like spiritualism, psychical research was very much a product of its culture. The relation of the various sciences to a philosophy of materialism concerned and even worried a good many twentieth-century Americans. Psychical researchers tried to transcend certain scientific biases they felt were endemic in their culture. As will be seen, however, in reacting to them they were also limited by them.

Before Hyslop died, he found a successor in Walter Franklin Prince. Prince was born in Detroit, Maine, in 1863. Like Hyslop, he grew up in a farming community in a strongly Methodist home. Prince, as he later told a friend, was reared on the Bible. When he was eighteen, he graduated from the Maine Wesleyan Seminary and began work as a Methodist minister, but he subsequently felt a need for more education and returned to school. He first went to Drew Theological Seminary and then to Yale where he received, with Phi Beta Kappa laurels, an A.B. at the age of thirty-three. Several years later, in 1899, Yale conferred on him a doctorate in psychology for a dissertation written on the subject of multiple personality.[3]

Though he did not leave the ministry, Prince's theological views underwent substantial liberalization. He became an Episcopal minister and directed his church work toward social gospel activities in which he could apply his expertise in abnormal psychology. In 1911, while serving as rector of All Saints Church in Pittsburgh, he met a disturbed young girl who suffered from a severe case of mental disassociation. Prince's own personal life was far from untroubled, and strong ties of love and dependence developed between the two. Prince had joined the ASPR in 1908, and this case gave him a specific reason to turn to Hyslop for advice. One of the girl's disassociated personalities, always referred to as "Sleeping Margaret," claimed to be a spirit voice. The clinical situation took a remarkable turn when Prince and his wife decided to take the girl into their home as their foster daughter.

Theodosia, the name they gave to this girl, was the "Doris

Fischer" of the well-known study of multiple personality that Prince published in the *Proceedings of the ASPR* in 1915. The report was important if only because so rarely does a trained psychologist bring a victim of a personality disorder within the intimate circle of his or her family. The strongly ambivalent bonds that normally developed between patient and analyst in psychoanalytic sessions were in this situation unusually accentuated. Prince missed most of the Freudian implications and felt that Theodosia had been cured when all the subconscious personalities except "Sleeping Margaret" had disappeared.[4]

Prince began a close collaboration with Hyslop after he moved to New York City to become director of the Department of Psychotherapeutics at St. Mark's Church. In 1917 he became a research officer of the ASPR and prided himself on his high standards of objectivity. Prince's formal training in abnormal psychology made him an ideal associate for Hyslop. Moreover, at the time he joined the ASPR in a research capacity, he was not, as Hyslop had been, a convinced spiritualist.

Prince's public attitude of skepticism toward all reports of the supernormal potentially carried some weight, although Prince proved no more able than Hyslop was to eschew speculating about his work in popular forums. At the least, Prince hoped that other scientists would accept him as the "excessively cautious" researcher he believed himself to be. Accuracy, he wrote, was a "religion" to him, and "minute analysis an obsession." A skilled magician in addition to his other talents, he was "alive by experience and study to various pitfalls of illusion, delusion, and deception."[5]

In 1920 Prince succeeded Hyslop as principal research officer of the ASPR and editor of its *Journal.* The transition happened to coincide with what looked like a lucky break for the fortunes of American psychical research—the arrival of William McDougall from England to head Harvard's Psychology Department. How the unorthodox Englishman ever got the nod from Harvard is something of a puzzle. Aside from his well-known interest in psychical research, he was a Lamarckian biologist who believed in the soul, an opponent of democracy, and a supporter of applied eugenics.[6] Each of these views eventually became bones of contention, making his years in Cambridge, Massachusetts, difficult ones. Some people apparently thought that the eccentricities of his professional interests made him a worthy successor to James, and in part this was so. As he admitted, however, he lacked the grace in controversy that his predecessor had had. "I have not been able," he wrote, "to acquire James' magic touch, which made all his readers his friends." [7]

Unlike most of the other early contributors to psychical research, McDougall had not been imbued at an early age with strong religious values. His father was a wealthy manufacturer who preserved "a friendly and respectful neutrality" towards all the leading Christian denominations. By sixteen, McDougall had settled into a mild agnosticism ("not militant, agressively negative, or hostile to religion") that raised few problems with respect to his studies. Christian orthodoxy was to him "a monstrous system of delusions," but he never made much of a fuss about it. He entered the University of Manchester at the age of fifteen, and upon graduation continued his biological and medical studies at Cambridge. What drew him eventually toward psychical research was his resistance to what he regarded as the prevailing reliance upon mechanistic explanations in science. Rather than falling under Huxley's spell, he became "a practicing disciple of Wordsworth." [8] Describing his intellectual development he wrote:

> I had come to see more and more clearly that the main defect of the psychologies with which I had struggled in the opening years of the century was their acceptance, or their compromise with, the mechanistic biology, and their consequent neglect of the purposive or teleological aspect of all mental life. I seemed to see clearly that, whatever theory of the relation of mind to matter . . . one might hold, any psychology that ignored, or failed to bring out clearly, the fundamental purposive nature of mental life, was doomed to sterility. . . . The most essential character of life-processes seemed to be their goal-seeking nature. [9]

Much influenced by James, McDougall approached psychical research through abnormal psychology. "Abnormal psychology," he wrote, "comprises a number of sub-departments, which in the main have been pursued independently by different bodies of workers; happily, in recent years these groups have come more closely together and are now giving mutual aid." He divided the sub-departments into "those that are concerned with minds in definitely morbid or pathological states" and "those concerned with distinctly unusual or abnormal states of mind which cannot fairly be classed as morbid." [10]

Like Hyslop, McDougall feared that the morbid aspects of abnormal psychology had received too much emphasis. Moreover, he disagreed with both Frederic Myers and Morton Prince, who McDougall thought had retained an essentially monistic interpretation of personality. That is, Prince regarded the multiple personalities of Miss Beauchamp as splintered parts of a once-united personality. In McDougall's opinion, secondary personalities, which Myers called subliminal selves, often had nothing to do with the original personality and originated outside the body altogether. They were autonomous and noncorporeal.

McDougall argued that his dualistic theory gave strong support to the spiritualistic explanation of such cases as Mrs. Piper and went far toward supplying a basis for a belief in the survival of human personality after death. [11] (So of course did Myers's theory, but McDougall felt that Myers had stated his case badly.) However, he was less concerned with demonstrating the reality of spirits than with defending what he called animism, his belief that some factor or principle resides in us that is different from body and can exist independently of it. He never regarded the empirical proof of animism as entirely conclusive, but as far as he was concerned, psychical research furnished the only possible source of evidence. McDougall never pretended that his quest for certain proof of animism was disinterested. "To believe in the transcendence of Mind," he said, "is a moral need of mankind in general." [12]

McDougall was forty-nine when he left his post at Oxford to come to Harvard. Almost immediately the board of trustees of the ASPR asked him to become the society's president and to use his prestige to form a scientific advisory committee. He consented and enjoyed good relations with Walter Franklin Prince, who bore the major responsibility for the research and publications of the ASPR. McDougall also sponsored work in psychical research at Harvard. As a memorial to Richard Hodgson, a group of his friends had given Harvard $10,000 in 1912 to be used "in any manner designed to encourage the investigation and study of mental or physical phenomena the origin or expression of which appears to be independent of the ordinary sensory channels." The first recipient of money from the Hodgson Fund was Leonard Troland, who promply employed it to write a report highly critical of existing psychical research. In the early 1920s, McDougall activated the Hodgson Fund to bring to Harvard two young men who made important positive contributions to the field. Gardner Murphy was a Hodgson fellow from 1922 to 1925 and G. H. Estabrooks from 1925 to 1926. They both conducted controlled experiments in telepathy that seemed to reverse John Coover's findings of the preceding decade.[13]

Unfortunately, and despite their credentials, McDougall and Prince found it impossible to maintain control over the ASPR. Neither could claim the absolute allegiance that had been Hyslop's, and both ran afoul of the wishes of major financial contributors to the society. World War I brought a renewed outburst of popular interest in spiritualism. The English scientist Oliver Lodge, a distinguished physicist who had been among the original sponsors of psychical research, published a volume of purported spirit communications from his son Raymond, who had been killed in the war.[14] The desire of many people to communicate with their war dead provided mediums with a lot of business. Lecturers on the subject of spiritualism also did well. In 1922, Arthur Conan Doyle made a triumphant tour across America, speaking on the philosophy of spiritualism. He filled the largest lecture halls in the country to overflowing, and repeated the trick on a second lecture tour, mostly along the West Coast, in 1923.[15]

Many people found it ironical that Sherlock Holmes's creator could not detect the outrageously fraudulent performances of many mediums he endorsed. One of those who questioned Doyle's credulity was Harry Houdini, who nevertheless remained a good friend of Doyle.[16] But, as we have previously seen, spiritualism had always been an appealing subject to those who fancied themselves good detectives and puzzle-solvers. Houdini spent as much time investigating mediums as Doyle did; he merely reached different conclusions concerning them. Americans should not have been surprised to learn early in the 1920s that Thomas Edison was working on a spiritual communication machine.[17]

As psychical researchers would learn again in the 1960s, the sudden popularity of subjects on which they were conducting experiments did not necessarily work to their advantage. McDougall and Prince both became alarmed at the number of credulous spiritualists who joined the ASPR but who were much more interested in popular demonstrations of spirit communication than in legitimate scientific experiment. In an address delivered in 1922, McDougall criticized Conan Doyle, saying: "Only by the methods of Science can we hope to combat effectively the errors of Science."[18] A year later the trustees dismissed McDougall as president and replaced him with Reverend Frederick Edwards. They also demoted Prince to associate editor of the *Journal* and named as a coordinate research officer a man with whom Prince could not work. In 1925, Prince finally resigned from his offices in the ASPR. Until his death in 1934 he ran a rival organization, the Boston Society for Psychic Research. In explaining his reasons for abandoning the ASPR, he wrote:

> The new president tried to "democratize" one of the most technical and difficult of all types of research, brought a "section" composed for the most part of credulous, vaudeville seeking amateurs, into the very building with the ASPR, made the contents of the *Journal* puerile, neglected American Research for the publication of foreign matter, in fact nearly stopped research in order to carry out his futile schemes, put research work, calling for expert judgment, under a lay committee, etc., etc.[19]

Prince was especially bitter because among the trustees who acquiesced in what Prince regarded as the destruction of the ASPR was George Hyslop, the founder's son: "One would have thought that he would have resented the new policies which would have roused his father's scorn, but I see no sign of it." [20]

The person whom Prince most blamed for the troubles of the ASPR was J. Malcolm Bird, an avid spiritualist and psychical researcher who happened to be an associate editor of *Scientific American*. Largely at Bird's urging, but also as a direct result of the interest in spiritualism that followed World War I, the popular scientific magazine in December 1922 offered to pay $2,500 to the first person who produced a "psychic photograph" or "visible psychic manifestation of other character" to the full satisfaction of a panel of judges. [21]

McDougall, Prince, and Houdini consented to serve on the panel. So did Daniel Comstock, a former professor of physics at the Massachusetts Institute of Technology, and Hereward Carrington, the author of a number of popular books on spiritualism and psychical research. Bird was to act as the nonvoting secretary of the committee, but he assumed a far more active role than this title suggested. He did most of the committee's preliminary search for promising subjects to investigate. He toured Europe, attending séances and photographing spirit-produced ectoplasm. In the end, he found what he was looking for much closer to home. In July 1924, Bird reported in the *Scientific American* that the committee had focused its serious attention on a "refined and cultured lady" who lived in Boston. In Bird's mind, as quickly became apparent, Massachusetts had produced a second Mrs. Piper. [22]

Mrs. LeRoi G. Crandon, which proved to be the name of the woman under investigation, was, however, not like Mrs. Piper at all. For one thing, she was the wife of a prominent Boston surgeon who never for a moment entertained the thought of becoming a professional medium or an employee of the ASPR. In fact, rather than accepting fees for her sittings, Margery, as Mrs. Crandon was known to the public, frequently fed investigators elaborate suppers and put them up for the night. Bird was a grateful recipient of her hospitality. Moreover, in contrast to Mrs. Piper, the most distinctive features of Margery's sittings were the physical manifestations.

While Mrs. Crandon was in trance, under the control of her brother Walter, who had died in 1911, tables lifted themselves, furniture moved, and partially materialized spirits poured out of various orifices of Margery's body. In one celebrated proof of his presence, Walter even left behind an impression of his thumbprint. Walter spoke through Margery as well, but the content of his messages aroused less interest than his personality. Walter joined a long list of witty, swaggering, and boisterous spirits who became popular by turning the afterlife into a rollicking and fun-filled land of naughty amusements.[23] In the Jazz Age, he made good copy for newspapers.

Aside from Bird, however, who leaked enthusiastic accounts of Margery to the press, the committee reserved judgment. Only Carrington, who had earlier championed the Italian medium Eusapia Palladino during a disastrous trip to America, was convinced that supernormal phenomena occurred at Margery's séances.[24] At the other extreme, Houdini, after a few sittings with Margery, charged her with deliberate fraud and left the other judges to continue the investigations. Prince, McDougall, and Comstock were suspicious of the physical manifestations, but they found it very difficult to decide what was going on.

Margery's renunciation in advance of the prize money left her with no apparent motive to cheat. On the other hand, the investigators always found their efforts to establish adequate controls to govern the séances blocked in one way or another. Often Walter required the sittings to take place in utter darkness or that Margery's husband be seated next to her. In either circumstance, the judges felt, it was impossible to verify whether Margery's limbs were completely motionless when the manifestations took place. After a considerable expenditure of time, the frustrated McDougall, Comstock, and Prince joined with Houdini in rejecting Mrs. Crandon's claimed proof of supernormal phenomena. In April 1925, the *Scientific American* printed the final report of the judges and declared the contest closed.[25]

As far as the leadership of the ASPR was concerned, however, the matter was not closed. With Prince and McDougall out of the way, and with Bird as the new research officer of the ASPR, the society continued to try to vindicate Mrs. Crandon. Though

with the exception of Houdini, the *Scientific American* committee had ducked the question of whether both the Crandons
were up to their ears in fraud, there seemed to be no other explanation of what happened in the séance room if the phenomena were not genuine. The psychological explanations that
many had used to explain Mrs. Piper's trances were difficult to
apply to physical manifestations. Unconscious secondary personalities could not produce ectoplasm without some help. Unfortunately for the ASPR, few outside the organization were
able to verify what Bird and his friends regarded as indisputable evidence. For example, in the spring and summer of 1925,
four Harvard instructors and a Harvard graduate student made
their own investigation of Mrs. Crandon. Their initial attitude
was skeptical but not hostile. One of them, Hudson Hoagland,
even contemplated doing his dissertation on Margery if either
the supernormal or the abnormal aspects of her psychological
makeup warranted analysis.[26]

Unfortunately, Hoagland was disappointed. In an article that
appeared in the *Atlantic Monthly*, Hoagland concluded that
Walter was an "unconscious impersonation" produced by
Margery while in a hypnotic state in response to her husband's
interest in psychical research.[27] That explanation, Hoagland
thought, might somehow save Margery and her husband from
the charge of conscious deception. But most of the Harvard people who came in contact with the Crandons regarded them both
as deceivers. In either case, the claims made by the ASPR in
Margery's behalf ended for a long time the society's flirtation
with the scientific community.

To judge from what Prince wrote, the rift in the society that
drove him up to Boston resulted from a quarrel between those
who regarded psychical research as an empirical science and
those who valued it as a ready demonstration of spirit communication. Anyone who had followed the work of the society
at all critically would have found that explanation only partially
satisfactory. The Margery case divided loyalties without necessarily separating scientists from blind fools. In keeping with its
nineteenth-century heritage, popular spiritualism in the twentieth century, and particularly that strain of it that became com-

mon in the affairs of the ASPR, continued to define itself as a scientific enterprise. True enough, once spiritualists were convinced of the genuineness of spirit communication, they saw no need to treat every séance as a scientific experiment. But they regarded their basic belief as readily enough demonstrable by scientific standards when the need arose. Their quarrel with Hyslop and later with Prince had little to do with any differences over the appropriateness of investigating mediums or even the reality of spirit voices. The dispute arose over whether séance controls might on some occasions be relaxed so that the spirits could be enjoyed.

And sometimes it was not even that. Certainly Bird, whom Prince fiercely attacked, regarded himself as a scientific investigator with the same general aims as those of his predecessor. In 1931 he resigned as research officer of the ASPR, giving the same reasons Prince had given. He charged the board of trustees with unwarranted interference in his work. Substituting an emotional for a scientific atmosphere, they had, in Bird's mind, allowed the society to degenerate into an organization propagating religious mysticism.[28]

The more one tries to understand the differences between Bird and Prince, the more confused one gets. Prince may well have been right in arguing that Bird was unforgivably taken in by the Crandons, but there were weak points in Prince's own armor. Publicly, Prince approached the whole area of experimental proof of survival after death with caution. It was, as he knew, the most "emotional" of all the subjects covered by psychical research. Even on the international scene Prince gained a reputation among psychical researchers for being unusually cautious about reputed cases of the supernormal, especially when they involved spirits.[29] Yet in some important instances Prince's skepticism, no matter what he said, lapsed. The most controversial case involved Theodosia.

As noted earlier, Prince regarded the psychological treatment of his foster daughter as successful when all the secondary personalities except "Sleeping Margaret" had disappeared. As his correspondence makes perfectly clear, Prince saw no explanation for the remaining alternate personality other than the spiri-

tualist one. A few residual doubts did not prevent him from
relaying spirit messages from "Sleeping Margaret" to his
friends.[30] Gardner Murphy remembered that a "half smile
played on his lips" when he discussed whether the "Sleeping
Margaret" personality was a "guardian spirit." [31] Perhaps, but
there is room to doubt whether the smile was a sign of Prince's
own skepticism. Whatever else may be true, Prince was overly
sanguine about the balance of Theodosia's psychological condition. When he died, her personality disassociation again became severe.[32] Rather than a spirit, "Sleeping Margaret" was
probably a shrewd area of Theodosia's subconscious mind that
succeeded in tying her already devoted stepfather more closely
to her.

Prince also risked his claim to impartial investigation in the
case of Patience Worth. In 1913, Mrs. Pearl Lenore Curran suddenly became a writer. An alternate personality who called herself Patience Worth spun out verses, tales, parables, and
aphorisms. Prince looked into the matter during the early twen-
ties, while he was still studying Mrs. Crandon. On the face of
things, he thought, nothing in Mrs. Curran's background, even
on the level of unconsciously absorbed experience, could explain her writing skills. The hypothesis of secondary personality or disassociation got him nowhere unless he assumed, as
McDougall did, an autonomous secondary personality that originated totally outside the individual.

In his study, Prince quoted McDougall on the Beauchamp
case and F. C. S. Schiller on Prince's own report of the Doris
Fischer case. Prince applied their argument for a supernormal
explanation of those earlier cases to Patience Worth. In the end
he refused to draw a firm conclusion. But since his presentation
attempted to refute the possibilities suggested by abnormal
psychology (as well as the mundane possibility that Patience
Worth was too poor a poet to need explanation), readers quite
properly viewed Prince's book as designed to bolster the case
for spiritualism or reincarnation. There was no question of
Prince's honesty, merely a question of whether the way he
chose to push the evidence indicated more settled convictions
than he admitted even to himself.[33]

Prince's problem with those who doubted the worth of his work was the same as that which plagued psychical research from its beginnings. Within the world of psychical research, one could distinguish degrees of competence and objectivity among various workers in the field. Prince had good reason to consider himself a more cautious man than Bird. But viewed from outside the world of psychical research, assertions of scientific objectivity made by psychical researchers counted as little more than ritual. In departing so recklessly from the scientific mainstream, again as judged from the outside, psychical researchers seemed more intent on contributing to a metaphysical position than to an ongoing process of scientific research. Many scientists argued that the only possible context for psychical researchers' work was philosophical, at least given the existing state of scientific knowledge. Among a band of people driving off the road, some individuals may correctly point to the superiority of their driving skills as measured against those of the others. But none of them can make a convincing case for their caution to the people who are still on the highway.

At the Boston Society for Psychic Research, Prince kept Hyslop's standards of scientific objectivity alive. But even those did not satisfy everyone with an interest in the field. Hudson Hoagland had a point in charging that too many psychical researchers, even those who sided with Prince in his dispute with Bird, regarded the discovery of a good mystery as an end in itself. In resigning from the council of the BSPR, Hoagland warned that the word "supernormal" by itself did not explain anything. Many people who in most ways were militantly secular valued the category not because it helped them to understand the phenomena shoved into it, but because it gave some meaning to their existence. It served for them the same emotional purpose that the word "supernatural" served for Christians.[34] Hoagland was not really being fair to Prince, who never used supernormal as a synonym for unexplainable or unlawful. But even without Hoagland's letter Prince knew that in the 1920s experimental psychical research had fallen on hard times. Clark University sponsored a symposium on psychical research in 1926, and Prince was a leading participant. But Clark failed to do for Prince what it had done for Freud.[35]

The BSPR passed away with Prince's death, and the ASPR remained in a state of decline until 1941. In that year a group of highly intelligent people in psychical research engineered what they later referred to as a palace revolt.[36] The rebels "regretfully" accepted the resignation of various members of the board of trustees and installed George Hyslop as president. Hyslop continued in that office until 1962. Prince would not have liked the choice, because Hyslop had disappointed him during his own period of troubles with the society during the mid-1920s. In the minds of the rebels, however, Hyslop had redeemed himself by submitting his own resignation to the board of trustees in the 1930s. In general, Prince, who had come in contact with most of the new dominating figures of the ASPR, would have applauded their actions. They included Laura Dale, Gardner Murphy, and a young woman Murphy had taught during a session of Harvard's summer school, Gertrude Schmeidler.

Murphy was the most important of the rebels. Of all the figures in American psychical research, he is the only one who bears intellectual comparison to James. Born in 1895, he grew up in Concord, Massachusetts. His father, who was an Episcopalian rector, saw to it that Murphy received an excellent education, first at prep school, then as an undergraduate at Yale, and finally as a graduate student at Harvard and Columbia. He received a doctorate in psychology from Columbia in 1923. At one point he had considered becoming a missionary, but his religious faith vanished at Harvard. His religious crisis was not very different from what Hyslop had experienced years before. Murphy wrote:

> I found myself in this year at Harvard thinking through with genuine desperation, headaches and insomnia, the question of religious values and meanings and whether they could be made to coincide with the monistic, or if you like, materialistic world view which Keller had made so absolutely convincing. I decided, after much writing, at 2:00 one March morn-

ing in 1917, that I would have to give up my religious faith.
My knowledge of psychical research, however, was at this
time considerable, and I made up my mind that I would pursue psychical research for its own intrinsic interest and for the
very considerable possibility that it might ultimately reverse
my decision regarding religion.[37]

After getting his doctorate, Murphy returned to Harvard as a
Hodgson fellow to work with McDougall. Psychical research,
however, did not consume the whole of his professional interests as it had Hyslop's and Prince's. Before the period of the
Hodgson fellowship, in 1920 and 1921, he allowed himself three
hours a day to study early work in the field. He devoted the rest
of his time to more orthodox concerns of academic psychology.
While psychical research took up more of his time during the
term of his Hodgson fellowship, he also taught elementary and
abnormal psychology at Columbia. For a period of nine years
after 1925, ill health forced a drastic curtailment of all his activities. Yet his publications brought him a national reputation and
academic appointments at Columbia, at the City College of New
York, and at George Washington University. For many years he
served as research director for the Menninger Foundation in
Topeka, Kansas. Few other Americans since James have found
the time to win a major academic reputation while following so
closely work in all phases of psychical research.[38]

Between the death of Prince and the resurrection of the ASPR,
however, another figure emerged in psychical research who
gave the field an alternate name, a new set of terms, and a
somewhat different direction. According to most sources, the
first spiritualists in America had had trouble interesting people
below the Mason-Dixon line in the investigations because of
the well-known opposition of spirits to slavery. If that is so,
Joseph Banks Rhine's move to Duke University at the end of the
1920s did a good bit to make up for the South's early indifference to psychical matters.

7

Joseph Banks Rhine and the First Ten Years of Parapsychology at Duke University

J. B. Rhine's intellectual development fit a pattern that by now should be familiar to the reader. Born in 1895 and reared in a small Ohio town, he learned religion before he learned anything else. As a young man his early ambition to be a minister faded along with his orthodoxy. However, he retained a broad religious faith and began to look outside the church for something to support it.[1]

With the intention of becoming professional foresters, he and his wife Louisa (née Weckesser) both studied at the University of Chicago and earned doctorates in biology. Louisa Rhine grew up in the same town as her husband, and from the beginning of their relationship their intellectual interests ran closely together. They dropped their forestry careers after a lecture by Arthur Conan Doyle turned their professional interests toward psychical research.

In 1923 Rhine wrote to McDougall at Harvard applying for a Hodgson fellowship. Since Gardner Murphy already had the post, Rhine took a job teaching biology at the University of West Virginia. Two years later, in 1926, he resigned that position and reapplied successfully to McDougall. In writing to McDougall he explained that his interests had shifted toward abnormal psychology, and investigational work in subjective metaphysics. Psychical research, he later recalled, represented for him the opportunity to find a philosophy of life that was both scientifically sound and responsive to questions about the nature of man and his relations to the universe.[2]

Although McDougall was away on a leave of absence, Rhine spent the academic year 1926–27 at Harvard. Walter Franklin Prince was by that time in Boston, and Rhine shared his disgust over the stand taken by the ASPR on the mediumship of Mrs. Crandon.[3] Nonetheless, the possibility of collecting scientific evidence of life after death fascinated Rhine, and he confessed to Prince his elation with the strong evidence psychial research had already made available. On the other hand, expressing a fear that would grow even stronger in the next decade, he wondered whether any philosophic certainties could ever emerge from collected evidence suggestive of life after death.[4]

The question of life after death—and the Margery case was only the latest example of the difficulty of coming to terms with that question—had often led psychical research into a maze of entangling suspicions. The early psychical researchers had hoped that in shifting attention from physical mediumship to Mrs. Piper and others like her they could pursue the question of spirit communication in an atmosphere free of fraud. But Mrs. Piper had given way to Margery; and even if she had not, the thousands of pages of transcripts of the Piper séances required substantial interpretation to be meaningful. Such evidence, Rhine believed with increasing conviction, did not, and could not under any foreseeable circumstances, lend itself to precise and unambiguous interpretation.

McDougall did not return to Harvard, but instead, commencing in the academic year 1927–28, assumed the chairmanship of the psychology department at Duke. Though he himself had little time for psychical research, McDougall still regarded the field as extremely important. Rhine saw an opportunity at Duke that existed at no other American university, and McDougall secured for him a regular faculty appointment in 1928. Rhine remained there until his retirement in 1965. The esteem that Rhine and McDougall had for each other was genuine. Rhine referred to McDougall as one of the greatest minds he had met,[5] and McDougall cited Rhine as a man who placed scientific rigor before everything else. When Rhine caught his chairman reading a book on metaphysics or religion, McDougall recounted, "he scratches his head and . . . wonders whether, after all, I, in my latter years, am becoming a renegade." [6] Whether Rhine was himself not a covert renegade has of course been a matter of much subsequent discussion.

When Rhine and his wife arrived in Durham, they were still primarily interested in collecting and interpreting evidence of postmortem communication. They in fact had in their possession a large number of stenographic notes that John. F. Thomas, the assistant superintendent of schools in Detroit, had made on séances conducted by several well-known mediums. [7] He had received communications in those sessions that he believed had come from his recently deceased wife.

With the help of the Rhines, Thomas turned his notes into a doctoral dissertation, which Duke accepted in 1933. He argued the case for survival after death but presented alternate explanations for the evidence as well. It was the first doctorate awarded by an American university for work in psychical research, and it was very nearly the last. [8] Rhine preferred to call the field parapsychology, a term he adopted from the German "parapsychologie."

In giving another name to the field, Rhine wanted to change the emphasis of the experimental work—in fact, to narrow it. [9] He and his wife remained interested in the question of life after death, and during the 1930s Rhine invited the English medium Eileen Garrett to come to Duke for a series of tests. [10] But in the early thirties Rhine decided for reasons already mentioned (and probably because of the inconclusiveness of the Thomas study) to shelve further inquiries into the possibility of life after death. He saw no way to eliminate the ambiguity from even the best evidence. Instead, Rhine began his lifelong quest to design simple and absolutely clear experiments to test what he called extrasensory perception (ESP, of which Rhine distinguished three types: telepathy, clairvoyance, and precognition) and psychokinesis (PK).

In trying to determine whether the mind could gain information through other than sensory channels (ESP) or could influence matter (PK), Rhine wanted tests in which the personal biases of the experimenter could not affect the interpretation of the data. He excluded from parapsychology the collection of personal testimony about "spontaneous cases" of supernormal phenomena because such evidence was at best suggestive. Rhine sought to systematize ESP and PK effects by producing them in planned laboratory experiments. He sought proof for their occurrence in the laws of statistical mathematics. Rhine's hope was to design experiments that could easily be repeated in many other testing centers. For that reason, among others, he made ordinary people the subjects of his tests rather than renowned psychics. As it turned out, Rhine had set for himself a hideously difficult task.

The first experiments Rhine adopted at Duke in the 1930s were new only in detail. Psychical researchers had conducted experiments in thought transference in the first years of the SPR's existence, and a number of experimenters had employed card-guessing techniques. That is, they had asked subjects to guess the faces of a series of cards placed face down, and had then compared the number of right guesses with what might have been expected from the laws of chance. A run of correct guesses well above the chance level was taken as evidence of thought transference. Charles Richet, John Coover, and Gardner Murphy had all done experiments using some variation of this approach.[11] Rhine standardized the experiment by adopting a specially designed deck of twenty-five cards that contained five cards each of five symbols (a Zener deck). The symbols were a square, a circle, a star, a cross, and wavy lines. In a complete run of one well-shuffled deck, a subject could be expected, by the laws of chance, to name five of the cards correctly. Naturally in any one run the number of correct guesses could exceed or fall below five without contradicting the laws of chance. However, Rhine argued that if in a series of many runs a subject piled up a record averaging significantly higher (or lower) than five, one had to assume that something other than guessing accounted for the result.

In his first experiments with Zener cards at Duke, Rhine was attempting to establish evidence for telepathy. That is, he was trying to determine whether one mind could receive information from another mind in the absence of sensory communication. In those experiments of the early 1930s the experimenter (percipient) picked up a card, noted the symbol, and waited for the subject to write down what he thought it was. Rhine devised various controls to ensure that no kind of communication, intended or unintended, could pass between subject and tester. In some experiments the two were in open view of one another, but in others they were separated by a partition or even placed in separate rooms.

The Duke investigators quickly obtained what they regarded as positive evidence for telepathy, but Rhine spotted an ambiguity in the experiment:while the achieved runs of high guesses indicated something more than chance was at work, that something was not necessarily telepathy. The high-guessing subject might have picked up information from the mind of the percipient, but he might also have picked up cues directly from the cards.

Therefore in most of the subsequent experiments no one looked at the cards. One by one they were laid face down on the table and checked against the guesses only at the conclusion of a run or a series of runs. Continued high scores convinced Rhine that at least some human minds could in extrasensory ways receive information from objects in the environment—in this case cards. He called this power clairvoyance and regarded it as a proven hypothesis even if telepathy remained in doubt. Also in the 1930s Rhine designed a number of experiments with cards to test precognition (the ability to foresee a future event) and others with dice to test psychokinesis (the ability of mind alone to affect the movement of a physical object). By the early forties Rhine argued that the occurrence of these various psi phenomena (a general term to cover both PK and ESP effects suggested by the British parapsychologist Robert Thouless) had, with the exception of telepathy, been verified beyond any doubt by his Duke experiments. [12]

One of the most encouraging aspects of Rhine's first Duke experiments (and, as it happened, one of the most enduring prob-

lems about the credibility of the research) was the almost immediate discovery of brilliantly successful ESP subjects among the
Duke student body. A. J. Linzmayer, an undergraduate student
in psychology, amazed Rhine by twice calling correctly on successive days nine cards in a row. While admitting that neither
experiment occurred under carefully controlled conditions
(Linzmayer could see both Rhine and the backs of the cards),
Rhine estimated the odds against guesswork accounting for the
result as two million to one. Later in a quick run through a deck
when the two men were seated on the front seat of Rhine's car,
Linzmayer called twenty-one of the twenty-five cards correctly.[13] Linzmayer never scored significantly above chance in
more formally conducted experiments, but Rhine found other
Duke students who did.

For example, in 1933 Hubert Pearce, a student in the divinity
school, became the subject of an experiment in which Pearce sat
in a small cubicle in the Duke library and guessed cards that
J. Gaither Pratt, Rhine's assistant, put face down on a table in
the Physics Building one hundred yards away.[14] Pratt and
Pearce synchronized their watches, and at an appointed hour
Pratt removed the top card of the deck and without looking at
its face placed it on the table before him. Removing the top card
every minute, he continued through the deck. Meanwhile
Pearce kept a close eye on the time and recorded his guesses
each minute. At the conclusion of a day's work, Pratt looked at
the cards to determine the actual order of the cards in the run
and compared his list with the list of cards Pearce had guessed.
The number of recorded "hits" greatly exceeded expectations
based on the laws of chance. Of all the early experiments at
Duke, Rhine considered the "Pearce-Pratt series" as having
given the most indisputable proof of clairvoyance.[15]

In retrospect it almost seemed that Rhine had been too successful in the early 1930s. At least researchers at other universities, even ones sympathetic to Rhine, had inordinate trouble
getting the impressive results Rhine had reported from Duke. In
the 1940s Gardner Murphy lamented that the ASPR in New
York City had never successfully repeated any of Rhine's major
experiments.[16] The Englishman S. G. Soal finally found two

subjects in Britain who he thought exhibited extraordinary psi abilities.[17] But, as Oxford philosopher C. D. Broad noted, Soal spent years finding two successful ESP subjects, whereas Rhine turned them up in large numbers as soon as he began to experiment. Broad was deeply interested in psychical research, and the disparity did not strike him as suspicious. He merely wondered whether English students possessed so little ESP capacity because they were underfed in comparison with American students and or because they were more worried about their work.[18] Many other scholars were inevitably less charitable in their thinking than Broad.

In any case, the problem of independent verification became an extremely difficult one for Rhine. To his considerable exasperation, his gifted subjects at Duke lost their powers of ESP the more they were tested. Rhine gave a name to the phenomenon—the "decline effect"—but that did not help very much.[19] The whole point of his innovations in parapsychology had been to control the capriciousness and spontaneity of psi phenomena. If they remained just as capricious in the laboratory as they were in everyday life—that is, if ESP started fading as soon as it was studied—then Rhine's laboratory was a questionable advance over the medium's parlor. Certainly a truly repeatable experiment would be impossible to design.

Another related problem concerning verification arose in Rhine's early experiments. Given his hypotheses, Rhine sensibly enough attributed the "decline effect" to the mind-numbing boredom of sitting through thousands of runs with Zener cards. But that conclusion led Rhine to a practice that opened him to the charge of carelessness. Rhine believed that the only possible antidote for the lowering of scores in a long series of tests was a high level of enthusiasm on the part of both the tester and the subject. Both should want high scores, and the investigator in particular had to exude enthusiasm and confidence. "A critical or fussy investigator," Rhine wrote, "would be as much out of place in this kind of work as he would be as cheerleader at a football game." [20]

Some years after Rhine's first work at Duke, Gertrude Schmeidler, a psychologist and parapsychologist at the City

University of New York, would offer some empirical justification for Rhine's statement. Her studies, Schmeidler argued, showed that subjects who believed in psi abilities scored significantly higher in runs with Zener cards than those who did not. In fact the goats, as she termed the disbelievers, scored lower than chance expectations, indicating some kind of negative psi ability or blockage.[21] If true, it was a fascinating demonstration of the Jamesian principle that we help our ideas become true. But most scientists managed to ignore Schmeidler's later findings and chose to view negatively Rhine's immediate pleas for cheerleaders in the laboratory. The attitude that Rhine prescribed for the experimenter seemed too closely related to the warnings of mediums that undue skepticism at a séance could frighten the spirits away.

Given the difficulties of his work, Rhine showed unseemly haste in the early 1930s in publishing claims about the reality of ESP. His first book, *Extra-Sensory Perception,* appeared in 1934; in it he tried to place the case for ESP beyond a statistical shadow of a doubt.[22] Walter Franklin Prince lived long enough to guide it through the press of the Boston Society for Psychic Research. Prince, though extremely pleased with Rhine's conclusions, was sharply critical of errors he found in tables in the manuscript.[23] (Curiously, for all of Rhine's efforts to establish his credentials as a painstaking researcher, he has won even among parapsychologists a reputation for a carelessness amounting at times to sloppiness.) To allay Prince's fears, Rhine promised to have a mathematician go over the statistical work. But the editorial help did not save what was basically a poor job of scientific reportage. Rhine rarely made clear enough in his book what controls he applied in experiments to prevent cheating and unintentional human error.[24]

Though he had promised to base his parapsychology on something more solid than anecdote, much of *Extra-Sensory Perception* amounted to little more than that. Rhine discussed informal experiments, some of which had produced spectacular results, even while admitting that the controls were inadequate. He justified their inclusion in his report because they were suggestive, he thought, within the context of the more stringently controlled work. Rhine admitted that rigorous formality produced less impressive statistical deviations from chance in an experimental run, but they were still, he believed, significant.[25] Since ESP could be proved in the most carefully controlled experiments, Rhine saw no harm in conducting and reporting more casual experiments even though by themselves they proved nothing. In doing so, however, Rhine risked yet another comparison with spiritualists who wanted to relax séance controls once the reality of spirits had been established. While in Rhine's mind the uncontrolled experiments were only the tail of the dog, his critics suspected that the tail was doing the wagging. In any case, a reading of *Extra-Sensory Perception* made it hard to tell.

Despite its monographic format, *Extra-Sensory Perception* received wide notice in the press. Waldeman Kaempffert, the science editor of the *New York Times,* became an enthusiastic admirer of Rhine.[26] An English professor at Columbia compared him to Copernicus.[27] Rhine's next book, *New Frontiers of the Mind* (published in 1937), was a Book-of-the-Month Club selection and contained no scholarly apparatus at all. He aimed most of his subsequent book publications at general audiences.[28] Rhine was much like Hyslop in this respect. He justified his popular writing by saying that anyone interested in reports of experimental work at Duke could consult the *Journal of Parapsychology,* which Rhine founded in 1937. McDougall and Rhine were the original editors.

However, the *Journal of Parapsychology* did not solve Rhine's problems in communicating with the scientific community. The very fact that he had to found a journal of his own to get his experimental work published only underscored the difficulties. Moreover, the *Journal* had trouble setting standards for itself. For example, after McDougall's death in 1938, Rhine made Gardner Murphy and Bernard Riess coeditors of the *Journal.* In an effort to increase respect for its contents among the members of the academic community, they set up an outside board of review, headed by Saul B. Sells of Brooklyn College, to read and criticize the articles submitted for publication.

Unfortunately for Rhine the board proved to be very harsh on his articles. In 1942, in a step reminiscent of Hyslop's bungled attempts to cooperate with other scholars, Rhine resumed editorship along with J. G. Pratt and C. E. Stuart, and dropped the review board. He expanded the format of the *Journal* to contain, in addition to technical accounts of experimental work, speculative discussions about the philosophical implications of ESP.[29] In 1950, conceding that there was not a sufficient clientele for a scientific journal of parapsychology, Rhine went one step further and announced that the articles would henceforth be pitched to an intelligent but nonscientific audience.[30]

Rhine had by that time grown quite used to addressing such audiences. For a revolutionary who claimed to be destroying the framework of existing science, Rhine seemed to have a strong desire for popular approval.[31] If his findings were so important, his critics said, and suggested the vast intellectual reorientation Rhine said they did, then he should have followed Darwin's example and left the public clamor to others. Rhine could not, however, keep quiet about his metaphysical preferences.

Rhine's appeal to popular forums in the 1930s got him into trouble at his home institution. Despite McDougall's support, other members of the Department of Psychology began to view him as an embarrassment. As a result of the controversy that swirled around the publication of his 1934 monograph, Rhine set up his Parapsychological Laboratory as a special division within the Department of Psychology. When McDougall was no longer around, Rhine and his assistants were virtually isolated from the rest of the academic staff in psychology. The department refused to give Pratt a regular teaching appointment and did its best in the next forty years to destroy the equation drawn in the public mind between psychology at Duke and Rhine.[32]

American psychologists in general were perhaps a bit kinder than Rhine's colleagues at Duke. Reflecting the historical ties that had been formed in the 1890s, psychologists showed more interest in Rhine's work than any other group of scientists. In fact, polls suggested that whatever members of the American Psychological Association thought of Rhine's methods, a growing number of them conceded the possibility of ESP.[33] At the end of the 1930s, Rhine's cause got a big boost when B. H. Camp, a Harvard professor and the president of the Institute of Mathematical Statistics, endorsed the methods and assumptions of Rhine's mathematical computations.[34] While most of the discussions of Rhine's work in the academic journals of American psychology were critical or hostile, at least psychologists paid attention to it.[35] In 1938 the American Psychological Association sponsored a round-table discussion of parapsychology. That year represented a peak of both scientific and popular interest in the Duke experiments. For over a decade thereafter, the controversy over parapsychology raised very little interest.

The attention that psychologists paid to his work was in one important sense neither useful nor pleasing to Rhine. He of course resented the criticism, but there was more to his growing dislike of psychology than that. Unlike the most important men in psychical research who had preceded him—James, Hyslop, Prince, McDougall—Rhine had no training and little interest in abnormal psychology. Hyslop, Prince, and McDougall insisted, to be sure, on a distinction between abnormal and supernormal psychology. They had wanted to show that supernormal mental capacities operated best in perfectly healthy, unexceptional individuals. However, their observations often suggested otherwise, and the relation of supernormal perception to non-normal states of consciousness (e.g., trance, hypnotic sleep, secondary personality) fascinated them.

By contrast, Rhine, though believing that psi processes were unconscious, shied away from the whole subject of subconscious or altered personality. At Duke in the 1930s he conducted a few experiments with drugs and trance mediums to determine if various sorts of non-normal consciousness improved powers of ESP in a subject. His conclusions were negative.[36] In fact, he said that the use of drugs impaired ESP ability. The ordinary students with whom he worked at Duke convinced him that ESP was a characteristic of all reasonably healthy people, a normal attribute of normality.[37] Rhine was of course left with the question of why such a common factor of everyday life was so difficult to verify, but he expected little help from psychology in

answering that question. At one point he even regretted coin-
ing the word "parapsychology." [38] But if parapsychology wasn't
psychology, then what kind of science was Rhine trying to
make it?

In 1879 Wilhelm Wundt had said some harsh things about
spiritualism's claim for scientific recognition. "I have looked in
vain," he wrote, "through the whole history of science for a
case in which a scientific authority came forward with the assertion of having discovered a new fact, at the same time adding to
this assertion the assurance that all natural laws were
overthrown by the fact, and that in the fact itself no kind of law
or order was to be perceived." [39] Very early in his work, Rhine
recognized as a problem the lack of any intelligible hypothesis
to account for ESP and PK.

By themselves, psi events did not make sense, and more important, they threatened to make nonsense out of everything
else. Rhine was trying to convince the world of facts that violated fundamental principles of natural causation and temporal
order. The various psi phenomena, as C. D. Broad pointed out,
seemed among other things to imply (1) that events could have
effects before they had taken place; (2) that events in one place
could produce effects in another without any lapse of time and
without a continuous causal chain between the two events; (3)
that persons could perceive physical events or material things
without the event or thing producing sensations in their minds;
and (4) that A could know of B's experiences without hearing or
reading B's words, without observing his gestures or facial expressions, and without access to any kind of record that B or
others might have left of his experience.[40] As James had said in
discussing white crows, it was not merely their rarity that discouraged scientific interest. Nor was it only the difficulty of
producing them on command in repeatable laboratory experiments. The real difficulty of white crows was their meaning-
lessness to existing research in terms of either clarifying a problem or pointing toward a line of profitable theoretical and
experimental work.

In fact, white crows of the sort Rhine was after were not even encountered in the normal course of scientific research. The whole search for psi went on precisely to challenge existing general theories of science—not because those laws ran into difficulty in the laboratory but because parapsychologists believed that they threatened morality. In other words, the search for psi began for reasons external to any problem encountered in experimental work. From the standpoint of most scientists, that fact made Rhine's challenge a gratuitous one and gave him a special obligation to come up with a general theory of his own.

Through Rhine thought that the terms "telepathy," "clairvoyance," and "precognition" referred to distinguishable phenomena, these were still only names. Classification helped to sort out material, but it did not of itself provide an explanation. And without the ability to explain, Rhine's taxonomy, as he found out, could quickly break down. In the 1940s Thouless's general term "psi phenomena," tended to replace Rhine's more specific categories (telepathy, clairvoyance, precognition, psychokinesis) because the links between a particular case of supernormal cognition and a particular hypothesis looked increasingly problematic. While Rhine had thought that his early experiments at Duke had established clairvoyance and precognition, there were other possible hypotheses to explain his facts even if they were accepted as correct. The subject might have foreseen what would be on the mind of the tester when he looked at the cards at the end of the experiment (precognitive telepathy). Or he might have mentally controlled the position of the cards in the pack as they were shuffled (psychokinesis). In fact, without an understanding of the actual process of supersensory information-gathering, the possibility that spirits had whispered the correct answer to the subject did exist.

In many ways parapsychology in Rhine's hands behaved like a textbook model of how a science should conduct itself. Researchers amassed facts and set up theories based on those facts. Experimental designs were continuously improved, and further tests served to verify, modify, or overturn existing theories. By the end of the 1930s, Rhine believed that his experiments had established some useful theories about the operation and nature of ESP. It was not, he said, subject to physical

laws. Its strength did not diminish over long distances (if anything, it got stronger); it was not blocked by physical substance;
and it did not respect the normal sequence of past, present, and
future. Moreover, it operated at an unconscious level and vanished when attempts were made to control it consciously.[41]

Later researchers would add other characteristics to it.
Among them, they noted that it was a common human trait. It
was intimately involved with the whole personality. It appeared
in animals.[42] But when the greater ignorance about what accounted for psi phenomena was taken into consideration, these
were scarcely more than incidental observations about the facts.
What was worse, many of the observations pointed to the conclusion (not reached by Rhine) that psi was immune to laboratory investigation. When he retired from the university in 1965,
Rhine referred to psi events as making increasing sense. A
number of laws, he said, had been attached to the mystery.[43]
But perhaps recognizing that those laws were not that much different from ones advanced by spiritualists in the nineteenth
century, Rhine continued to regard a fundamental explanation
of psi phenomena as the most pressing challenge of parapsychology.[44]

Even in the absence of a satisfactory hypothesis, one important development in the scientific world did lend a certain plausibility to Rhine's work in the 1930s. Just as the new psychology
gave an important stimulus to psychical research in the 1890s,
the new physics accounted for much of the interest in Rhine's
early work at Duke. The influence in the latter case was far less
reciprocal than in the former. However, in suggesting the limitations of the Newtonian descriptions of causality, the physics
of Niels Bohr, Albert Einstein, and Werner Heisenberg seemed
to some nonphysicists to be the basis for a revolution in
thought that would yield a scientific framework in which psi
phenomena possibly would make sense. The blurring of the
distinctions between space, time, and matter in the new physics served in many minds to destroy the basis for materialistic,
mechanistic, and deterministic philosophies. And that was precisely what Rhine hoped to accomplish with the demonstration
of ESP.[45]

At the Clark University conference on psychical research in 1926, several participants noted the possible contribution which the new physics might make in understanding the supernormal, but the suggestions were not very precise. Oliver Lodge, the only physicist to give a paper, delivered some remarks about telepathy and spirit communication becoming comprehensible once more was known about the interaction of ether and matter.[46] In talking about the ether, Lodge managed mainly to demonstrate how out of touch he was with the new physics. F. C. S. Schiller, the Oxford philosopher, was more to the point. The overturning of many of the certainties of Newtonian physics and Euclidean geometry had, he said, created an atmosphere favorable to psychical research. "Modern science," he wrote, "would no longer seriously boggle at what I should take as the first canon of psychical research, viz. that nothing is incredible if the evidence for it is good enough." [47]

Rhine's *Extra-Sensory Perception* appeared a few years after the publication of the first popular expositions of the new physical theories that had overturned the Newtonian world view. Sir Arthur Eddington's 1927 Gifford Lectures were published in 1928. *The Nature of the Physical World* as well as Eddington's *New Pathways in Science* (his Messenger Lectures at Cornell University) both reached a wide American audience in the late 1920s and early 1930s.[48] At the same time Sir James Jeans, another distinguished British scientist, turned his hand to popular accounts of the new physics.[49] Aside from attempting to render relativity and quantum mechanics intelligible to nonscientists, Eddington and Jeans gave their opinions about the philosophical and religious implications of recent scientific theories.

Both questioned whether matter could any longer be regarded as a primary reality. They threw determinism out the window, insisting that it, along with so much else, no longer served as a useful characterization of natural processes. Eddington's thought edged into mysticism, and Jeans embraced an idealistic philosophy that reduced human reality to a thought in the mind of a Creator-Mathematician. There were many dimensions to reality, it seemed, that science would never reveal. Parapsychologists took heart in knowing that scientists knew less than they had formerly thought they knew. They also saw as a favorable sign the preface that Albert Einstein contributed to Upton Sinclair's *Mental Radio* in 1930. Einstein endorsed the importance of Sinclair's account of what the novelist regarded as successful experiments in telepathy between himself and his wife.[50]

If Rhine could have seen in the writings of Jeans and Eddington a metaphysical posture in some ways similar to his own, he might also have discovered in the new physics methodological problems arguably analogous to those he encountered in working with psi. For example, Heisenberg's uncertainty principle suggested that physicists inevitably distorted the phenomena they tried to observe. As soon as they attempted to measure the velocity of a small particle, they lost sight of its location. Prediction of subatomic events could get no further than the laws of probability.

After World War II, parapsychologists continued to receive encouragement from a few prominent physicists. Henry Margenau and Pascual Jordan, respectively Sterling Professor of Physics at Yale University and professor of physics at the University of Göttingen, viewed the loosening of laws of causality into laws of statistical probability as a scientific development favorable to the recognition of psi events.[51] Contemporary physicists postulated all kinds of unobservable entities that possessed neither mass nor spatial location and acknowledged an innate indeterminacy within things themselves. The affinity between parapsychology and modern physics was, as Arthur Koestler later remarked, more intuitive than logical. But since Koestler, in his many iconoclastic writings, has argued for the importance of intuition in all discovery, he regarded the affinity as potentially of great value.[52]

Rhine remained curiously indifferent toward speculation of this sort during the 1930s and throughout the rest of his career. Apparently he viewed his own notion of scientific revolution as a step beyond even anything suggested by Einstein or Heisenberg. At the same time, Rhine's indifference suggested that his common-sense approach to science had trapped him.

Twentieth-century physicists frequently maintained that the

truth of their fundamental propositions lay in their simplicity. Rhine apparently shared something of that viewpoint, for he reduced his experimental designs and his conclusions to simple sequential statements modeled on textbook exposition. Unfortunately, however, he was not trained to appreciate the simplicity of higher mathematical equations. His nonmathematical language could therefore not touch in any significant way the most exciting developments in twentieth-century science. Partly by choice and partly by necessity, Rhine adopted the stance of a "nonassimilationist." That is, he did not wish to see parapsychology absorbed by some other scientific field.[53]

Like Hyslop and Prince before him, Rhine became overly content with the pursuit of parapsychology as an absolutely separate discipline, a scientific field with its own subject matter and its own method. During a generation when boundaries between other scientific disciplines were breaking down, this sort of confidence in independence was surely misplaced.

Ironies abound in Rhine's career. Despite his professed modernism, he was a dualist of the most old-fashioned sort. (Of course, the adjective "old-fashioned" should not suggest isolation. Plenty of twentieth-century Americans saw the world in the same terms.) There was mind (spirit, soul) on the one hand and matter (body) on the other. To be sure, they interacted, and for that reason Rhine called his dualism a relative one. His qualification to absolute dualism, however, was scarcely new.

What was important to Rhine was the proof of two separate realms. The idea that psi phenomena might somehow be explicable by the same laws that applied to ordinary physical matter went against all the conclusions he reached in the 1930s. Psi, he thought, operated according to no known physical laws, including as far as he could see the physical laws that controlled the movement of subatomic particles. Thus in a decade when scientists and philosophers were wrestling with new and puzzling relationships between space, time, and matter, Rhine was promoting a vague sort of dualism as the new frontier in science.

Potentially Rhine's work in the 1930s represented a radical critique of the Western faith in science. His work suggested that objectivity was a myth, that scientific vocabularies were not revolutionary enough even for science's own discoveries, and that the whole modern conception of scientific verification kept human beings from acknowledging crucial aspects of their experience. But despite some grumbling about the experimental rigor forced upon him, Rhine never drew these conclusions or any others remotely resembling them. It was as if Rhine, in choosing to go out on a limb, selected one that was beginning to rot rather than a freshly sprouted one.

Compared to Eddington and Jeans, Rhine's belief in the use of laboratory scientific procedures to penetrate nature's mysteries (or, indeed, to prove a metaphysical position) was straight out of the nineteenth century.[54] He went assiduously about his task of trying to knock holes in physicalist theories of the universe with the experimental tools of a behaviorist. He would have been delighted to measure psi ability, make telepathy predictable, and build clairvoyant machines. Again, one is reminded of the ambiguous struggle that nineteenth-century spiritualists waged against the monster materialism.

Rhine wanted to revolutionize science, but he could not revolutionize his manner of perceiving reality. In trying to escape the limits of contemporary thought, he remained bound by some of its most conventional categories of ordering reality. Rhine appeared to be little bothered by the possibility that psi was fundamentally incomprehensible given the way most people understood law and causation. Rhine's laws of psi sounded strange because he wrote them down with little appreciation of the point that they destroyed any basis for laws. His ability to promise new reality in the ordinary language of the old reality (however confusing the mixture) made his writings understandable and exciting to a general audience. But it won less admiration from professional scientists, who followed Einstein in exploring a new language and a new reality. A few of them, nonetheless, retained an interest in parapsychology even if Rhine had missed its most important implications.

Rhine left no disciples at Duke. When he retired from teaching in 1965, the university disowned his Parapsychology Laboratory and the Department of Psychology hired no one to replace him. In anticipation of these reactions, Rhine had founded prior to his retirement an independent organization in Durham through which he could carry on his work. He conceived the Foundation for Research into the Nature of Man (FRNM) in broad terms, but its basic research unit, the Psychical Research Foundation, continued to pursue Rhine's aim of establishing parapsychology as an experimental science. As of 1965 Rhine thought that this research was moving at a disappointing rate when compared with other fields of science and that it did not show the signs of liveliness expected of a thriving new branch of inquiry.[55] Rhine had a point, but he was not being particularly generous about the work of some of his successors in parapsychology, who had come to regard Rhine's own experiments as the labor of Sisyphus. To them the problem of modern thought was not materialism and mechanism, which any sensible person could see were irrelevant issues after the new physics, but a scientism that had apparently outlasted them and infected even their own field.

8

Conflicting Developments in Parapsychology Since World War II

However vulnerable the Duke University work of the 1930s proved to be, it entirely eclipsed the previous experiments in psychical research as foundations for future inquiries. Rhine set the course of basic experimental research in parapsychology for the next forty years. Convinced that his early labors had demonstrated the reality of psi phenomena beyond a reasonable doubt, his work in the 1940s and thereafter focused on identifying the variables that affected psi phenomena occurrence. Most other people who wished to contribute to the field followed his lead.

Particularly in the years after World War II, researchers in parapsychology tried to specify the personality types of successful ESP subjects. This work spilled over into experiments with blind people, children, twins, and animals.[1] Parapsychologists wrote dozens of articles seeking to confirm Rhine's belief that such subjective factors as the attitude of a subject toward an experiment had far greater impact on psi ability than the physical variables in the experiment. Distorted symbols on the Zener cards, for example, did not seem to affect ESP success, nor did the distance between the subject and the tester or the physical barriers between them. But the emotional atmosphere in which the experiment was carried out did.

At the same time, after 1940 Rhine was no longer the only important voice in American parapsychology. A good deal of what happened in the field after Rhine's first decade of work at Duke served either implicitly or explicitly to cast doubt on Rhine's methods and assumptions. A certain disillusionment was inevitable once it became clear that Rhine had not conceived a perfectly repeatable experiment acceptable to the scientific community.[2] If confining the scope of inquiry to laboratory work had not worked to convince the skeptical, then plenty of people were ready to open the field up again beyond the boundaries Rhine had tried to set for it. The individuals who engineered the "palace revolt" at the ASPR in 1941 saw no reason, as Rhine had, to shelve further work on the question of life after death.[3] While recognizing the value of Rhine's statistical studies, they solicited for their journal articles about mediums, philosophy, and "spontaneous" psi events (i.e., psi events that happened in life rather than in the laboratory).[4] In 1944 the English parapsychologist G. N. M. Tyrell gave a firm "no" to the question of whether measurement was essential to psychical research.[5] His mood was shared by most members of the ASPR: in a poll conducted that same year they expressed a much stronger interest in the nonquantitative evidence used to sustain arguments for life after death than in Rhine's experiments.[6]

Jamesian eclecticism and tolerance became the standard not only for the reorganized ASPR but for most other American parapsychological organizations founded after World War II. The Parapsychology Foundation, which was organized in 1951, represented perhaps the most significant postwar effort to release psychical research from its dependence on Zener cards and automatic dice-throwing machines.[7] Launched by Eileen Garrett with the financial support of a wealthy Congresswoman, Francis Bolton, the foundation supplied funds over the next several decades for publications, experiments, and international conferences.[8]

Garrett was herself a charismatic and innovative person. A trance medium who was genuinely puzzled about her abilities, she stressed far more than Rhine did the relation between psi phenomena and abnormal mental states or altered states of consciousness.[9] For reasons that were important to him, Rhine had opted to emphasize the normality of psi. The great majority of his experiments had therefore dealt with people in ordinary wakeful mental states. High-scoring ESP subjects, he and his assistants concluded, were extroverted, self-confident, nonaggressive, and well-adjusted.[10]

Garrett, who had been tested at Duke in the 1930s, never quite agreed. While she was in fact extroverted and well-adjusted, she was not much like the average Duke student. Without regarding herself as "mentally ill," she recognized that her spirit controls might be split-off parts of her personality.[11] She suspected that the most interesting aspects of supernormal cognition were not only unconscious (as Rhine believed) but most active when normal consciousness was in abeyance. In the 1950s she experimented with LSD.[12] In 1958, well before mind-expanding drugs had received much attention, her foundation sponsored an international conference on parapsychology and psychedelics.[13] It also contributed money to Timothy Leary's and Richard Alpert's experimental work at Harvard.[14]

Aside from the Parapsychology Foundation, there were other significant postwar efforts to keep parapsychology tied in a meaningful way to the field of psychology. Heartened by the interest that Freud had taken in telepathy, Jan Ehrenwald and Jule Eisenbud began in the early 1940s to report cases of telepathic exchange between themselves and their patients.[15] They also argued that their patients' dreams contained much material that was telepathically received. Since those telepathic elements were disguised in the same manner as the other latent content of dreams, dream interpretation in their minds was a more difficult and probably more subjective business than Freudians generally suspected.

Most American psychoanalysts paid little attention to Ehrenwald and Eisenbud (or to Nandor Fodor and Emilio Servadio, who held similar views), but the writings of these researchers stimulated some important lines of experimental inquiry in the field of parapsychology. Montague Ullman, a New York psychiatrist whose interest in psychical research dated back to the 1940s, made the most sophisticated attempts to confirm the reality of telepathic dreams. In 1962 he succeeded in establishing a Dream Laboratory at the Maimonides Medical Center in New York City. His work during the next few years was impressive enough to gain a grant from the federal government. For a parapsychologist, this recognition was almost unprecedented.

The interest of these new researchers in altered states of consciousness and dreams conflicted with what had been Rhine's major concerns in the 1930s, but even so, they had more in common with Rhine's work than the many new experiments designed to prove survival after death had. When Rhine left Duke in the mid-sixties, the question he had tried to shove further into the background was receiving more attention in supposedly scientific centers than at any other time since the days of Mrs. Piper.

In 1960, William G. Roll launched the Psychical Research Foundation in Durham, North Carolina, with the exclusive purpose of promoting scientific studies of survival of the human personality after death. And in 1968 the University of Virginia School of Medicine established a Division of Parapsychology within its Department of Psychiatry. Ian Stevenson, a psychiatrist with a strong interest in reincarnation, became the first holder of a chair in the Virginia School of Medicine whose incumbent had to devote at least 50 percent of his or her time to parapsychology, including research directed at proving the reality of life after death.[16] In 1967 a bewildered judge in Arizona had the dubious privilege of watching a number of scientific organizations, parapsychological and otherwise, squabble over which one of them could best carry out the wishes of James Kidd. At stake was a substantial sum of money the virtually unknown Arizona miner had left in his will to someone conducting research to prove the survival of the human soul.[17] Arthur Ford, Ena Twigg, and Uri Geller were a few of the mediums who gained almost celebrity status in the years after 1960 because of the sudden burst of fresh investigations into spiritualist claims.

Of course Rhine had many things in common with the new parapsychologists who emerged between 1940 and 1970. They disagreed, but not necessarily in ways that indicated mutually exclusive points of view. Parapsychologists who found Rhine's work dull and rigid (or else excessively popularized) had two different (though sometimes overlapping) bones to pick with him. First, they felt that Rhine's conception of a scientific experiment was overly restrictive and unimaginative. Second (a criticism which was much less important in parapsychological circles until roughly the middle of the 1960s), they blamed Rhine for paying too much attention to science or even any attention to it at all.

Obviously, the former argument was less divisive than the latter, because the parapsychologists who criticized Rhine for his restrictive conception of an experiment had every intention of being scientific themselves. They merely thought of ways to be cautious and systematic without using Zener cards and without necessarily working in a laboratory. The mathematics of long odds remained the most popular mode of confirmation in parapsychology. For his part, Rhine had recognized the great usefulness of many kinds of work that he did not designate as scientific parapsychology. (Such work included the investigation of mediums, poltergeists, and ghostly apparitions.) Rhine remained a spokesman for quantification. That had to come first. But he also appreciated for their suggestiveness books on subjects he considered beyond the reach of experimental proof. For that matter, he justified experiments in his own laboratory that he admitted were too informal to meet scientific standards of verification.[18]

We must later return to the second quarrel, for it struck at the roots of what psychical research had tried to be since its inception. But for the moment we must not lose sight of the obvious. Although the fields of parapsychology and psychical research became increasingly splintered after World War II, especially when compared to the period of Hyslop's monolithic leadership, most people dedicated to them, whatever their attitude toward Rhine, continued to assign a very high priority to scientific acceptance. With respect to that quest, they could record some noteworthy progress.

Parapsychology emerged from World War II with a more impressive list of scholarly supporters than in any other period since before World War I. The list was not long, but it contained some important names. For example, Margaret Mead's fieldwork in primitive cultures gave her a strong feeling for the significance of the kinds of events studied by parapsychology. She was elected a trustee of the ASPR in 1942 and appointed to its research committee in 1946.[19] Harvard's distinguished sociologist P. A. Sorokin and two internationally known Yale biologists, G. Evelyn Hutchinson and Edmund W. Sinnott, worked actively to promote psychical research.[20] Yale, in fact, was the home of a cluster of scholars who in the 1940s and 1950s tried to boost the scientific standing of parapsychology. Henry Margenau in physics, Ralph Linton in anthropology, and Brand Blanshard in philosophy added their endorsements of parapsychology to those of Hutchinson and Sinnott.[21] Each of these men, aware of wartime misapplications of scientific knowledge, argued for a scientific perspective that refused to view life processes as blindly unintentional. While to them parapsychology could not prove the existence of cosmic purpose, it could at least help overthrow the inevitably destructive scientific attitude based on an assumption of the lack of it. For an academic publisher, Yale University Press was unusually receptive in the late 1940s and 1950s to books about parapsychology.[22]

In 1969, in what many parapsychologists regarded as the climax of almost a century of effort, the American Association for the Advancement of Science (AAAS) accepted the Parapsychological Society as a member organization. Because the Parapsychological Society, which Rhine founded in 1957, had a membership restricted to people who had actually done experimental work in parapsychology, it had a better claim on the AAAS than the other psychical research societies. Coming at almost the same time that Montague Ullman received support for his Dream Laboratory from the National Institute of Mental Health, acceptance by the AAAS seemed more than symbolic. Even the American space program got involved with parapsychology. The astronaut Edgar Mitchell did ESP experiments on a trip to the moon and later received support from the Stanford Research Center to do further work in parapsychology. Mitchell now heads his own organization in Palo Alto, the Institute of Noetic Studies.[23]

Despite this progress, any suggestion that parapsychology has won general scientific acceptance is wrong. As parapsychologists would be the first to admit, certain important things have not changed in a long stretch of time since World War II. The flurry of organizational activity, especially during the 1960s, did little to establish inroads for parapsychology in American universities. Without question there were many more undergraduate courses devoted to parapsychology in 1970 than in 1940, but the amount of university research, especially considering the demise of Rhine's Parapsychology Laboratory at Duke, did not grow. The number of regular university faculty who contributed to parapsychology in the period from 1940 to 1970 was very small. To the list of Murphy, Schmeidler, Rhine, Pratt, Eisenbud, and Stevenson, one could add E. Douglas Dean of the Newark College of Engineering, R. A. McConnell of the University of Pittsburgh, Charles Tart of the University of California at Davis, and Thelma Moss of the University of California at Los Angeles.

Further, while parapsychology established itself as a Ph.D. field at a few American universities, the experimental work for the most part went on outside the academy. Aside from Ullman's grant from the government, it depended upon private funding. The ASPR, for example, would have been hard pressed to continue its work without the gifts of Chester Carlson, the inventor of the Xerox copying process.[24] Nothing in recent years has altered the estrangement between higher learning and parapsychology. While many parapsychologists today are in no strict sense amateurs, professional opportunities in parapsychology remain limited, as do the ways to attain recognized competence in the field.[25]

In most respects, the standard criticisms of parapsychology have never changed. The charge of fraud is still made as frequently as at any past time and with telling effect. Parapsychologists have maintained with justice that their severest critics have almost willfully misrepresented the experiments they have attacked. In general, if one wants to make a case against parapsychology, the publications of its shrillest opponents make a poor place to begin. They come as close to the mark as those writings which in the nineteenth century assaulted spiritualism as the work of Satan.[26] Nonetheless, both cheating and carelessness did intrude into the work of parapsychology often enough to raise legitimate suspicions. And unfortunately, given his well-established fame in the field, the charges were often directed at Rhine.

The British psychologist C. E. M. Hansel outraged parapsychologists when in 1966 he published an account of how the successes obtained at Duke in the early 1930s might have resulted from cheating.[27] The key part of the book was in fact largely an unconvincing reconstruction of events Hansel argued might have happened. Yet in 1974, when the experimental safeguards in parapsychology were supposedly far tighter than thirty years back, during Rhine's early career, Dr. Jay Levy, the twenty-six-year-old director of Rhine's Institute for Parapsychology, was caught faking results.[28] Neither Hansel's book nor the newspaper accounts of Levy's exposure accused Rhine of bad faith. But the former explicitly and the other implicitly held him guilty of inexcusable gullibility.

The continuing failure of parapsychologists to establish the credibility of their research was related less to real or suspected fraud than to another problem already broached in these pages. In 1951, D. O. Hebb, a Canadian psychologist influenced by behaviorism, made clear what little progress parapsychologists had made in solving the problem of how to revolutionize science with white crows. Rhine and others, Hebb conceded, had offered evidence for ESP that was good enough to convince scientists about most things. But, Hebb noted, he would continue to reject ESP because it made no sense. His attitude, he admitted, constituted prejudice, but without prejudice of this sort he did not see how science could go forward.[29] For the foreseeable future he had to react as Thomas Henry Huxley had to claims of spirit communications: if the dead come back and mutter inanities, so what? Parapsychologists have frequently cited Hebb's article, just as they have cited Thomas Kuhn's more recent *Structure of Scientific Revolutions.* [30] In both they have found an explanation for how work that is to them so potentially explosive could continue to be neglected by so much of the scientific community. Yet no facts in modern history that finally won acceptance within some scientific framework have waited so long for recognition as psi phenomena. Given the fact that in 1969 parapsychology did not matter in the slightest to most scientists, acceptance by the AAAS only accentuated its isolation. It won recognition as a separate discipline, but separateness was always its most grievous problem.

If parapsychologists have failed to find a theoretical explanation that makes psi events comprehensible within new or old scientific paradigms, it is not because they have paid no attention to the question. Rhine had little inclination for philosophy or abstract thought of any kind, yet he recognized very clearly the need to explain psi. It emerged as a major concern, perhaps the major concern, of parapsychologists in the 1940s and thereafter. Gardner Murphy in particular emphasized the importance of putting ESP in a context that made it discussable, not merely recordable. His own line of thought favored explaining ESP as a force analogous to the one advanced by physical field theory. [31] Just as magnets created invisible fields of force, Murphy speculated, the unconscious mind creates a field that hooked up to fields formed by other unconscious minds. Ideas are not transmitted from one person to another. There is rather a fusion of ideas in an interpersonal system of force. The notion of a fusion, which was analogous to something recognized by physics yet was not quite physical, proved to be a popular one. In 1946 the English psychical researcher Whately Carington, in a book very much admired by Murphy, posited a psychon unit of mind in elaborating a complicated and, as far as he was concerned, nonphysical explanation of telepathy. He wished to suggest how two ideas linked together in the mind of A might get linked in the mind of B through a commingling of their unconscious minds. [32] Both Murphy's and Carington's ideas bore some relation to Jung's speculation about the collective unconscious. Much later Aniela Jaffé, Jung's prolific interpreter, suggested that people caught in what she called an archetypal situation showed strong telepathic bonds. No "mechanism" explained what happened. Telepathy was in Jungian exposition an acausal process doubling a thought content in two separate persons.[33]

Although parapsychologists in recent decades have paid more attention to the new physics than Rhine did in the 1930s, they have not found borrowing from it an easy matter. After all, what exactly did physical mean? And if ESP was not a physical process, as Murphy, Carington, and Jung seemed to suggest, then what possible help could physics be? Most of the attempts to furnish theoretical explanations of psi floundered on these questions, however important, that made parapsychology more a debating ground for philosophers than a testing ground for scientists. Certainly philosophers, and mostly British philosophers, made the most important contributions to the theoretical literature of parapsychology, which gained currency after World War II.

Reading theoretical discussions about psi (and some of them are very intelligent) is a little like reading Eddington and a little like reading P. D. Ouspensky. They all challenge the suitability of our most common intellectual categories for understanding psi. In fact, the number of parapsychologists who have argued the case for a physical explanation of ESP has been small. Adrian Dobbs was one of the few who suggested that parapsychology would never get anywhere until it talked about things located in physical space time, which interacted according to laws recognized either in classical physics or in relativity or quantum theory.[34] Dobbs felt that he was not arguing for materialism. Modern physics, he believed, had dispensed with nineteenth-century notions about the primacy of matter and dealt regularly with quantities and operations that were either undetectable with present apparatus or intrinsically unobservable.

However, most parapsychologists sought explanations characterized by a more clear-cut psycho-physical dualism than Dobbs offered, though not necessarily of the kind described by Rhine. H. H. Price, who was the Wykeman Professor of Logic at Oxford until 1959, doubted the wisdom of pursuing a physical theory of psi.[35] J. R. Smythies, a psychiatrist at the University of Edinburgh who shared Price's general perspective, opted for a non-Cartesian dualism in which a number of substantive minds extended in mental space interacted with physical things extended in physical space.[36] C. D. Broad, the Oxford philosopher, also argued for the interaction of independent space-time realities, only some of which were physical.[37] These discussions engender a healthy respect for the present confusion surrounding the word "physical," but they are not very successful in solving the ancient problem of dualism—how exactly two discontinuous, independent, and absolutely distinct things can interact.

In 1974, J. G. Pratt was still making notes for a future Einstein of parapsychology.[38] The theoretical debate over thirty years had settled nothing—least of all the relations between parapsychology and the new physics. As one parapsychologist noted, vague applications of principles drawn from quantum physics could not make illogical theories of psi phenomena logical.[39] In addressing parapsychologists in 1966, Henry Margenau advised them to strike out on their own and not expect to find their theory ready-made for them by physicists.[40] Those who sought to track ESP, he said, should remind themselves of the early difficulties physicists encountered in tracking radiation. Their struggle would be comparably difficult. However, the best help Margenau could offer from physics was analogy, and by the late 1960s analogy had been exploited for all it was worth and had still been found wanting. Over the preceding years philosophers had presented some highly abstract ideas about what might constitute the nature of reality if telepathy did indeed demonstrate itself to be a fact.[41] But they had not furnished either operational models or any other models of how telepathy worked. Inevitably it occurred to some people that the explanation, and indeed the proof, of psi lay beyond the power of language or of any of the analytical tools of human beings.

That second quarrel with Rhine now becomes relevant to our discussion. If scientific respectability remained the dominant goal of parapsychology, a countercurrent that had more serious implications for future work than, say, the takeover of the ASPR by the Margery clique back in the 1920s had developed. Anti-scientism, as it was adapted into a critique of Rhine's work, had nothing to do with the credulity of spiritualists, who were as apt to praise science as anybody else.

Of course it was not always apparent whether one of Rhine's critics was quarreling with his restricted view of what qualified as scientific experiment or was countering his positivist tendency to recognize science as the only source of certitude. Even if clearly doing the latter, the critic was not necessarily intending to demean science. To criticize Rhine for seeming to place *exclusive* reliance on scientific proof was not the same as criticizing Rhine for placing *any* reliance on scientific proof. For example, while Robert Thouless regarded as silly Rhine's view that the only justification for religion was concrete evidence of the kind offered by parapsychology, he clearly respected science as a legitimate and necessary sort of inquiry.[42] He merely wanted to keep people mindful of the legitimacy of other sorts of inquiry.

In many cases the point of an argument could as likely go in one direction as another, depending on the persuasion of the person who was exposed to it. Jule Eisenbud criticized Rhine for thinking that psi phenomena could be proved only by observation in a laboratory. Since psi was not like anything else and operated at an unconscious level, it was folly, Eisenbud thought, to believe that all variables could be identified, much less controlled, in an experimental situation.[43] In saying this, Eisenbud meant no attack on objectivity and systematic thought. On the contrary, he was trying to identify instances in which the illusion of those things could interfere with observation and hence the scientific aim. However, while Eisenbud intended to liberalize the conditions that Rhine had set on a scientific approach to the supernormal, he brought into question the appropriateness of modeling parapsychology on science. If psi events were unsystematic and unlawful, then could any conceivable scientific procedure pin them down? The first American spiritualists had stormed the ramparts of scientific respectability with the claim of having made the unnatural natural. But what if by nature psi events were unnatural? That question seemed to pose a dilemma for scientific parapsychology in the last half of the twentieth century.

The dilemma was arguably semantic, but if so, no easy way out of it suggested itself. Either parapsychologists had to systematize psi or they had to give up trying to be scientists. In trying to make the unlawfulness of psi one of its laws, they arguably had turned the quest for scientific status into a will-o'-the-wisp and expended hours doing things that were a complete waste of time. For example, in their most obviously unfinished enterprise of the past forty years, they had looked vainly for a repeatable experiment. Not that Rhine's experiments could not be done over again, but the results were completely unpredictable. Karl Popper would have seen in that complication a more fundamental difficulty.

By Popper's analysis, a hypothesis such as ESP was scientific only if it was susceptible to falsification. And falsification to have some experimental meaning required a regular pattern of occurrence. For example, the hypothesis that oxygen supports combustion can be shown to be wrong by experimental procedures if in fact it is wrong. Merely demonstrating that oxygen supports combustion every time it has been tried has no scientific standing without the possibility that someone could come along and show that what supported the combustion was a separable component of oxygen. But what if the combustion itself were irregular and the hypothesis was that oxygen supported combustion occasionally, in certain unspecified and unpredictable situations? At the very least, that would enormously complicate the possibility of falsification.

Indeed, with respect to ESP one can question whether there is any experimental way to falsify the claim that on a given odd day, someone used ESP to name correctly the faces of twenty-five cards in a row. It would really not even matter whether the subject performed the feat successfully on five days in a row in five different laboratories. Parapsychologists believe that ESP is a fact because using the mathematics of long odds they have "verified" its occurrence. In Rhine's mind, if a case of ESP never happened again, it would not change things. The once-recorded fact (the once-spotted white crow) remained an enduring entity that science would have to accommodate. Aside from proving trickery or carelessness (extra-experimental procedures), there is no way to falsify a unique demonstration of telepathy. But without the possibility of falsification, Popper feels that there can be no verification.

In the 1940s Gardner Murphy saw the creation of a repeatable experiment as crucial to the future of psychical research. So of course did Rhine. But Murphy later changed his mind. The very failure to find such an experiment suggested to him that no orderly pattern bound and structured psi phenomena.[44] At least human beings, given the limitations of their senses and their categories of understanding, could not perceive one. That possibility did not put psi entirely beyond the range of science. After all, present concepts of space and time, which did not explain psi, might in time be replaced by others that did. Pointing to the relative elements in our language and frames of reference, as Poincaré had demonstrated, in no sense constituted an attack on science. On the other hand, many parapsychologists grew doubtful as to whether the dissecting operations of human reason could ever devise categories of understanding sufficient to grasp the mystery of psi.

Ironically, Ian Stevenson, the only holder of an academic chair in parapsychology in America, made some of the boldest statements questioning the utility of science for parapsychology. Though located in a medical school, he had relatively little use for the laboratory. Reincarnation, a subject of great interest to him, did not lend itself to controlled experimental investigation. One simply had to look into such reported cases as there were.

Stevenson's approach to cases of telepathy was empirical, but he had no particular use for Rhine's methods of statistical computation. The need to apply statistical analysis, he said, immediately signaled to him that the effects under study were trivial.[45] In a far more radical statement, he suggested that the very existence of extrasensory perception offered the possibility of transcending the scientific method altogether. A direct and nonrational acquisition of knowledge, such as would be ours if we learned how to use ESP, would obviously make other forms of cognition irrelevant. That possibility, Stevenson argued at the end of the 1960s, explained the inclinations of many parapsychologists toward mysticism.[46]

Lawrence LeShan's book *The Medium, the Mystic, and the Physicist* furnished the most intelligent example of the inclination to which Stevenson referred. Writing in the mid-1960s, LeShan assembled quotations seeking to link the metaphysical systems of spiritualist mediums, religious mystics, and Einsteinian physicists. That metaphysical system, which according to LeShan differed in fundamental ways from the one that governed normal awareness or the historical consciousness of the majority, enabled the three types of people he discussed to visualize a world in which psi made sense. Not that they carried around such a metaphysical perspective all the time. For LeShan, "sensory reality" (based on distinctions, parts, and separateness) and "clairvoyant reality" (based on sameness, wholeness, and oneness) were both valid modes of perception, and the usefulness of each depended upon what one wanted to accomplish at a particular moment. Unfortunately, since the scientific revolution of the seventeenth century Westerners had given such exclusive attention to "sensory reality" that they did not even suspect the existence of "clairvoyant reality." Hence their difficulties in accepting ESP.[47]

LeShan's argument that telepathy, clairvoyance, and precognition made sense within the metaphysical perspective of modern physics reflected his concern for maintaining a scientific attitude.[48] He even offered proof of his thesis in the form of a personal narrative. While himself in a mental state ruled by "clairvoyant reality," he discovered that he could heal people using a process reminiscent of mesmerism.[49] LeShan's arguments harked back to the expansive views of the unconscious that had circulated in America at the turn of the century.

Within each of us lies buried a repressed kind of knowledge that can produce great and, by our present understanding, supernormal effects if we learn to use it. Encouraged by Eileen Garrett, LeShan demonstrated to his satisfaction how people in altered states of consciousness did things that were observable in the normal world but inexplicable by its standards. In his case he healed people by nonmedical techniques, while others gained clairvoyant powers. LeShan believes that these things proved the existence of white crows, though mere observers would never understand them until they learned to alter their own consciousness.

Acquiring the metaphysical perspective of "clairvoyant reality" required a leap beyond what most people in the twentieth century called reason. And once there, the proof that one had landed safely was an intensely personal one. In LeShan's case, only he and the person he healed were likely to share his interpretation of what had happened. Those who remained unaltered by the experience, either because they had not changed their metaphysical perspective or because they had not felt the cure, would most likely, as LeShan knew, find an excuse to ignore his story. LeShan had no illusions that his "general theory of the paranormal" would excite the community of American physicists. It did, however, as he was surely aware, speak to a mood that was noticeable in America especially in the 1960s.

That parapsychology should grow popular among the American student counterculture has been one of the more interesting twists in its fate. Its founders had mostly been people of conservative tendencies. Walter Franklin Prince was assistant secretary of the Connecticut Law and Order League.[50] J. B. Rhine was a fierce cold warrior who had in the 1950s stressed the importance of psi phenomena as a refutation of Communist materialism.[51] Suddenly parapsychology became part of a political (left-wing and veering toward anarchism) attack on science and on what many assumed to be the requirements of rational inquiry. Not since the nineteenth century had the supernormal (in that case spirits) proved so useful to radicals. But there was a big difference in the rhetoric.

In a decade in which irrationalism and romanticism were seriously explored in America for the first time since the post–World War I era, altered states of consciousness became a deliberate means of refilling the world with wonder and mystery. Most parapsychologists who conducted experiments with drugs or yoga meditation in the 1960s intended to further scientific knowledge.[52] In other hands, however, psychedelics and meditation were, just as ritual witchcraft often was, ways of rebutting or simply ignoring Western science and liberalism. The student counterculture, having discovered parapsychology, quickly decided that the people who possessed the most matter-of-fact knowledge of psi phenomena lived in Asia. In their minds it figured. Western science and technology could not grasp psi because its approach to nature was a predatory one. What it could not harness and put to work it ignored. And it dropped bombs on people who viewed the world differently. The logic of radicals was not impeccable, but generally it was not intended to be.

The upsurge of occultism and mysticism as objects of serious interest among certain parapsychologists did not of course surprise those who had always inveighed against investigations of the supernormal. They had never imagined that parapsychology was the scientific enterprise it claimed to be. Behind whatever parapsychologists said or even whatever they thought was their real wish to preserve a realm of human experience beyond all scientific categories and beyond all rational comprehension—a realm that was important to humankind precisely because it was not comprehensible. In the 1960s Rhine and others of his persuasion protested the attitude of those who leaped on every opportunity to hold parapsychology guilty by association. But they also worried.

Parapsychology as a matter of necessity had long relied on the support of people who had no particular interest in science. In the middle of the 1960s important researchers in the field appeared unconcerned when the labels "occult" or "mystical" were applied to their work. The latter considered their work empirical, but they also believed that Rhine spent too much time trying to distinguish parapsychology from various and sundry other enterprises that the majority of American academics rejected as pseudoscience. Taking the word "supernormal" seriously required a tolerance for almost any mode of investigation. Parapsychology might just learn something from the things to which it was linked in the popular mind. It was time to stop denying associations that could not be escaped anyway and to see what profit there might be in them.

9

Spiritualism, Parapsychology, and the Occult:
Some Summing Up

In 1970, speaking to an international conference devoted to psychical research, the Englishman E. J. Dingwall explained why he had lost interest in the field.[1] The speech, and the accusations that were laced into it, naturally unsettled the audience. Dingwall had as long a record of service to the SPR as anyone in the room. His disappointment with what had been accomplished after so many decades served to remind people that the history of parapsychology constituted a long record of frustration. Despite recognition by the American Association for the Advancement of Science, psychical research enjoyed no more prestige among respected scientists in 1970 than it had in 1890. Which is to say, parapsychology remained a marginal activity.

Dingwall might have been cheered by the amount of publicity showered on parapsychology during the 1960s (public attention unmatched during any time period since the 1930s); but that publicity, as it happened, only deepened his disillusionment. His belief in supernormal occurrences remained strong. What he had come to doubt was whether parapsychology could successfully combat the wealth of literature linking it with what journalists in the 1960s had dubbed "the occult revival." Over the years too many parapsychologists had been closet occultists

who used the name of science to promote a preconceived religious position. In the 1960s they had turned their attention to
drugs, astral projection, reincarnation, and Eastern forms of
meditation—all in the name of tracking psi phenomena. Some
of the new work in parapsychology was in Dingwall's opinion
legitimate, but most of it merely served to encourage a rampag-
ing public superstition.

Events in the 1960s convinced Dingwall that magical categories of thought still strongly appealed to the human mind.
And parapsychologists were just as susceptible to the appeal as
anyone else—perhaps the more so because their work carried
them into areas where it was very difficult to keep one's imagination under control. Dingwall thought it too bad, for without a
firm commitment to rationalism and scientific naturalism,
parapsychology was not in his mind worth anybody's time.

Not many people in the 1960s stopped to define exactly what
they meant by the word "occult," and Dingwall himself did not
adequately distinguish between an occult enterprise and what
he regarded as legitimate investigations of supernormal phenomena.[2] He was surely correct, however, in thinking that popular associations during the 1960s made the task of establishing
the reputation of parapsychology as a laboratory science all the
more difficult. In that decade an amazing range of people found
it possible to explore witchcraft (black and white), telepathy,
Zen, astrology, and alchemy (all while smoking dope) with no
sense of having opened an oddly mixed bag of things. In the
minds of some people Zener cards took on the same magical
significance as Tarot cards.

Many American parapsychologists shared Dingwall's concern
over these developments, but their journals nevertheless dealt
increasingly with subjects widely identified with the literature
of irrationalism marketed to the American counterculture.[3] The
middle-class people who had worked over the years with Rhine
watched with bewilderment as their conclusions were used to
sustain left-wing political and social ideas. Along with a good
many other things that at first glance had nothing in common
with one another, parapsychology was adopted as a "relevant"
subject by people who had grown suspicious of words and ver-

bal communication. Young students who imagined themselves at war with the rational technology and oppressive social system of the West cited telepathy and clairvoyance as proof that human beings discovered truth intuitively rather than by a process of logical analysis.

No doubt the majority of the people who in the 1960s subscribed to the journals lumped together under the classification "occult" led thoroughly bourgeois lives and harbored no revolutionary plans whatever for American society.[4] On the other hand, anything that seemed to challenge the dominant traditions of Western intellectual life could in the decade of the Vietnam War take on political significance. The possibility that people might communicate without language, thus avoiding the inevitable distrust and misunderstanding bred by words, encouraged many in the 1960s to try to construct utopian communities out of love, ecological metaphor, and Consciousness III.

Parapsychology was supposed to revolutionize science without falling victim to the all-encompassing revolutionary designs of a cultural avant-garde. Most parapsychologists in the almost one hundred years of psychical research activities had hoped to turn Western science away from what they regarded as its materialistic preoccupations. However, the morality and social arrangements that they wished to protect by their efforts were unremarkable by traditional Christian standards. Like the nineteenth-century American spiritualists, most of them believed that their ideas were misapplied when they were used to promote irrationality, sexual freedom, and calculated acts of social rebellion.

Of course, as Dingwall argued, the problem he bewailed in 1970 was an old one. Dingwall blamed parapsychologists, while most parapsychologists blamed their critics. The leaders of psychical research societies in America had usually been unhappy with much of the lay support they attracted. They were terribly upset when the labels "occult" and "magical" were applied to their work, but the connection had been made many times prior to the 1960s. Spiritualists in the nineteenth century had experienced the same difficulty in trying to get their claims recognized by science. People kept equating their interest in spirit voices with mysticism or occultism or magic (or all three), whereas they insisted that it had nothing to do with any of those things.

On most formal grounds, as we have seen, theirs was a proper enough statement. They were not with much logic classed with mystics because they made no claim to sudden divine illumination. The only truth important to all was the outward fact of the spirit manifestations. Nor did they have any relation to occultism if occultism is presumed to involve: (1) some degree of exclusiveness and secrecy; (2) a reliance on ancient texts or teachings that are often heretical by Christian standards; (3) a monistic conception of an interrelated universe in which the most significant causative forces are not mechanical ones. Finally, spiritualists were not magicians because, with the possible exception of healing mediums, they professed no power to bend cosmic forces to their will. Mediums summoned spirits who would appear if conditions were right. But everything in the spiritualist tradition went toward asserting the powerlessness of mediums over their spirit controls. They had not penetrated into any mysteries of the universe that were not generally accessible to anyone who was willing to go to a few séances. From the spiritualist perspective it made no more sense to call mediums magical because they attracted spirits than to call magnets magical because they attracted iron filings or Christian ministers magical because they invoked the Holy Ghost.

Obviously, such distinctions applied with even more force to parapsychology. However, while they are crucial to our getting straight the history of spiritualism and parapsychology, there is more to be said. On most occasions critics who insisted that there was a straight line of descent from primitive magic to Renaissance occultism to spiritualism and parapsychology deliberately misunderstood behavior and misused words.[5] For all that, their criticism did raise some serious issues that spiritualists and parapsychologists would have been well advised to think through more clearly than they normally did.

The spirit messages in the 1850s and 1860s, for example, commonly contained teachings about affinities and correspondences that arguably descended from the world view of the Renaissance magus. Many of them attributed a magical significance to numbers. As we have seen, the vocabulary spiritualists absorbed during the American antebellum period included both romantic and positivist elements. Spiritualists may have reached an audience by praising empirical science; but some, like S. B. Brittan in the following passage, also used a language that was traceable to occultist roots: "The empire of being is not peopled with separate forms and distinct entities, but every thing, from the Universe to the ultimate particles of matter, and from the realms of angels and men down to the plane of the animalculae, sustains specific relations to other objects or conditions of being. . . . The Universe, though infinitely complex is One, and a mutual dependence and reciprocal action characterize all gradations of being. . . . Hence there may be some elements of truth in astrology." [6] It did spiritualists little good in the nineteenth century to proclaim their scientific intentions if they wanted all along to practice the science of Giordano Bruno.

Moreover, it was not merely confusion that placed Swedenborg and Davis, who both had an important influence on the spiritualist movement, in the tradition of Western mysticism. Most nineteenth-century people may have paid little attention to the contents of spirit messages and may have denied the medium the status of a divinely inspired seer. But in a movement as eclectic as spiritualism was, spiritualists were bound at times to find themselves at cross-purposes. In view of some of the sources from which spiritualism derived, their scientific critics quite properly wondered whether spiritualists did not hide something from themselves with their professions of scientific modernism. At least one can find a considerable range of attitudes among individual believers.

The historical question appropriate to ask of spiritualism and psychical research is not whether the founders of those movements intended to practice magic or occultism or mysticism. By any conceivable definition of those words, most of them did not. Nonetheless, it is appropriate to ask why, despite their best efforts, they so often failed (the 1960s being only the latest instance) to keep people both within and without their camps mindful of the distinctions they wanted to make. It is equally appropriate to ask why spiritualism and parapsychology often appealed to persons who later joined an occult society or fell under the sway of an Eastern religion. It is easy to say that Zen Buddhism, Theosophy, and the American Society for Psychical Research require different sorts of commitments from Americans and make distinguishable intellectual demands. But it is relatively easy to find historical cases of ordinary people who dabbled in all three without any sense of self-contradiction. Without trying to collapse spiritualism and parapsychology into things they claimed not to be, one must say something about those cases.

Naturally a good deal of the historical traffic in and out of marginal social and religious groups had nothing to do with what we might call matters of substance. That is, membership in or an association with such groups was not necessarily valuable to adherents because of the particular intellectual position represented by the group. Rather, affiliation helped them adjust to (and even overcome) their sensed alienation from society— often through the promise of some kind of powerful knowledge that could help them deal with adversity.

One can, no doubt, overemphasize the degree of social deviance that fringe religious movements encouraged. The sense of loyalty that spiritualists and parapsychologists felt to middle-class social values was usually very strong. For that matter, the amount of behavioral deviance stirred by the rituals of contemporary witchcraft cults is far less than much popular lore would suggest. Nonetheless, the participants in a fringe activity did see themselves as freed from certain of the attitudinal norms of everyday society. They did not have to be "sensible" about a whole range of reported supersensible phenomena that their society apparently wanted either to deny or to put beyond human reach. Hence an interest in groups devoted to "odd" beliefs could become almost an experimental posture of life.

When people believed (as did the spiritualist and the parapsychologist) that their most important ideas had been rejected out of hand, the temptation arose for them to make common cause with the champions of other rejected ideas. How often the temptation actually influenced belief and behavior is a matter of conjecture. But certainly the average American spiritualist in the twentieth century was apt to know something about the Rosicrucians, New Thought, Yoga, Hermetics, faith healing, pyramidology, Scientology, and flying saucers. Marginality in various historical contexts may encourage associations that make little sense on strictly intellectual grounds. Dingwall learned that sad lesson in the 1960s.

On the other hand, there were solid enough intellectual connections between the subjects considered in this book and other subjects that might more appropriately be labeled as occult or magical (with a descriptive, not a pejorative, intent). However different the forms of practice may have been, occultists, spiritualists, and psychical researchers often spoke about issues in terms that were familiar to each of them. After all, spiritualists and psychical researchers aimed at scrutinizing many of the things that concerned occultists, albeit with the methods and assumptions of contemporary empirical science and without occultist theoretical constructs.

The single case of Theosophy suggests something of the complexities and contradictions that anyone inevitably encounters in trying to fathom the overlapping appeal of movements that claimed to be doing quite different things. The Theosophical Society, which Madame Blavatsky founded in 1875 in New York City, was occult by anyone's definition of the word.[7] It also contained elements of magic and Hindu mysticism. The amount of secrecy claimed by the society varied in the early years. Despite the beliefs that could be extracted from Blavatsky's lengthy writings, Theosophy never developed into a strongly dogmatic religious organization. It had, however, a password, a handshake, rites of initiation, and a set of worship practices reserved for advanced members. Full induction into the mysteries of Theosophy was a process potentially requiring years. During her many travels, Blavatsky had picked up knowledge of Russian, Egyptian, and Eastern secret orders. She was acquainted with Renaissance magic and a variety of modern occult teachings. The organization of the society distinguished an inner and an outer circle of adherents and was in all respects hierarchical.

Until a series of schisms split the movement, it was ruled at the
top by Blavatsky, who possessed a marvelously charismatic personality.

In short, Theosophy was everything nineteenth-century
American spiritualists said they wanted nothing to do with.
Unlike the truth of spirit communication, occult secrets were
not intended for everyone. To the spiritualist way of thinking,
the Theosophical organization was a rigid sect claiming to teach
truths that lay beyond common-sensical and empirical demonstration. Spiritualist publicists therefore dutifully sounded the
alarm. Theosophy, one spiritualist warned, in seeking to tap
"the penchant of mankind to dabble in mysterious things,"
threatened "to load spiritualism with the incubus of mysticism." [8] "Occultism," according to the *Banner of Light*, "is the
old, old story. . . . Establish a system of religion or philosophy
invested with this; place it in the keeping of a priesthood or
brotherhood claiming to hold secrets which God has revealed to
them and withheld from everybody else, but a knowledge of
which at the same time is requisite for the salvation of all, sub-
stantiating their claims by the working of divine 'miracles' or
occult 'wonders' and you have the power that has in all past
times held mankind in mental bondage and consequent physical slavery." [9] In line with its past argument, the *Banner of Light*
wrote that a "true spiritual science" had to be one that could be
"tested, proved and admitted by all competent persons." [10]

The secrecy of the Theosophical Society undercut the traditions of Western liberalism that spiritualism enthusiastically
supported. When Madame Blavatsky moved the headquarters of
the Theosophical Society to India in 1879, American spiritualists
drew what to them seemed an obvious conclusion. Her supposedly spiritual philosophy was suitable only for a people who
had "remained through all these centuries in a nearly stagnant,
semi-barbarous condition, the victims of ignorance, superstition, poverty . . . and physical degradation." [11] One should
keep this last quotation in mind as an indication of how distant
spiritualist concerns were from more radical cultural perspectives, which, beginning at the end of the nineteenth century,

would view the wisdom of India as an antidote for Western materialism. [12]

The characterizations that spiritualists made of Theosophy were about as fair as the ones that their enemies made of them. But they did manage to pinpoint significant areas of disagreement that would have prevented any crossover between the two movements had they been the only relevant points. They of course were not the only relevant points, and Theosophy without question gathered the limited support it did in the United States from people who already believed in spirit communication. In fact both Madame Blavatsky and Henry Steel Olcott, a New York lawyer who became her close associate, had been deeply involved with spiritualism immediately prior to the formation of the Theosophical Society. Even before anyone had heard of Blavatsky, spiritualist newspapers recognized the potential appeal that occultism might have for its readers. One of them wrote: "It is a lamentable fact that there are large numbers of Spiritualists . . . to whose palates Spiritualism in its simplicity, is becoming stale and nauseating. . . . These, impelled by the aspirations of vanity, have essayed to elevate themselves a few inches above the heads of their peers, by the establishment of a secret order. . . ." [13]

Vanity may have had something to do with it. But in many ways an interest in the mysteries supposedly unveiled by an occult society was a logical graduation for spiritualists who took seriously the caveat, posed again and again by leading figures in the movement, that they ought to do something more than merely go through the dry exercise of watching mediums' performances. Those who took the substance of the spirit messages seriously could find plenty in them that resembled the secret teachings of Theosophy. Although Andrew Jackson Davis would never have admitted it, his books were a good preparation for the study of Blavatsky's *Isis Unveiled*. [14] Some believers in spirit communications thought they found in Theosophy the knowledge that their exposure to mediums had prepared them to receive.

Olcott, for example, justified his absorption in Theosophy as

a natural culmination of the steps he had begun with spiritualism to escape the materialistic concerns of American life. Spiritualism was fine as far as it went. But its break with Western assumptions went only halfway, and it was on that account
confused. American spiritualists were unable to imagine the future life as anything more than an extension of this one in time.
In their obsession with individuality (as opposed to Oneness)
they let their imaginations be bounded by earthly existence.

Blavatsky, Olcott said, had not asked him to give up the spiritualist hypothesis, but had showed him that the spirit manifestations, in which he had formerly taken delight, were "an abhorrent proof that the dead are not happily dissevered from
earthly concerns, and thus are hampered in their normal evolution towards the condition of pure spirit." Moreover, in reveal-
ing to him that the communications of earthbound spirits
formed but a small part of the realm yet unseen by most human
beings, she had turned spiritualism into a true science. Theosophy revealed secrets that if studied carefully would give people the practical wisdom to control their lives both here and in
the hereafter. Americans who called themselves spiritualists
had not in Olcott's mind "discovered a system by which spirits
may be evoked or physical phenomena complled at will. Not a
medium that I have ever met or heard of possesses a mantram of
Yidya (scientific method) for those purposes, such as are common and have been known for ages in all Eastern countries." [15]
Lacking a system such as Theosophy, they would never get
beyond a cheap sensationalism and grasp the true importance
of the Fox family rappings. As Blavatsky wrote: "The difference
between us is that the mediums sell spirits and their phenomena for money and the spiritualists buy them as they would
sweet candy, while we occultists regard the subject as a religion
which should not be profaned." [16]

Theosophy's claim to be scientific and to provide practical
knowledge was familiar rhetoric to spiritual listeners. To be
sure, what Blavatsky meant by science was considerably more
complicated (and esoteric) than what nineteenth-century spiritualists said they had in mind when they used the term. The
phrase "occult science" suggested a method that fell somewhere

between the empirical methods imitated by spiritualists and the inward illumination sought by mystics. The German philosopher Rudolph Steiner broke with Theosophy to form his own Anthroposophical Movement after he decided that the former had taken too much from Hinduism, a tradition alien to Western thought.[17] However, his conception of occult science (he called himself "a scientist of the invisible") was roughly equivalent to that of Blavatsky.

Steiner regarded occult discoveries, which penetrated into the supersensible realm that human beings associated with magic, as empirical, objective, and subject to pragmatic verification. In saying that, he paid his respects to the natural science of his own day and the conception of science entertained by most spiritualists. But the mere fact that truth was empirical and verifiable did not mean that everyone could appreciate it. Steiner and other occultists put their science in a form unfamiliar to most spiritualists when they asserted that the ineffable nature of the highest truths bound the occultist to silence before those who were not qualified to receive them.

Unlike the mystic, the occultist did not regard the noetic state of penetrating depths of truth unplumbed by discursive intellect as an end in itself. But he did share with the mystic the belief that the highest forms of knowing had nothing to do with ordinary intellect. Truth was reserved to the person whose soul had been transformed and whose whole perception of the world had changed. Occult science therefore could not be transmitted in the systematic fashion appropriate to the natural sciences.

While this occult conception of science was presumably too mysterious to meet spiritualist standards, some spiritualists nonetheless felt an empathy with the metaphysical claims of the Theosophists. As with most other things about the spiritualist movement, much depended on whether an individual who believed in spirit communication was inclined to interest himself in philosophy. As we have seen, philosophy (other than an ill-defined antimaterialism) had very little to do with the appeal of the movement. In fact the more spiritualists in the nineteenth century strayed from their straightforward claims about the facts of spirit communication, the more they lost a general audience. It hardly needs emphasizing that Theosophy or any other form of occultism never commanded the public interest in America that spiritualism did (except when they discarded secrecy—witness the popularity of newspaper horoscopes).

On the other hand, by virtue of the fact that occultism claimed to pose an alternative to the mechanical and materialistic assumptions of Western science it struck a responsive chord among spiritualists. Many spirit messages in the nineteenth century taught a metaphysics that was indistinguishable from the one that scholars have most commonly associated with occultism.[18] They portrayed the universe as an interrelated and mutually responsive system where distant events in the macrocosmic area of space determined what happened in the microcosmic world of man. Contact was irrelevant to causation. Blavatsky borrowed more from Far Eastern sources than from the traditions of Neoplatonism and Renaissance magic. But she was apparently familiar with the Hermetic tradition that man not only could understand the complex sympathies, antipathies, and correspondences that animated the cosmos, but also could manipulate them to his own advancement. Spiritualists, insofar as they paid attention to Swedenborg, were heirs to part of that intellectual tradition. At the very least, they had picked up words and phrases of the ancient wisdom Blavatsky tried to systematize.

However disinclined spiritualists were to accept Theosophy's claim to have gained a comprehensive understanding of the human situation (to them Theosophy reversed their efforts to simplify belief), nineteenth-century occultism in America corresponded in broad ways with the liberal theology to which spiritualists were dedicated. The organization of the Theosophical Society was rigid when compared to the congregational structure of spiritualism, but Theosophy formed part of the nineteenth-century revolt against the authority of American Protestant churches. In fact, without the background of that revolt, Blavatsky's attempt to implant her version of Hinduism in America would have had no significance. Like spiritualism, Theosophy rejected predestination and original sin, made God an impersonal presence in Nature, and proclaimed everyone's real self to be divine. The mastery of church doctrine became unimportant, and the experience of the power of religious belief in one's life became everything.

Because Blavatsky opted for the doctrine of reincarnation and the soul's ultimate release from personal identity, her scheme of salvation differed in important respects from the spiritualist one. However, the differences were not as profound as they might seem upon first glance. A number of American spiritualists, influenced by the French spiritualist Alain Kardec (Leon Rivail), judged reincarnation to be indistinguishable from their own theory of advancement through the spheres. True enough, the spiritualist doctrine posited no future corporeal existences beyond this life. But the earthlike quality of life in the heavenly spheres as described by spiritualists came very close to the same thing. In spiritualist belief, people worked out their own salvation without the assistance of divine grace. The same was true of Theosophy. Both assumed that the evolutionary process of attaining the highest spiritual advancement would cover a time span of many lifetimes. And neither recognized the possibility of backsliding. While Theosophy held up the disappointing prospect that spirits faced a series of rebirths into earthly life, it also guaranteed that the karma of individuals would improve in each of their lives. Advancement in successive existences was just as assured as it was in the spiritualist spheres. The optimistic faith of Universalism found a place in Theosophy as surely as it had in spiritualism.

By their revolt against American Protestantism, both spiritualists and Theosophists sought to expand the limits of the natural world. The common rejection of the word supernatural, perhaps more than anything else, made the line between spiritualism and occultism a relatively easy one to cross. It gave spiritualists and Theosophists one important bit of shared language that they used time and again to criticize American science and religion. The Calvinist tradition, they believed, had tried to place a transcendent order of nature beyond the reach of immediate and personal experience by calling it supernatural. Therefore Calvinism had to attribute the spirit manifestations, like other extraordinary effects in nature, to the special intervention of either divine or demonic forces. In the case of the spirit manifestations, American Protestant leaders much preferred the demonic explanation. The practical result of that belief was to encourage people to leave the supersensible world alone (God had preserved a realm of knowledge that humans should not try to understand) and concentrate on material things. In the process, the concept of spirit became an abstraction that had no meaning in everyday life.

To Theosophists and spiritualists, nineteenth-century science only narrowed further the range of acceptable human inquiry. Most nineteenth-century scientists, at least prior to Darwin, retained the category supernatural but placed it beyond the range of what empirical methodology could deal with. The result was not only to eliminate the supersensible world as an object of human knowledge, but, worse, to limit the accepted modes of experiencing the world (i.e., what could not be seen by a community of observers was not real). One scholar has recently written: "The Occult world offers an alternative for those who, usually by dint of some uncanny experience in their own lives or their need for a more immediate and direct religious consolation, are not able to encase themselves in a 'contentment with the finite,' nor, on the other hand reconcile themselves to a concept of the infinite that seems (a) remote and (b) potentially hostile." [19] Surely the attitude described in this passage applied to the nineteenth-century Americans who were attracted to Theosophy and spiritualism.

Spiritualists remained much more rigidly (narrowly?) empiricist than the Theosophists and never pretended to get anywhere near the latter's comprehensive vision of the unseen world. Occultists charged that the halfway measures of spiritualists only increased the materialist malaise of America they sought to cure. But spiritualists and occultists agreed that the boundaries of the natural order encompassed the material and the spiritual, the seen and the unseen, the finite and the infinite. Nothing, in theory, lay beyond the reach of human minds. That belief gave Blavatsky the confidence to promise "a mathematical demonstration" of God and the spirits and to affirm that "there are no such uncompromising believers in the immu-

tability and universality of the laws of nature as students of occultism." [20]

To reiterate, most American spiritualists rejected the secrecy
and the systematization that were essential to occult philosophy
and occult science. Spiritualism was not, as one student of the
movement said, an attempt to make "trafficking with the occult
respectable." [21] The word "occult" as used in that phrase means
nothing, and one could with as much accuracy say that Epis-
copalianism attempted to make trafficking with the occult respectable. Any historian of spiritualism must bear in mind that
a far greater percentage of Americans who believed in spirit
communication became (or remained) Methodists than Theosophists. However there were sufficient parallels in the self-jus-
tifying phrases uttered by spiritualists and occultists to mini-
mize the discontinuity one would feel in passing from the
company of the first to the company of the second. Almost the
same parallels suggest why some spiritualists in the late nineteenth century gravitated toward Christian Science.

Cora Richmond, one of the leading trance mediums of the
nineteenth century, wrote that occultism and spiritualism
worked together to open "to the comprehension and mind of
man the existence of a world of magic, of spiritual powers and
gifts, of an underlying spiritual science which belongs to
human life, exists in connection with embodied human spirits,
and occupies a great portion of the lives of humanity, even
though they are unaware of it." [22] Many spiritualists would
have regarded Richmond's use of the word "magic" as ill-advised, but they would have had no trouble getting her point.

Virtually every new American religion of the nineteenth and
twentieth centuries has offered to prove itself by empirical and
objective standards. A far-from-exhaustive list would include
Mormonism, Christian Science, Theosophy, American versions
of Zen Buddhism, Transcendental Meditation, Scientology,
New Thought, and contemporary witchcraft. Insofar as spiritualism was the first popular movement in America to insist on
empiricism as the exclusive foundation of religious thought, it
was bound to be associated with many other movements that
sought to copy its example. This was doubly so given the ecu-

menical and nonsectarian nature of spiritualist teachings. Believers in spirit communication were free to apply that belief in any way that made sense to them.

Nineteenth-century spiritualists quite understandably wanted to avoid labels, like "occult," that were so easily used to make their work appear zany and exotic. Their refusal throughout the nineteenth century to accept a marginal status for their ideas (occultists bore their marginality with considerably more equanimity; it was in fact an essential part of their identity) left them with little choice but to join in the general damnation of occultism. Nonetheless, empiricism proved to be an invitation to many sorts of experience, and spiritualists should not have been surprised to see people sliding from one allegedly empirical (and rational) religion into another. Their critics were not.

The problems that spiritualists had in denying unwelcome associations did not go unnoticed by psychical researchers. In making a fresh start with the scientific investigation of the supernormal, psychical researchers in England and America tried very hard to learn from the mistakes spiritualists had made. Almost by reflex, they made the required statements disclaiming interest in the theoretical teachings of any occult, magical, or religious system. With absolute appropriateness, one of the first important studies undertaken by the SPR condemned Madame Blavatsky.[23] Though spirit communication was one choice among the proposed areas of investigation, psychical researchers were careful to distinguish themselves from those who made spiritualism their religion. What they proposed was a fresh and cautious inquiry into certain kinds of puzzling and apparently nonphysical facts that had no ready explanation within existing scientific systems. They successfully sought support from people whose opinion carried weight in the scientific community.

Unfortunately, the SPR and the ASPR had no choice but to encourage amateur support (which included the support of many people who already had a less-than-neutral attitude toward the phenomena the societies proposed to investigate) and to solicit reports of supernormal occurrences from the general public. These two factors certainly compromised their scientific standings from the beginning. But the establishment of psychical research societies at least produced a group of men and women who could lay claim to a special professional expertise in the investigation of supernormal (again they avoided the word supernatural as prescientific) events. Devoting much of their adult lives to the field, they designed experiments, worked out statistical methods of verification, and published their findings in journals modeled after existing scientific publications. What psychical researchers most wanted to avoid was the democratic tolerance of the nineteenth-century spiritualist investigators. They did not deny that some spiritualists had done careful investigations, but as a movement spiritualism had failed to enforce the kind of rigorous standards it would take to convince skeptics.

In the United States, Hyslop and Prince turned the need to maintain scientific standards into an obsession of psychical researchers. Their pleas had a strong effect on Rhine, who in the 1930s tried to move parapsychology completely into the laboratory. As we have seen, despite his constant reiteration of the point that he and his coworkers meant to revolutionize the base of modern science, he held unusually conventional notions of scientific experimentation. He delighted in emphasizing the drudgery of the work at Duke University, as if the drudgery in itself was evidence of scientific method. While he frequently played up spectacular instances of ESP that he witnessed under poorly controlled experimental conditions, Rhine and his assistants spent most of their time conducting card experiments that over the years produced results only slightly above chance expectations. Compared to a good mind-reading act, the work in the parapsychology lab at Duke produced few wonders.

The public interest in Rhine's early work may have had something to do with a general desire for mystification. But if so, that desire in the pre–World War II years was better satisfied by the spectacular advances in twentieth-century technology. In those years, machines were still classed as marvels. Upton Sinclair referred to ESP as Mental Radio, but it did not turn on and off with the predictability of a radio. When the American public realized that, most of their interest in Rhine's work disappeared. It did not reappear until technology itself became dull.

Yet despite everything that leading parapsychologists said and wrote and did, they had only slightly better luck than nineteenth-century spiritualists in freeing themselves of the occultist association. The association in itself would not have been important had it been entirely a product of the imaginations of people who saw parapsychology as mere foolishness. But, as was the case with spiritualism, parapsychology inevitably reflected some of the concerns that motivated modern occult movements.

Consider again, for a moment, the perplexing dilemmas encountered by Rhine in his work. Rhine refused to recognize matter as the primary or the single stuff of reality. Yet he aped a science that, though it was no longer in the twentieth century ruled by mechanistic or materialistic assumptions, sought to uncover predictable laws governing entitites that had some sort of physical reality. In this case, as in many others, Rhine was limited by his language. He apparently did not believe that principles of mechanical causation applied to psi (which is not to say that he believed in a universe ruled by correspondences and sympathetic influences), but he and his followers used a language of mechanics because they could not think of another. They spoke, for example, of thought transference, of displacement, of psi hits, and of psi misses. Psychical research began as an attempt to undermine the assumptions of natural science using the methods of natural science. In Rhine's hands, that endeavor looked more and more questionable.

The more Rhine worked, the more he convinced some parapsychologists that if psi was, as he postulated, an invisible force acting according to no known physical laws, a laboratory science of parapsychology had a limited potential. One could not even hope to demonstrate the occurrence of psi through controlled experimentation, because objections could always be found to block the acceptance of experimental results that could not be put into some lawful framework.[24] Besides, it was boring to demonstrate something over and over again. Those parapsychologists disappointed with Rhine often turned for help to various occult teachings because these seemed to furnish a more radical alternative to prevailing scientific approaches. For them, occult science, while not to be swallowed uncritically, suggested better ways to understand and investigate psi than the models Rhine had emulated with such frustrating results.

Rhine, of course, disclaimed responsibility for the conduct of parapsychologists who strayed from the straight and narrow path of scientific experimentation. On the other hand, Rhine might have done better to admit that his own scientific quest was less marked by a cool detachment than by what James had called the "will to believe." The admission would have opened him to the charge of subjectivity. But he was open to the charge anyway. Rather than as a detached observer, Rhine was viewed by his detractors as a man who had yielded to the desire to understand the world in intensely personal terms. In their minds, to yield to that need was human. But from a more dispassionate position it made parapsychology similar to astrology. The latter sought not to understand the motion of the stars (a legitimate scientific aim) but to prove that the motion of the stars had a mysterious influence on the destinies of individual men and women.

The suggested similarity in motive explained why parapsychologists chose to investigate things not because they had importance for any established area of scientific research but because they were believed to be important to morality. In defending themselves against that criticism, parapsychologists correctly pointed out that the people who took the most interest in Rhine's work were agnostics or atheists who denied the existence of a personal God. But that answer was not relevant to the argument, particularly in view of the fact that most parapsychologists, from the very time they lapsed into agnosticism, began searching for evidence to sustain the view that individual life held meaning.

Whether Rhine admitted it or not, parapsychology's attempts to become scientific were bound to produce ambivalence and tension within the movement. Parapsychology recognized that a science of material substances and mechanics was the most fantastically successful strategy of human thought and activity ever devised. Yet at the same time it argued that science needed

to reach beyond itself by incorporating back into its structure
categories of experience it had deliberately, and at one time correctly, excluded. As necessary as positivism had been to the advancement of knowledge, it had become a constricting vision.
Like the writers of some science-fiction pieces, psychical researchers tended to mix their admiration for technological marvels produced by normal scientific activity with a prophetic
vision that our present concepts of "rationality" were not adequate to grasp what lay ahead in future decades. At some point
those categories would require dramatic reshaping. If nothing
else, parapsychology gave forewarning of the necessity and in-
evitability of that moment. However, in trying to get science to
recognize facts it had no present way of handling, parapsychologists could not pretend to be ordinary laboratory technicians. At least William James did not think so. Nor did a
number of other part-time parapsychologists, including Henri
Bergson, Carl Jung, Gardner Murphy, and Arthur Koestler.

None of the men just mentioned thought they were arguing
for irrationalism or any other epistemological position that was
contemptuous of modern scientific procedure. However, they
regarded the science of their own day as an intellectual strait-
jacket when it was taken as the sole determinant of the truth of
every proposition. They were as concerned as a Hyslop or a
Rhine that parapsychology be granted scientific standing. But
they were convinced that psychical researchers should spend
less time trying to prove their hardheadedness and skepticism
and more time rethinking the problem of what exactly constituted objectivity. It was out of this problem that they tried to
devise a philosophical position which avoided a choice between
romantic idealism and scientific positivism.

In one way or another, James, Bergson, and Jung were all suspicious of the quest for certainty. True, they made room in their
philosophies for intuition as a possible source of knowledge. To
them, intuition was in an existential sense as real a mode of experiencing the world as sensory observation. Moreover, psychical research suggested that it might even have a kind of priority. Ian Stevenson was probably thinking of James when he
suggested that the ESP phenomena studied by parapsychology

could make traditional methods of empirical observation obsolete. So was Lawrence LeShan when he attempted to define a world view common to the medium, the mystic, and the physicist.[25]

But Jung and James knew no way to prove finally that visions of mystics and clairvoyants originated in a transcendent ground of reality. Where they differed from most scientists, and indeed from Rhine, was in refusing to think that the so-called subjectivity of the experience disqualified it as an object of scientific inquiry. James in particular argued that the unique, deeply felt personal experience was as much an objective fact as routine transformations in the physical world that were demonstrated in laboratories and subsumed under general laws. The parapsychologists were perfectly justified in approaching such facts with as many systematic procedures as they could think of. But in striving for scientific credibility, they risked making the misleading assumption that experimental ingenuity inside the laboratory could establish the certainty of a fact which behaved elusively outside the laboratory. The experience of genuine psychic powers was perhaps inseparable from the context of the everyday world. A proper science had to allow for that possibility and adjust its standards of proof accordingly.

The critiques of science that formed part of the literature of parapsychology did not make parapsychology an occult science. But it helps explain why Jung could become deeply interested in both alchemy and extrasensory perception. From his study of them as well as from a number of bizarre episodes in his own life, he derived his concept of synchronicity.[26] Jung believed that significant relationships existed between events that were described in everyday language as coincidences. Those relationships defied explanation according to the rules of mechanical causation, but they were not on that account illusory. In Jung's mind the principle of synchronicity gave scientific status to psi events (and some of the macrocosmic/microcosmic connections recognized by occultists) at the same time it forced science to rethink its procedures of verification.

For Jung, as well as for James and for Bergson, much of the failure of the modern scientific imagination stemmed from its insistence that nothing could be understood until it was broken down into parts. Arguably Rhine's work merely repeated that mistake. That is, it tried to isolate psi under conditions inimical to its appearance. The holism that was central to occultist teachings could not tell Rhine how to design a better experiment, but it could tell him what was lacking in his approach. The relevance of occultism to parapsychology was to remind the latter that its goal was to correct the analytic categories of modern science, not to mimic them.

To get back to Dingwall, he need not have worried quite so much about the uses to which parapsychology was put in the 1960s. So long as parapsychologists define their task as directing the American mainstream away from impersonal and materialistic habits of thought, they will attract attention from many diverse sorts of individuals. They might even find themselves flirting with a few genuine social revolutionaries. As many people interested in parapsychology have recognized, however, parapsychology does not necessarily lose anything in the encounter. Besides, whatever reactions professional parapsychologists have had against Rhine's efforts to make the field scientifically rigorous, they showed no sign of transforming themselves into a band of secret occultists.

What will keep parapsychology qualitatively different from occultism will be its loyalty to the principle that the world should not be packaged in falsely coherent ways. That same conviction kept most American spiritualists out of the Theosophical Society in the late nineteenth century. From the standpoint of many psychical researchers who have worked in America, science and occultism have been equally guilty of placing a greater value on coherence than on recognizing the baffling complexities of human experience. The coherence of natural science left no room at all for the supernormal. Modern occultism left plenty of room for it, but was not content to leave it unexplained.

The task of the parapsychologist was best stated by the American writer Charles Fort. Fort, who was born in Albany in 1874, deeply distrusted scientific categories because of what he believed they excluded. He developed a tireless energy for pursuing facts that interested no one else. In doing so, he presumed to act as "a horsefly that stings the scalp of knowledge to prevent it from sleeping." [27] If parapsychology ever requires an epitaph, Fort's line might serve.

Notes

Chapter 1

1. The number of historical studies of nineteenth-century spiritualism has increased in recent years. Among scholarly works, see Geoffrey K. Nelson, *Spiritualism and Society* (London: Routledge and Kegan Paul, 1969); Howard Kerr, *Mediums and Spirit Rappers and Roaring Radicals: Spiritualism in American Literature, 1850–1900* (Urbana: University of Illinois Press, 1972); Burton Gates Brown, Jr., "Spiritualism in Nineteenth-Century America," Ph.D. dissertation, Boston University, *1973*; Mary Farrell Bednarowski, "Nineteenth-Century American Spiritualism: An Attempt at Scientific Religion," Ph.D. dissertation, University of Minnesota, 1973. Katherine H. Porter, *Through a Glass Darkly: Spiritualism in the Browning Circle* (Lawrence, Kan.: University of Kansas Press, 1958), remains in many ways the best book on the subject. Anyone interested in the historical origins of spiritualism in America should consult Ernest Isaacs, "A History of American Spiritualism: The Beginnings, 1845–1855," Master's thesis, University of Wisconsin, 1957.
2. Garrison's first statement on the subject can be found in the *Liberator*, March 3, 1854. The *New York Tribune*, June 8, 1850, reported on a famous séance attended by Bryant, Willis, Cooper, Greeley, and Bancroft. For Harris's interest in spiritualism, see Kurt F. Leidecker, *Yankee Teacher: The Life of William Torrey Harris* (New York: Philosophical Library, 1946), p. 56. On Roebling, consult Alan Trachtenberg, *Brooklyn Bridge: Fact and Symbol* (New York: Oxford University Press, 1965), p. 60.

3. Russel B. Nye, *George Bancroft, Brahmin Rebel* (New York: Alfred A. Knopf, 1944), p. 188.

4. E. W. Capron, *Modern Spiritualism: Its Facts and Fanaticisms, Its Consistencies and Contradictions* (Boston: Bela Marsh, 1855), p. 191.

5. John Weiss, ed., *Life and Correspondence of Theodore Parker* (London: Longmans, Green, 1863), vol. I, p. 428.

6. Allan Nevins and Milton H. Thomas, eds., *The Diary of George Templeton Strong* (New York: Macmillan, 1952), vol. II, pp. 244–245.

7. Alice Felt Tyler, *Freedom's Ferment* (Minneapolis: University of Minnesota Press, 1944); Nelson, *Spiritualism and Society*.

8. Just after the death of a son and a year before he and his wife began attending séances, Horace Greeley wrote to his author-friend Bayard Taylor, also a spiritualist investigator, that "the world looks very dark to me. . . . I do not hope that it will ever again wear the old line of gladness." Letter of August 16, 1849, Horace Greeley Collection, New York Historical Society.

9. On this point I have found helpful Neil Harris's discussion of the "operational aesthetic" in *Humbug: A Biography of P. T. Barnum* (Boston: Little, Brown, 1973).

10. For a use of Festinger, see Edwin Boring's introduction to C. E. M. Hansel, *ESP: A Scientific Evaluation* (New York: Scribner's, 1966), pp. xiii–xxi. A more sympathetic application of "cognitive dissonance" to explain spiritualist belief can be found in the Bednarowski dissertation.

11. Hugo Münsterberg, "Psychology and Mysticism," *Atlantic Monthly* 83 (January 1899), 67–85; Charles K. Mills, "Occultism with Particular Reference to Some Phases of Spiritism," *American Journal of the Medical Sciences* 157 (July 1921), 115; Joseph Jastrow, "The Modern Occult," *Fact and Fable in Psychology* (Boston: Houghton Mifflin, 1900).

12. John Senior, *The Way Down and Out: The Occult in Symbolist Literature* (Ithaca, N.Y.: Cornell University Press, 1959); Perle Epstein, *The Private Labyrinth of Malcolm Lowry: Under the Volcano, and the Cabbala* (New York: Holt, Rinehart, 1969); George Wilson Knight, *Neglected Powers: Essays on Nineteenth and Twentieth Century Literature* (London: Routledge and Kegan Paul, 1971); James Webb, *The Flight from Reason* (London: Macdonald, 1971). For extended discussion of this idea, see chap. 9.

13. The earliest accounts of the Hydesville events are: *A Report of the Mysterious Noises Heard in the House of Mr. John D. Fox, in Hydes-*

ville, Arcadia, Wayne County, Authenticated by the Certificates, and Confirmed by the Statements of the Citizens of the Place and Vicinity (Canandaigua, N.Y.: E. E. Lewis, 1848); Eliab W. Capron and Henry D. Barron, *Explanation and History of the Mysterious Communion with Spirits, Comprehending the Rise and Progress of the Mysterious Noises in Western New York, Generally Received as Spiritual Communications* (Auburn, N.Y.: Finn and Rockwell, 1850); and D. M. Dewey, *History of the Strange Sounds of Rappings, Heard in Rochester and Western New York* (Rochester, N.Y.: Dewey, 1850).

14. Earl Wesley Fornell, *The Unhappy Medium: Spiritualism and The Life of Margaret Fox* (Austin: University of Texas Press, 1964) is an unreliable biography, but it does recount the charges against the Fox girls. Adelbert Cronise collected a number of inaccessible details about the sisters in "The Beginnings of Modern Spiritualism In and Near Rochester," *Rochester Historical Society Publications Fund Series* 5 (1926), 1–22.

15. *Tribune,* June 5, 1850; *Weekly Tribune,* August 17, 1850.

16. T. K. Oesterreich provides encyclopedic coverage of the topic in *Possession, Demonical and Other, Among Primitive Races in Antiquity, the Middle Ages, and Modern Times* (New Hyde Park, N.Y.: University Books, 1966).

17. Another widely cited work besides Kerner's *The Seeress of Prevorst* was Johann Heinrich Jung-Stilling's *Theory of Pneumatology, in Reply to the Question: What Ought to be Believed or Disbelieved Concerning Presentiments, Visions, and Apparitions, According to Nature, Reason, and Scripture* (translated into English in 1834). Also see Henry C. Blinn, *The Manifestation of Spiritualism among the Shakers* (East Canterbury, N.H., 1899).

18. On the origins of mesmerism, see Robert Darnton, *Mesmerism and the End of the Enlightenment in France* (Cambridge, Mass.: Harvard University Press, 1968).

19. Slater Brown, *The Heyday of Spiritualism* (New York: Hawthorn, 1970), pp. 1–64.

20. Robert W. Delp, "Andrew Jackson Davis: Prophet of American Spiritualism," *Journal of American History* 54 (June 1967), 43–56.

21. Reviews in *Harbinger,* September 11 and October 2, 1847.

22. Letter of September 15, 1847, Sarah Helen Whitman Collection, Brown University Library. Bush, *Mesmer and Swedenborg or, The Relation of the Developments of Mesmerism to the Doctrines and Disclosures of Swedenborg* (New York, 1847).

23. Harris emerged as the most interesting of these figures. See Herbert W. Schneider and George Lawton, *A Prophet and a Pilgrim* (New York: Columbia University Press, 1942).

24. S. B. Brittan, *Univercoelum and Spiritual Philosopher* 2 (February 12, 1848); T. L. Harris, *Univercoelum and Spiritual Philosopher* (September 30, 1848).

25. "To Our Patrons," *Univercoelum and Spiritual Philosopher* 2 (June 3, 1848), 116.

26. Ibid.

27. "Knowledge through Obedience," *Univercoelum and Spiritual Philosopher* 2 (August 12, 1848), 168.

28. See J. R. Jacob, "LaRoy Sunderland: The Alienation of an Abolitionist," *Journal of American Studies* 6 (April 1972), 1–17.

29. Isaacs, "History of American Spiritualism . . . ," p. 105.

30. Kerr, *Mediums and Spirit Rappers* . . . , pp. 59–60.

31. Statistics for such figures derive mainly from early histories written by spiritualists, but the notion of a rapid increase in interest in spiritualism is well supported in newspaper accounts.

32. The best-known of these volumes published during the 1850s were Edmonds and Dexter, *Spiritualism* (New York: Partridge and Brittan, 1853–55); Robert Hare, *Experimental Investigations of the Spirit Manifestations* (New York: Partridge and Brittan, 1855); Charles Linton, *The Healing of Nations* (New York: Society for the Diffusion of Spiritual Knowledge, 1855); S. C. Hewitt, *Messages from the Superior State Communicated through John M. Spear in the Summer of 1852* (Boston: Bela Marsh, 1853); Reverend C. Hammond, *Light from the Spirit World: The Pilgrimage of Thomas Paine and Others to the Seventh Circle in the Spirit World* (Rochester, N.Y.: D. M. Dewey, 1852); Josiah Brigham, *Twelve Messages from the Spirit of John Quincy Adams Through Joseph D. Stiles, Medium* (Boston: Bela Marsh, 1859). In addition, all spiritualist periodicals published messages.

33. Letter to Frank J. Garrison, January 18, 1867, Boston Public Library.

34. *Beyond the Valley: A Sequel to 'The Magic Staff.' An Autobiography of Andrew Jackson Davis* (Boston: Colby and Rich, 1885), p. 145.

35. "Modern Spiritualism. Its Truths and Its Errors; A Sermon Preached in London, January 15, 1860."

36. James, "Modern Diabolism," *The Atlantic* 32 (August 1873), 219–224; *The Pythonism of the Present Day: The Response of the Ministers of the Massachusetts Association of the New Jerusalem to a Resolution of that Association Requesting their Consideration of What is

Usually Known as Modern Spiritualism (Boston: G. Phinney, 1858).

37. Giles B. Stebbins, *Upward Steps of Seventy Years* (New York: John W. Lovell, 1890), p. 262.

38. John Higham, *From Boundlessness to Consolidation: The Transformation of American Culture, 1848–1860* (Ann Arbor, Mich.: William L. Clements Library, 1969).

39. *Spirit World,* July 26, 1851.

40. *Explanation . . . of the Mysterious Communion with Spirits . . . ,* p. 6.

41. Introduction to John Edmonds and George T. Dexter, *Spiritualism.*

42. Edmonds, "Personal Experience," *Shekinah* 1 (New York, 1852), 265–271. Edmonds, *Letters and Tracts on Spiritualism* (London: J. Burns, 1874), p. 2.

43. Edmonds, "False Prophesying," *Spiritual Tracts* (New York: Partridge and Brittan, 1858). Edmonds and Dexter, *Spiritualism* vol. I, app. F.

44. Emma Hardinge, *Modern American Spiritualism: A Twenty Years' Record of the Communion between Earth and the World of Spirits* (New York: published by the author, 1870), pp. 532–536. Since Emma Hardinge married only after her career was well established, her maiden name is retained in the text.

45. James Hackett Fowler, *New Testament 'Miracles' and Modern 'Miracles'; The Comparative Amount of Evidence for Each* (Boston: Bela Marsh, 1856), p. 4.

46. *Banner of Light* (hereafter *BL*), August 20, 1857.

47. The issue was complicated because some spiritualists' messages distinguished between soul and spirit, the latter being less continuous with matter than the former. However, the spiritualist imagination was not abstract. It gave material shapes to almost everything in the afterlife that it tried to describe. Charlotte Fowler Wells, whose family publishing firm printed many phrenological and spiritualist tracts, compiled an interesting set of spirit teachings in late 1850 and early 1851; her fifty-page manuscript is in the Cornell University Regional History Collection. Defining soul as the perfection of matter (p. 7), the spirits dictated: "If the objection of materialism be urged, my answer is, of *what is soul formed,* or, if it has *no* formation, if it be *not* a *material* body, how *can* it have an existence?"

48. "The New York Conference," *Telegraph Papers* 4 (February 28, 1854), 216.

49. Capron and Barron, *Explanation . . . of the Mysterious Communion with Spirits . . .* , p. 35.

50. Robert Peel, *Mary Baker Eddy: The Years of Discovery* (New York: Holt, Rinehart, 1966), p. 153.

51. "Letter to Prof. Hermann Ulrici," *Popular Science Monthly* 15 (September 1879) 593.

52. Davis, *The Approaching Crisis: Being a Review of Dr. Bushnell's Recent Lectures on Supernaturalism* (New York, 1852), p. 45.

53. Bushnell, *Nature and the Supernatural, as Together Constituting the One System of God* (New York: Scribner's, 1858), p. 110.

54. Barbara Novak, *American Painting of the Nineteenth Century* (London: Pall Mall Press, 1969), pp. 109, 122, 163, 146–149. The painters mentioned by Novak are William Sidney Mount, Fitz Hugh Lane, and George Caleb Bingham. Epes Sargent, *The Proof Palpable of Immortality* (Boston: Colby and Rich, 1876), p. 25; John B. Wilson, "Emerson and the 'Rochester Rappings,' " *New England Quarterly* 41 (June 1968), 248–258; Moncure Conway, *Autobiography, Memories, and Experiences of Moncure Daniel Conway* (Boston: Houghton Mifflin, 1904), vol. I, p. 149.

55. For the relations of scientists and theologians in America up to midcentury, consult George H. Daniels, *American Science in the Age of Jackson* (New York: Columbia University Press, 1968), especially pp. 51–56, 191–200.

56. R. G. Collingwood, *Idea of History* (Oxford: Oxford University Press, 1946), pp. 21–22.

57. For an account of the rebuff given a scientist other than Hare who tried to present spiritualist evidence at a scientific convention in Springfield, Mass., see *BL,* September 3, 1859.

58. *Discovery and Explanation of the Source of the Phenomena Generally Known as the Rochester Knockings* (Buffalo, N.Y.: George H. Derby, 1851).

59. For Faraday's views, see his letter to the *Times,* June 30, 1853, p. 4; his report in *Athenaeum,* July 2, 1853, pp. 801–803; his letter to the *Times,* November 8, 1864, p. 7; and the letter of John Tyndall to the *Pall Mall Gazette* 7 (May 9, 1868), 1750.

60. Editorial, *New York Times,* June 12, 1852.

61. "Impostures and Delusions," *National Intelligencer,* April 25, 1853.

62. Strong, *Diary . . .* , vol. II, pp. 15–16, 93, 119, 125.

63. Charles Beecher, *A Review of the Spiritual Manifestations* (New York: G. P. Putnam's Sons, 1853).

64. Some pamphlets and books of the 1850s sustaining Beecher's argument include: John C. Bywater, *The Mystery Solved; or a Bible Exposé of the Spirit Rapping, Showing that They are not Caused by the Spirits of the Dead, but by Evil Demons or Devils* (Rochester, N.Y., 1852); William Ramsey, *Spiritualism, a Satanic Delusion, and a Sign of the Times* (Rochester, N.Y.: H. L. Hastings, 1857); The Reverend William Henry Corning, *The Infidelity of the Times as Connected with the Rappings and Mesmerists* (Boston: J. P. Jewett, 1854); William R. Gordon, *A Three-Fold Test of Modern Spiritualism* (New York: Scribner, 1856); J. W. Daniels, *Spiritualism versus Christianity or, Spiritualism Thoroughly Exposed* (New York: Auburn, Miller, 1856); Z. Campbell, *The Spiritual Telegraphic Opposition Line; or, Science and Divine Revelation against Spiritual Manifestations* (Springfield, Mass., 1853); Joseph F. Berg, *Abaddon, and Mahanaim; or, Daemons and Guardian Spirits* (Philadelphia: Higgins and Perkinpine, 1856); Charles Munger, *Ancient Sorcery as Revived in Modern Spiritualism Examined by the Divine Law and Testimony* (Boston: Deger, 1857); James Porter, *The Spirit Rappings, Mesmerism, Clairvoyance, Visions, Revelations, Startling Phenomena and Infidelity of the Rapping Fraternity Calmly Considered and Exposed* (Boston: George C. Rand, 1853); William M. Thayer, *Trial of the Spirits* (Boston: J. B. Chisholm, 1855); J. A. Seiss, *The Empire of Evil, Satanic Agency, and Demonism* (Baltimore: James Young's Steam Printing Estab., 1856).
65. A Citizen of Ohio (David Quinn), *Interior Causes of the War: The Nation Demonized and its President a Spirit-Rapper* (New York: M. Doolady, 1863).
66. Bushnell, *Nature and the Supernatural, as Together Constituting the One System of God,* pp. 124, 360.
67. Peel, *Mary Baker Eddy,* pp. 153–154.
68. John Bovee Dods, *Spirit Manifestations Examined and Explained, Judge Edmonds Refuted; or, an Exposition of the Involuntary Powers and Instincts of the Human Mind* (New York: DeWitt and Davenport, 1854), p. 29.
69. Karl, Baron von Reichenbach, *Researches of Magnetism, Electricity, Heat, Light, Crystallization, and Chemical Attraction, in their Relations to the Vital Force* (London: Taylor, Walton and Maberly, 1850).
70. E. C. Rogers, *Philosophy of Mysterious Agents, Human and Mundane* (Boston: J. P. Jewett, 1853).
71. *Modern Mysteries Explained and Exposed* (Boston: John P. Jewett, 1855); *The Phenomena of Spiritualism Scientifically Explained and Exposed* (New York: A. S. Barnes, 1876).

72. *National Magazine,* "The Spirit Rappings Again," July 1853, p. 86; "The Spirit Rappings," August 1853, p. 184.

73. Letter to Lydia M. Child, February 6, 1857, Boston Public Library.

74. George Fisher, *Life of Benjamin Silliman* (Philadelphia: Porter and Coates, 1866), vol. II, pp. 253–256.

75. Brittan to Hare, January 30, 1857, Hare Papers, American Philosophical Society (APS).

76. Partridge to Hare, January 17, 1857, APS.

77. There is a long rough draft of Hare's reply to Silliman among his papers at the APS.

78. *Philadelphia Inquirer,* July 27, 1853; *New York Times,* July 29, 1853.

79. Hare to Silliman, rough draft, Hare papers, APS.

80. *Life and Correspondence of . . . Parker,* vol. I, p. 331.

81. For a reference to Eustis and some other Harvard professors, see Lester Ward, *Glimpses of the Cosmos* (New York: G. P. Putnam's Sons, 1913), vol. I, pp. 59–62.

82. *Life and Correspondence of . . . Parker,* vol. I, p. 332.

83. *Spiritualism Shown as It Is. Boston Courier Report of the Proceedings of Professed Spiritual Agents and Mediums in the Presence of Professors Peirce, Agassiz, Horsford, Dr. B. A. Gould* (Boston: Courier, 1859).

84. Gardner to Robert Hare, July 23, 1857, Hare papers, APS.

85. Allen Putnam, *Agassiz and Spiritualism, Involving the Investigation of Harvard College Professors in 1857* (Boston: Colby and Rich, ca. 1874).

86. *Spiritualism Shown as It is . . . ,* p. 13.

87. Hardinge, *Modern American Spiritualism,* p. 187. Hardinge's volume contains a full defense of the spiritualists at this Cambridge confrontation.

88. Gardner to Hare, June 8, 1857, Hare papers, APS.

89. *Spiritualism Shown as It Is . . . ,* p. 12.

90. "Fruits of Spiritualism," December 2, 1856, p. 4. See also "Suicide of a Spiritualist," *New York Daily Tribune,* Dec. 1, 1856, p. 3; the *Tribune* had by this time lost its former sympathy for spiritualism and blamed Fairbanks's death on temporary insanity caused by his beliefs.

91. Daniels, *American Science in the Age of Jackson,* p. 56.

92. *The Spirit-Rapper: an Autobiography* (Boston: Little, Brown, 1854), p. 125.

93. *An Exposition of Views Respecting the Modern Spirit Manifestations* (Liverpool: Edward Howell, 1853), pp. 57–58.

94. James H. Hyslop, a professor of philosophy at Columbia University and a pioneer in American psychical research, made this point

in all his books on the subject. To be convincing, Hyslop felt, the spirits had to cite small details relating to the lives of the people they visited. To the community at large these were bound to seem banal, but spirits had to worry about proving their identity. Discussions of moral philosophy, which were beyond the talents of most spirits anyway, could not have done that job.

95. "How I Came to Study Spiritual Phenomena: A Chapter of Autobiography," *Atlantic Monthly* 34 (November 1874), 578–590.

96. Bushnell," *Nature and the Supernatural, as Together Constituting the One System of God,* pp. 457–458.

97. *Passages from the French and Italian Notebooks* (Cambridge, Mass.: Riverside, 1883), p. 394.

98. Brown, "Spiritualism in Nineteenth-Century America," p. 92.

99. A Searcher After Truth, *The Rappers or the Mysteries, Fallacies, and Absurdities of Spirit Rapping, Table-Tipping and Entrancement* (New York: H. Long, 1854), p. 266.

100. William Dean Howells, *The Undiscovered Country* (Boston: Houghton Mifflin, 1880), p. 193.

101. From *A Coney Island of the Mind* (New York: New Directions, 1968).

Chapter 2

1. "Spiritism and Spiritists," *The Catholic World* 9 (June 1869), 289–302; "Spiritualism," *Christian Advocate* 186 (November 20, 1856), 186; "Communing with Spirits," *Boston Review* 1 (November 1861), 568–579; "Spiritualism Tested by Science," *The New Englander* 16 (May 1858), 225–70; "The Necromancy of the Nineteenth Century," 12 (February 1854), 33–44; "The Agency Employed in the So-Called 'Spiritual Manifestations,' " *Christian Review* 18 (October 1853), 582–603; "Review Article," *Church Review* 8 (July 1855), 169–188; Austin Phelps, "Ought the Pulpit to Ignore Spiritualism," *The Congregationalist* (July 20, 1881). These articles are representative. For selected books attacking the religion of spiritualism, see chap. 1, note 64.

2. "The Drift Period in Theology," *The Christian Examiner* 79 (July 1865), 12. For Frothingham's analysis of possible dangers of spiritualist belief, see "Spiritualism and Superstition," *The Index,* July 8, 1871.

3. "The Professor at the Breakfast Table," *Atlantic Monthly* 3 (January 1859), 90.

4. Emma Hardinge, *Modern American Spiritualism: Twenty Years'*

Record of the Communion between Earth and the World of Spirits (New York: published by the author, 1870).

5. The substance of her later criticism can be found in her letter to the *BL*, November 25, 1876. For a time she found Madame Blavatsky's Theosophical Society an alternative to spiritualism.

6. *The Drama of Life after Death* (New York: Henry Holt and Co., 1932), p. ix. Lawton's book remains for many reasons a valuable assessment of spiritualist practices as he encountered them, but his assessment of the place of spiritualism within American religious thought is seriously misleading.

7. Editorial, *Brittan's Journal of Spiritual Science, Literature, Art, and Inspiration* 1 (1873), 391.

8. *New England Spiritualist Association. Constitution and By-Laws, List of Officers, and Address to the Public* (Boston, 1854), p. 14.

9. *BL*, June 25, 1857.

10. Edmonds letter to *BL*, June 1, 1867.

11. For the Adventist position on spiritualism, see J. S. Waggoner, *The Nature and Tendency of Modern Spiritualism* (Battle Creek, Mich.: Steam Press, 1860).

12. Scott Trego Swank, "The Unfettered Conscience: A Study of Sectarianism, Spiritualism, and Social Reform in the New Jerusalem Church, 1840–1870," Ph.D. dissertation, University of Pennsylvania, 1970.

13. The Fox conversion is covered in the Fornell biography. Also see George W. Corner, *Doctor Kane of the Arctic Seas* (Philadelphia: Temple University Press, 1972). The Home conversion is potentially more interesting, but like most aspects of his life, it awaits adequate telling.

14. An interesting book by a Jesuit about the relations of his church and spiritualism is Herbert Thurston, *The Church and Spiritualism* (Milwaukee: Bruce Publishing Co., 1933).

15. Cited in Charles S. Braden, *These Also Believe: A Study of Modern American Cults and Minority Religious Movements* (New York: Macmillan, 1949), pp. 350–351.

16. Consult chap. 1, note 64. Commonly cited Scriptural passages included Exod. 22:18; Deut. 18:10–12; Lev. 20:6, 27; 1 Sam. 28:6–19; Acts 16:16–18; Rev. 21:8..

17. Thomas L. Nichols, *Forty Years of American Life* (London: Longmans, Green, 1874), p. 271.

18. Manuscript journals of Ella Gertrude Thomas, entry of October 2, 1870, Duke University Library. The nature of spiritual gatherings

could acquire legal significance. In a Massachusetts Supreme Court case, reported in *BL*, June 24, 1871, the right of the spiritualist plaintiff to recover damages from a public carrier hinged on whether she was traveling on Sunday to a place of amusement or a religious ceremony. Especially in the last two decades of the nineteenth century, attempts to ban mediums along with fortune-tellers or to license them as entertainers made the question of religion a vital one.

19. "Modern Spiritualism," *Cornell Review* 2 (December 1874), 116.
20. *The Telegraph Papers* 2 (1853), 119; *BL*, November 6, 1858.
21. J. W. Edmonds, "Uncertainty of Spiritual Intercourse," *Spiritual Tracts* (New York 1858), p. 10.
22. Owen, "Some Results of My Spiritual Studies: A Chapter in Autobiography," *Atlantic Monthly* 34 (December 1874), 722; Epes Sargent, *Planchette; or, The Despair of Science* (Boston: Roberts Brothers, 1869), p. 300.
23. *BL*, August 17, 1861.
24. Epes Sargent, *Planchette . . .* , p. 300.
25. Letter dated September 18, 1853, J. S. Williams manuscript journals, vol. IV, bk. 1. Wisconsin State Historical Society.
26. Smith, *Lectures on the Religion of Reason* (Petersboro, N.Y.: C. A. Hammond, 1864), pp. 39–40.
27. Isaac Rehn, "Has Spiritualism a Basis?" *BL*, December 16, 1865. Significantly, the Society for the Diffusion of Spiritual Knowledge, supposedly an organization of Christian spiritualists, counted no ministers of any denomination among its officers.
28. Those who know Whitney R. Cross, *The Burned-Over District: The Social and Intellectual History of Enthusiastic Religion in Western New York, 1800–1850* (New York: Harper & Row, 1965), will recognize both my debt to it and my disagreements with it.
29. E. W. Capron, *Modern Spiritualism: Its Facts and Fanaticisms* (Boston: Bela Marsh, 1855), p. 379.
30. "The Errors of Old Theology," *BL*, May 26, 1866.
31. "Is God a Principle or a Person," *BL*, July 7, 1860.
32. "Proceedings of the Third National Convention of Spiritualists," *BL*, September 8, 1866.
33. "The Bible and the Soul," *The Shekinah* 2 (1852–53), 253.
34. Asaph Bemis Child, *Whatever Is, Is Right* (Boston: Berry, Colby, and Co., 1861), p. 4.
35. John W. Edmonds and George T. Dexter, *Spiritualism* (New York: Partridge and Brittan, 1853), p. 360.

36. Sargent, *The Scientific Basis of Spiritualism* (Boston: Colby and Rich, 1881), p. 346.

37. Ann Douglas, "Heaven Our Home: Consolation Literature in the Northern United States, 1830–1880," *American Quarterly* 26 (December 1974), 496–515.

38. Josiah Brigham, *Twelve Messages . . . John Quincy Adams,* (Boston: Bela Marsh, 1859), p. 81.

39. Edmonds and Dexter, *Spiritualism,* pp. 380–381.

40. Prof. William Denton, "Orthodoxy False, Since Spiritualism is True," *BL,* June 11, 1870.

41. See note 1 for examples.

42. *BL,* April 25, 1857.

43. Denton, "Orthodoxy False, Since Spiritualism is True."

44. For example, see Warren Chase, "Spiritualism and Social Discord," *BL,* May 12, 1860.

45. Ibid.

46. Child, *Whatever Is, Is Right,* p. 2.

47. Davis, *The Approaching Crisis: Being a Review of Dr. Bushnell's Recent Lectures on Supernaturalism* (New York, 1852), pp. 100, 111.

48. Waggoner, *Nature . . . of Modern Spiritualism,* p. 120.

49. Higginson, *The Results of Spiritualism* (New York: S. T. Munson, 1859), p. 20.

50. Sargent, *The Proof Palpable of Immortality* (Boston: Colby and Rich, 1876), p. 199.

51. *The Index,* May 20, 1871; July 8, 1871.

52. Letter from Morris Einstein, *The Index,* October 7, 1871.

53. There are a number of books on American Protestant liberalism, but see especially William McLoughlin, *The Meaning of Henry Ward Beecher* (New York: Alfred A. Knopf, 1970).

54. Lester Ward, *Glimpses of the Cosmos* (New York: G. P. Putnam's Sons, 1913), vol. I, pp. 96–98.

55. For this phrase and for a great deal else I am indebted to Frank Miller Turner, *Between Science and Religion: The Reaction to Scientific Naturalism in Late Victorian England* (New Haven: Yale University Press, 1974).

56. Beard, "The Psychology of Spiritism," *North American Review* 129 (July 1879), 65, 78.

57. Joel Tiffany, *Spiritualism Explained* (New York: Graham & Ellinwood, 1856), p. 111.

58. Sargent, *Planchette . . .*

59. Most accounts of the social gospel movement in America contain

biographical information about Savage. The career of Newton is covered in a Cornell University dissertation, Richard B. Dressner, "Christian Socialism: A Response to Industrial America in the Progressive Era," 1972. For a summary of Macintosh's investigation, see his article, "The Hope of Immortality," *Religion in Life* 7 (Spring 1938), 163–181.

60. Richard W. Leopold *Robert Dale Owen: A Biography* (Cambridge, Mass.: Harvard University Press, 1940), pp. 400–405.

61. See Reuben Briggs Davenport, *The Death-Blow to Spiritualism, Being the True Story of the Fox Sisters as Revealed by Authority of Margaret Fox Kane and Catherine Fox Jencken* (New York, 1888).

62. See chap. 5.

63. Burton Brown, "Spiritualism in Nineteenth-Century America," Ph.D. dissertation, Boston University, 1973, pp. 186–189.

64. H. D. Barrett and A. W. McCoy, eds., *Cassadaga: Its History and Teachings* (Meadville, Penn., 1891).

65. *Proceedings of the Sixth Annual Convention of the National Spiritualist Association, October 18–20, 1898,* p. 98.

66. Brown, "Spiritualism in Nineteenth-Century America," p. 178.

67. *Proceedings of the Sixth Annual Convention of the National Spiritualist Association, October 18–20, 1898,* p. 18.

68. Brown, "Spiritualism in Nineteenth-Century America," pp. 155—156.

69. For the best account of twentieth-century spiritualism, see J. Stillson Judah, *The History and Philosophy of the Metaphysical Movements in America* (Philadelphia: Westminster Press, 1967). Also the appropriate chapters of Irving I. Zaretsky and Mark P. Leone, *Religious Movements in Contemporary America* (Princeton: Princeton University Press, 1974).

70. The phrase is lifted from a spiritualist hymn. See *The Spiritualists' Hymnal* (Cincinnati: Light of Truth Publishing Co., 1894).

71. *BL,* April 18, 1857.

72. *BL,* December 11, 1869.

Chapter 3

1. Gerrit Smith, *Lectures on the Religion of Reason* (Petersboro, N.Y.: C. A. Hammond, 1864), pp. 39–40.

2. Dean Clark, "An Address to the Spiritualists of America," *BL,* September 7, 1867; *BL,* September 21, 1872.

3. Samuel Bernstein, *The First International in America* (New York: A. M. Kelley, 1962).

4. Many of the shorter-lived spiritualist journals carried the word "reform" as part of the title. Both the *Banner of Light* and the *Religio-Philosophical Journal* devoted many columns to the support of various reform causes. The sympathy for Indians was a particularly interesting theme, for many of the spirit guides purported to be Indian braves or squaws. See the citation to Cora Richmond (Cora Daniels Tappan) in Linda Kerber, "The Abolitionist Perception of the Indian," *Journal of American History* 62 (September 1975), 295.

5. For an interesting account of the treatment of spiritualism in nineteenth-century American literature, consult Howard Kerr, *Mediums and Spirit Rappers and Roaring Radicals* (Urbana: University of Illinois Press, 1972).

6. From a resolution adopted by the California State Spiritualist Association, September 1898. *Proceedings of the Sixth Annual Convention of the National Spiritualist Association, October 18–20, 1898,* p. 124.

7. "Spiritualism and Spiritualists," *BL,* March 9, 1901.

8. *Proceedings of the Fourth Annual Convention of the National Spiritualist Association, October 20–22, 1896,* p. 4.

9. See, for example, editorial in the *Los Angeles Times,* May 5, 1888.

10. J. Stillson Judah, *The History and Philosophy of the Metaphysical Movements in America* (Philadelphia: Westminster Press, 1967). Judah's book contains a good account of twentieth-century institutional developments in the spiritualist church.

11. The fullest intellectual biography of Garrison is contained in John L. Thomas, *The Liberator: William Lloyd Garrison. A Biography* (Boston: Little, Brown, 1963).

12. Aside from Thomas, the best books on Garrison's antislavery thought are Aileen Kraditor, *Means and Ends in American Abolitionism* (New York: Pantheon, 1967), and Lewis Perry, *Radical Abolitionism: Anarchy and the Government of God in Antislavery Thought* (Ithaca, N.Y.: Cornell University Press, 1973).

13. Rev. C. Hammond, *Light From the Spirit World. The Pilgrimage of Thomas Paine, and Others to the Seventh Circle in the Spirit World* (Rochester, N.Y.: D. M. Dewey, 1852), p. 140.

14. Emma Hardinge, *Modern American Spiritualism* (New York: published by the author, 1870), p. 540.

15. *BL,* February 9, 1861. For difficulties that reformers in general faced in coming to grips with force, see George Fredrickson, *The Inner Civil War* (New York: Harper & Row, 1965).

16. "Spiritual Reformation," *BL*, September 17, 1857.

17. I have discussed several individual examples in this chapter. See also J. R. Jacob, "LaRoy Sunderland: The Alienation of an Abolitionist," *Journal of American Studies* 6 (April 1972), 1–17.

18. Whitney Cross, *The Burned-Over District* (New York: Harper & Row, 1965), pp. 284, 341–352.

19. Letter from John F. Grey, *The Shekinah* 3 (1853), 190.

20. Davis, "The Emergence of Immediatism in British and American Antislavery Thought," *Mississippi Valley Historical Review* 49 (September 1962), 209–230.

21. *The Liberator*, December 17, 1852.

22. See chap. 2.

23. Child, *Whatever Is, Is Right* (Boston: Berry, Colby, and Co., 1861), p. 144.

24. Statement of S. B. Brittan, *BL*, August 17, 1872. In a séance reported in the Charlotte Fowler Wells material at Cornell University, one spirit was quite specific about numbers: "Those who would wish to obviate the evils of society, can do so, to a very great extent, and ultimately to the fullest extent, by forming into circles, at first admitting but few, and gradually increasing in number to as many as twelve or twenty-four or forty-eight, never thirty-six." For information on connections of the Fowler family to spiritualism and reform, consult Madeline B. Stern, *Heads and Headliners: The Phrenological Fowlers* (Norman: University of Oklahoma Press, 1971).

25. W. S. Courtney, "Individual Sovereignty," *The Telegraph Papers* 2 (1853), 301.

26. *BL*, December 29, 1860.

27. See, for example, Davis's statement of his beliefs in *Beyond the Valley: A Sequel to 'The Magic Staff': An Autobiography of Andrew Jackson Davis* (Boston: Colby and Rich, 1885), pp. 133–134.

28. Epes Sargent, *The Scientific Basis of Spiritualism* (Boston: Colby and Rich, 1881), p. 327.

29. *Beyond the Valley . . .* , p. 267.

30. Child, *Whatever Is, Is Right*, p. 80.

31. Davis, *The Approaching Crisis: Being a Review of Dr. Bushnell's Recent Lectures on Supernaturalism* (New York, 1852), p. 202.

32. See Robert E. Riegel, *American Feminists* (Lawrence: University of Kansas Press, 1963), p. 191. His list of feminists who were interested in spiritualism and Theosophy includes Anthony, Stanton, and Willard plus Caroline Dall, Paulina Davis, Eliza Farnham,

Abigail Foster, Sarah Grimké, Isabella Beecher Hooker, Harriet Hunt, Mary Ashton Rice Livermore, Mary Gove Nichols, Mary Wright Sewell, Mary Elizabeth Walker, and Elizabeth Oakes Smith.

33. See his autobiography *Upward Steps of Seventy Years* (New York: John W. Lovell, 1890).

34. Dean Clarke, "The Children's Progressive Lyceum," *BL,* April 8, 1899.

35. John Shoebridge Williams Manuscript Journals, Wisconsin State Historical Society, vol. I, bk. 1, p. 40.

36. See Hardinge's letter to *BL,* November 9, 1861.

37. *Beyond the Valley . . .* , p. 149.

38. James H. Hyslop, *Enigmas of Psychical Research* (London: G. P. Putnam's Sons, 1906), pp. 426–427.

39. J. O. Barrett, *The Spiritual Pilgrim: A Biography of James M. Peebles* (Boston: William White and Co., 1871), p. 157.

40. John Humphrey Noyes thought that a unified religious sentiment was at the base of every successful communitarian venture. However, for a somewhat contrary view, see Charles Nordhoff, *The Communistic Societies of the United States* (London: John Murray, 1875), p. 408.

41. Maren Lockwood Carden, *Oneida: Utopian Community to Modern Corporation* (New York: Harper & Row, 1971), pp. 122–123.

42. Léon Denis, *Here and Hereafter* (New York: Brentano's, n.d.).

43. Ward, *Young Ward's Diary* (New York: G. P. Putnam's Sons, 1935), pp. 273, 277–278, 281–282, and *passim.*

44. Arthur Mann, *Yankee Reformers in the Urban Age* (New York: Harper & Row, 1966); Allen J. Matusow, "The Mind of B. O. Flower," *New England Quarterly* 34 (December 1961), 492–509.

45. Garland, *Forty Years of Psychic Research* (New York: Macmillan, 1936).

46. Miles Menander Dawson, "Religious and Ethical Implications of the Spiritualistic Hypothesis," *Psychical Review* 1–2 (May 1894), p. 253.

47. "Report of the Convention of the Massachusetts State Spiritualist Association," *BL,* June 11, 1870.

48. Higginson, *Contemporaries* (Boston: Houghton Mifflin, 1900), p. 329.

49. *The Life-Line of the Lone One* (Boston: Bela Marsh, 1858); *Forty Years on the Spiritual Rostrum* (Boston: Colby and Rich, 1883).

50. *Life-Line . . .* , pp. 18–19 and *passim.*

51. Ibid., p. 147.

52. Ibid., pp. 168, 170–171.

53. For biographical information, see A. E. Newton, ed., *The Educator: Being Suggestions, Theoretical and Practical Designed to Promote Man-Culture and Integral Reform with a View to the Ultimate Establishment of a Divine Social State on Earth. Comprised in a Series of Revealments from Organized Associations in the Spirit Life Through John Murray Spear* (Boston: Office of Practical Spiritualists, 1857), and N. B. Lehman, "The Life of John Murray Spear: Spiritualism and Reform in Antebellum America," Ph.D. dissertation, Ohio State University, 1973.

54. Lehman, "Life of John Murray Spear . . . ," pp. 73, 81; Newton, *The Educator . . .* , p. 15.

55. Newton, *The Educator . . .* , p. 28.

56. Slater Brown, *The Heyday of Spiritualism* (New York: Hawthorn Books, 1970), p. 175.

57. Lehman, "Life of John Murray Spear . . . ," p. 201.

58. Newton, *The Educator . . .* , p. 30.

59. Lehman, "Life of John Murray Spear . . . ," p. 202.

60. Ibid., p. 111.

61. Ibid., p. 184.

62. William S. Heywood, ed., *Autobiography of Adin Ballou, 1803–1890* (Lowell, Mass.: Thompson and Hill, 1896).

63. Ibid., pp. 86, 88, 147, 176.

64. Ibid., pp. 224–225.

65. Perry, *Radical Abolitionism . . .* , p. 139.

66. Ballou, *An Exposition of Views Respecting the Modern Spirit Manifestations* (Liverpool: Edward Howell, 1853).

67. The charge of free love was leveled at many reformers besides the spiritualists. See, for example, John B. Ellis, *Free Love and its Votaries; or, American Socialism Unveiled* (San Francisco: A. L. Bancroft, 1870). Only chap. 24 deals specifically with spiritualists.

68. Lehman, "Life of John Murray Spear . . . ," p. 265.

69. *Autobiography of Ballou . . .* , pp. 459, 339.

70. Richard Leopold, *Robert Dale Owen* (Cambridge, Mass.: Harvard University Press, 1940), pp. 407–410.

71. A convinced spiritualist would often go to inordinate lengths to vindicate "exposed" mediums. The exposer was often assailed for having endangered the medium's life. And even if the medium admitted to some specific fraud, that did not necessarily convince a spiritualist that everything about the medium was fraudulent. People who duplicated mediumistic displays (with the intention of ex-

posure) were frequently credited by spiritualists with genuine powers. Their denials did no good.

72. Editorial, *New York Times,* October 20, 1853.

73. Kiddle's Address to Second Society of Spiritualists, *New York Times,* January 5, 1880.

74. For statements on Debs, see *Proceedings of Third Annual Convention of the National Spiritualist Association, October 15–17, 1895,* pp. 26, 101.

75. *Proceedings of the Sixth Annual Convention of the National Spiritualist Association, October 18–20, 1898,* p. 30.

Chapter 4

1. For the most convincing attempt to provide a sociological explanation of the rise of spiritualism, see Geoffrey Nelson, *Spiritualism and Society* (London: Routledge and Kegan Paul, 1969). The information provided there, however, is not nearly detailed enough to provide an adequate sociological portrait of the Americans who turned to spiritualism. At the moment, any attempt to provide such a portrait would far outshoot the available data.

2. Vanderbilt's interest in spiritualism was a result of both his advancing age and his affection for Victoria Woodhull.

3. Emerson, *Journals* (Boston: Houghton Mifflin, 1912), vol. 8, p. 574. John B. Wilson, "Emerson and the 'Rochester Rappings,' " *New England Quarterly* 41 (June 1968), 248–258.

4. For a summary of the issues and two opposite points of view, see Emma Hardinge, "Compensation of Mediums," *BL,* October 22, 1859, and the letter from A. C. Robinson, *BL,* May 5, 1866.

5. Letter from Emma Hardinge to *BL,* July 27, 1861.

6. Quoted in Ernest Isaacs, "A History of American Spiritualism," Master's thesis, University of Wisconsin, 1957, p. 180.

7. Uriah Clark, ed., *The Spiritual Register for 1859—Facts, Philosophy, Statistics of Spiritualism* (Auburn, N.Y.: U. Clark, 1859).

8. Slater Brown, *The Heyday of Spiritualism* (New York: Hawthorn Books, 1970), pp. 243–245.

9. Mortimer Thomson, *Doesticks What He Says* (New York, 1855), quoted in Howard Kerr, *Mediums and Spirit Rappers and Roaring Radicals* (Urbana: University of Illinois Press, 1972), p. 40. The stereotyping probably increased with time. Four-fifths of the mediums Lawton encountered in the course of his study of twentieth-century spiritualist religion were women.

10. For an analysis of another professional role identified with women, see Dee Garrison, "The Tender Technicians: the Feminization of Public Librarianship, 1876–1905," *Journal of Social History* 6 (Winter 1972–73), 131–159. Other professional roles for women included nursing and teaching. On the problem of professional women, also see Ann Douglas Wood, "The 'Scribbling Women' and Fanny Fern: Why Women Wrote," *American Quarterly* 23 (Spring 1971), 3–24.

11. For nineteenth-century images of women, see Carroll Smith-Rosenberg and Charles Rosenberg, "The Female Animal: Medical and Biological Views of Woman and Her Role in Nineteenth-Century America," *Journal of American History* 60 (September 1973), 332–356; Carroll Smith-Rosenberg, "The Hysterical Woman: Sex Roles and Role Conflict in Nineteenth-Century America," *Social Research* 39 (Winter 1972), 652–678; Ann Douglas Wood, "The Fashionable Diseases: Women's Complaints and Their Treatment in Nineteenth-Century America," *Journal of Interdisciplinary History* 4 (Summer 1973), 25–52.

12. The theme of self-sacrifice is a central concern in Kathryn Kish Sklar, *Catherine Beecher: A Study in American Domesticity* (New Haven: Yale University Press, 1973). See also Barbara Welter, "The Cult of True Womanhood, 1820–1860," *American Quarterly* 18 (Summer 1966), 151–174, and Carroll Smith-Rosenberg, "Beauty, the Beast and the Militant Woman: A Case Study in Sex Roles and Social Stress in Jacksonian America," *American Quarterly* 23 (October 1971), 562–584.

13. Vieda Skultans, *Intimacy and Ritual: A Study of Spiritualism, Mediums and Groups* (London: Routledge and Kegan Paul, 1974). Skultans's study does not touch at all on nineteenth-century America, but there are parallels between his findings and those of the present study. In Skultans's mind, the weekly repetition of spiritualist activities in the community he studied constituted a ritual of reconciliation to a situation that did not permit any radical alterations. Rather than a cause of marital unhappiness, spiritualist practices among women were a response and adjustment to it. In nineteenth-century America, as we shall see, adjustment and reconciliation represented only one side of the coin.

14. *Autobiography of Emma Hardinge Britten,* Margaret Wilkinson, ed. (London: John Heywood, 1900), 22–26.

15. "Biography of Miss Ellen D. Starkweather," *BL,* November 27, 1858.

16. Lydia W. Allison, "Obituary of Mrs. Piper," *Journal of the ASPR* 45 (January 1951), 38.

17. "Normal speaking" meant that one spoke from one's own prepared text. In one count, most of the men listed as spiritualist orators fell into the category "normal speakers." However, 100 of the 121 listed women were "trance speakers." Clark, *The Spiritual Register for 1859* . . .

18. *New York Times,* March 29, 30, 31, April 1, 2, 3, 1888.

19. D. D. Home, *Incidents in My Life,* vol. I (New York: Carleton, 1863), vol. II (New York: Holt and Williams, 1872); Jean Burton, *Heyday of a Wizard: Daniel Home, the Medium* (New York: Alfred A. Knopf, 1944).

20. Letter of A. B. Child to *BL,* July 31, 1868. A wealth of other material in the *BL* and other spiritualist publications, including advertisements, gives general support to the modest level of fees.

21. Emma Hardinge, *Modern American Spiritualism: A Twenty Years' Record of the Communion Between Earth and the World of Spirits* (New York: published by the author, 1870), p. 273.

22. For example, Augusta A. Currier wrote to the *BL,* December 23, 1865, that she had yet to see "the first medium who has been able to earn a decent competency by the exercise of his or her spiritual gifts." The level of fees became a matter of professional jealousy. Lita H. Barney charged that famous mediums set too high a fee, leaving nothing for the rest of them, whose spiritual gifts were just as great. *BL,* September 21, 1861.

23. Autobiographical and semi-autobiographical accounts of nineteenth-century female mediums include Amanda T. Jones, *A Psychic Autobiography* (New York: Graves Publishing Company, 1910); Reuben Briggs Davenport, *The Death Blow to Spiritualism: Being the True Story of the Fox Sisters* (New York: G. W. Dillingham, 1888); *Autobiography of Emma Hardinge Britten,* Margaret Wilkinson, ed.; Harrison D. Barrett, *Life Work of Cora L. V. Richmond* (Chicago: Hack and Anderson, 1895); Mrs. Nettie Colburn Maynard, *Was Abraham Lincoln a Spiritualist? or, Curious Revelations from the Life of a Trance Medium* (Philadelphia: Rufus C. Hartranft, 1891); Abram H. Dailey, *Mollie Fancher, The Brooklyn Enigma* (Brooklyn: Press of Eagle Book Printing Dept. 1894); Anne Manning Robbins, *Past and Present with Mrs. Piper (New York: Henry Holt* 1921); Francis H. Green, *Biography of Mrs. Semantha Mettler, The Clairvoyant* (New York: Harmonial Association, 1853). These should be compared to the memoirs of twentieth-century female mediums; for example, Mrs Cecil M. Cook, *The Voice Triumphant: The Revelations of a Medium* (New York: Alfred A. Knopf, 1931); Eileen J. Gar-

rett, *Many Voices: The Autobiography of a Medium* (New York: G. P. Putnam's Sons, 1968); Gladys Osborne Leonard, *Brief Darkness* (London: Cassell and Co., 1942); Estelle Roberts, *Fifty Years a Medium* (New York: Avon, 1972). There is also a long list of autobiographical material concerning male mediums.

24. Maynard, *Was Abraham Lincoln a Spiritualist?* . . . , pp. 4, 72.

25. Dailey, *Mollie Fancher*, p. 47–48; G. Stanley Hall, "A Medium in the Bud," *American Journal of Psychology* 29 (April 1918), 144–158.

26. Report of a séance, conducted by Mrs. James A. Bliss, *BL*, July 26, 1884. Many mediums had in fact worked in the theater. Emma Hardinge is the most obvious nineteenth-century example. The theater background is more common in the twentieth century. Note, for example, the lives of Eileen Garrett, Hester Dowden, Gladys Leonard, and Jeanne Dixon. The parallels between acting and mediumship can be read in Anna Cora Mowatt (Ritchie), *The Autobiography of an Actress; or Eight Years on the Stage* (Boston: Tickner, Reed and Fields, 1854), p. 158.

27. Suzy Smith, *The Mediumship of Mrs. Leonard* (New Hyde Park, N.Y.: University Books, 1964), p. 48.

28. Judith Gussler, "Social Change, Ecology, and Spirit Possession Among the South African Nguni," in *Religion, Altered States of Consciousness and Social Change*, ed. Erika Bourguignon (Columbus: Ohio State University Press, 1973).

29. Henri Ellenberger, *The Discovery of the Unconscious* (New York: Basic Books, 1970), pp. 173–174.

30. Lenora Greenbaum, "Possession Trance in Sub-Saharan Africa: A Descriptive Analysis of Fourteen Societies," in *Religion . . . and Social Change*, ed. Bourguignon. Also see Keith Thomas, *Religion and the Decline of Magic* (New York: Scribner's, 1971), p. 48; Vieda Skultans, *Intimacy and Ritual . . .* ; Gail Parker, "Mary Baker Eddy and Sentimental Womanhood," *New England Quarterly* 43 (March 1970), 13–24.

31. See, for example, David Potter, "American Women and American Character," in *History and American Society* (New York: Oxford University Press, 1973), pp. 278–303.

32. Burton Brown, "Spiritualism in Nineteenth-Century America," Ph.D. dissertation, Boston University, 1973, p. 218.

33. For Davis's justification of his actions, see his autobiographies, especially *Beyond the Valley*, pp. 94–96.

34. *Autobiography of Emma Hardinge Britten*, pp. 77, 217.

35. *Life Work of Cora L. V. Richmond*, pp. 106ff. Walter M. Merrill,

Against Wind and Tide: A Biography of William Lloyd Garrison (Cambridge, Mass.: Harvard University Press, 1963), pp. 257–60.

36. *Autobiography of Emma Hardinge Britten,* p. 88.
37. *Life Work of Cora L. V. Richmond,* p. 225.
38. *Autobiography of Emma Hardinge Britten,* p. 198.
39. Ibid., p. 170.
40. *Life Work of Cora L. V. Richmond,* p. 183.
41. One of the best sources for information about itinerancy are the advertisements placed by mediums in the *BL.* On Mrs. Stowe, see *BL,* April 14, 1866.
42. For conflicting opinion on the wisdom of speakers settling down, see the editorial on "Itinerancy," *BL,* April 28, 1866, and D. W. Hull, "Settled Speakers," *BL,* March 4, 1871.
43. For the impact of mobility on various types of Americans, I am indebted to George Wilson Pierson, *The Moving American* (New York: Alfred A. Knopf, 1973).
44. Most spiritualist conventions in the nineteenth century were local and regional rather than national, but they were frequent and well attended. The declaration in favor of women received strong support from the spirits. See *Twelve Messages from the Spirit of John Quincy Adams Through Joseph D. Stiles, Medium, to Josiah Brigham* (Boston: Bela Marsh, 1859), pp. 348–349.
45. Letter from Warren Chase, *BL,* May 7, 1862.
46. The language is drawn from a resolution of a spiritualist convention in Rutland, Vermont, in the summer of 1858, reported in BL, July 10, 1858.
47. *Los Angeles Times,* August 17, 1888. For literary works other than *The Bostonians* that drew connections between spiritualists, feminism, and/or free love, see Kerr, *Mediums and Spirit Rappers . . .*
48. Benjamin F. Hatch, *Spiritualists' Iniquities Unmasked, and the Hatch Divorce Case* (New York, 1859), pp. 5–6, 13–15, and *passim.*
49. Wm. Bailey Porter, *Spiritualism as It Is: Or the Results of a Scientific Investigation of Spirit Manifestations* (New York, 1865), p. 20. Also Warren Chase, "Spiritualism and Social Discord," *BL,* May 12, 1860.
50. Lizzie Doten, "A Plea for Working Women," *BL,* May 10, 1862; "Lottie Fowler," *BL,* April 22, 1899; letter from Augusta Currier, *BL,* December 23, 1865.
51. "Lottie Fowler," *BL,* April 22, 1899; *Life Work of Cora L. V. Richmond,* p. 725.
52. *BL,* June 23, 1866; "Mediumship and Morality," *BL,* June 22, 1878.

53. Thomas R. Hazard, "Mediums and Mediumship," *BL,* December 9, 1871.
54. Biography of Mrs. J. H. Conant, *BL,* May 22, 1875.
55. "Mediumship and Morality," *BL,* June 22, 1878.
56. "Review of Modern Spiritualism," *Ladies Repository* 16 (February 1856), 92.
57. *BL,* September 25, 1858; *BL,* May 29, 1858; Hardinge, *Modern American Spiritualism,* p. 201; Dailey, *Mollie Fancher . . . ,* p. 2; *BL,* February 12, 1870.
58. *Life Work of Cora L. V. Richmond,* p. 471.
59. Hatch, *Spiritualists' Iniquities Unmasked . . . ,* pp. 32–41.
60. Ibid.
61. A. B. Child, "Cora L. V. Hatch," *BL,* July 17, 1858.
62. Hatch, *Spiritualists' Iniquities Unmasked . . . ,* p. 36.
63. Green, *Biography of Mrs. Semantha Mettler . . .*
64. *Autobiography of Emma Hardinge Britten,* pp. 218–219.
65. Reports in *BL,* April 7, April 21, 1866.
66. D. H. Rawcliffe, *Illusions and Delusions of the Supernatural and Occult* (New York: Dover, 1959), pp. 167ff.
67. *Autobiography of Emma Hardinge Britten,* p. 3.
68. Hardinge, *Modern American Spiritualism,* p. 319.
69. *BL,* February 9, 1861.
70. For a biased but interesting account of the network of fraud that grew up among professional mediums (a network complete with a supporting industry manufacturing props), see David P. Abbott, *Behind the Scenes With the Mediums* (Chicago: Open Court Publishing Co., 1908), pp. 270–273 and *passim.*
71. *BL,* January 9, 1892.
72. Brown, "Spiritualism in Nineteenth-Century America," p. 147.
73. *Proceedings of the Third Annual Convention of the National Spiritualist Association,* p. 16.
74. George Beard, "The Psychology of Spiritism," *North American Review* 129 (July 1879), 67. One twentieth-century commentator who has subjected mediums to Freudian scrutiny has concluded, among other things, that normal sexual activity is extremely rare among them. See George Lawton, *The Drama of Life After Death: A Study of the Spiritualist Religion* (New York: Henry Holt, 1932), pp. 48off.
75. "Mrs. R. I. Hull," *BL,* June 10, 1882.
76. Hardinge, *Modern American Spiritualism,* p. 371.
77. William Hammond, "The Physics and Physiology of Spiritualism," *North American Review* 110 (April 1870), 257.

78. Carroll Smith-Rosenberg in "The Hysterical Woman" provides an excellent discussion of a related historical problem.
79. Jones, *A Psychic Autobiography.*
80. Lawton, *Drama of Life After Death,* p. 480ff.

Chapter 5

1. The information on Chanler was derived from the John Armstrong Chaloner papers, Duke University Library.
2. Statement of Dr. Horatio Curtis Wood, December 10, 1900, Chaloner papers, Duke University Library.
3. "Spiritualism Tested by Science," *New Englander* (May 1858), 243.
4. William A. Hammond, *Spiritualism and Allied Causes and Conditions of Nervous Derangement* (New York: G. P. Putnam's Sons, 1876), p. 216. Note that the compatibility of spiritualism with phrenology suggests that phrenology was not intended to buttress a materialistic philosophy. See John Davies, *Phrenology, Fad and Science: A Nineteenth-Century American Crusade* (New Haven: Yale University Press, 1955).
5. William B. Carpenter, *Mesmerism, Spiritualism, etc. Historically and Scientifically Considered* (New York: D. Appleton, 1877), p. 109.
6. George Beard, "The Psychology of Spiritism," *North American Review* 129 (July 1879), 76–77, 67–68.
7. The best discussion of Beard is Charles Rosenberg, "The Place of George M. Beard in Nineteenth-Century Psychiatry," *Bulletin of the History of Medicine* 36 (May–June 1962), 245–259.
8. Sampson, *Physical Media in Spiritual Manifestations. The Phenomena of Responding Tables and the Planchette, and Their Physical Causes in the Nervous Organism* (Philadelphia: Lippincott, 1869), p. 154.
9. Hammond, *Spiritualism . . . and Conditions of Nervous Derangement,* pp. 74–75, 256.
10. Marvin, *The Philosophy of Spiritualism and the Pathology and Treatment of Mediomania* (New York: Asa Butts, 1874). For an equally detailed discussion of spiritualism and mental derangement, see Marcel Viollet, *Spiritism and Insanity* (London: Swan Sonnenschein, 1910).
11. Marvin, *Philosophy of Spiritualism . . . ,* pp. 42, 47, 51–58.
12. Morton Prince, *Clinical and Experimental Studies in Personality* (Cambridge, Mass.: Sci-Art Publishers, 1929), p. viii.
13. I am indebted for this account to Alan Gauld, *The Founders of Psychical Research* (London: Routledge and Kegan Paul, 1968).

14. Ibid., p. 140.
15. The presidents of the SPR in the period before 1920 included Balfour Stewart, William James, William Crookes, Charles Richet, Andrew Lang, Henri Bergson, F. C. S. Schiller, and Gilbert Murray.
16. London Dialectical Society, *Report on Spiritualism* (London: Longmans, Green, 1871).
17. Trevor Hall, *The Spiritualists: The Story of Florence Cook and William Crookes* (London: Duckworth, 1962).
18. "Report of the Committee Appointed to Investigate Phenomena Connected with the Theosophical Society," *Proceedings of the SPR* 3 (May–June 1885), 201–400.
19. William F. Barrett, Edmund Gurney, F. W. H. Myers, "Report on Thought-Reading," *Proceedings of the SPR* 1 (1882–83), 13–34, 70–97, 161–215; Malcolm Guthrie and James Birchall, "Record of Experiments in Thought-Transference," *Proceedings of the SPR* 1 (1882–83), 263–283; Oliver Lodge, "An Account of Some Experiments in Thought-Transference," *Proceedings of the SPR* 2 (1884), 189–200; "M. Richet's Recent Researches in Thought-Transference," *Proceedings of the SPR* 2 (1884), 239–264.
20. *Presidential Addresses to the SPR, 1882–1911* (Glasgow: Robert Maclehose, 1912), p. 35.
21. See especially Gauld, *Founders of Psychical Research*, pp. 32–65 and Frank Turner, *Between Science and Religion*, (New Haven: Yale University Press, 1974), pp. 1–37.
22. For a summation of Janet's attitude, see his letter of 1905 to Hyslop, *Proceedings of the ASPR* 1 (1907), 53–73.
23. A list of the original members can be found in *Journal of the ASPR* 1 (1907), 61–69.
24. "Address of the President," *Proceedings of the ASPR* 1 (July 1886), 63–86.
25. C. S. Peirce, "Criticism of *Phantasms of the Living*," *Proceedings of the ASPR* 1 (December 1887), 150–157; Edmund Gurney, "Remarks on Professor Peirce's Paper," *Proceedings of the ASPR* 1 (December 1887), 157–180; "Mr. Peirce's Rejoinder," *Proceedings of the ASPR* 1 (December 1887), 180–215. E. Gurney, F. Myers, and F. Podmore, *Phantasms of the Living* (London: Trubner, 1886).
26. A. T. Baird, *Richard Hodgson: The Story of a Psychic Researcher and His Times* (London: Psychic Press, 1949). In the early 1890s a group of men in Boston (including T. E. Allen and Hamlin Garland) founded the American Psychical Society. The society published two volumes of *The Psychical Review* (1892–94). Its members tended

to be more hospitable to spiritualism than the original officers of the ASPR. The organization had no connections to either the original ASPR (founded by James) or the subsequent one founded by Hyslop.

27. G. Stanley Hall, "Review of Some Literature in Psychic Research," *American Journal of Psychology* 7 (1894–95), 135–142. The objection Hall raised was repeated many times in subsequent years.

28. Thomas S. Kuhn, *The Structure of Scientific Revolutions* (Chicago: University of Chicago Press, 1962).

29. "Presidential Address of William James to SPR. January 31, 1896," *Presidential Addresses to the SPR . . . ,* pp. 81, 83.

30. James's best-known discussion of this point is found in his first lecture on Pragmatism.

31. James's Presidential Address, p. 84.

32. Ibid., p. 81.

33. William James, *The Varieties of Religious Experience: A Study in Human Nature* (New York: Longmans, Green, 1902). These were James's Gifford Lectures delivered in Edinburgh in 1901 and 1902. Also see his famous essay "The Will to Believe."

34. James, "Certain Phenomena of Trance," *Proceedings of the SPR* 6 (1890), 652.

35. James's Presidential Address, p. 80.

36. For biographical information on Mrs. Piper, see Anne Manning Robbins, *Past and Present with Mrs. Piper* (New York: Henry Holt, 1921), and M. Sage, *Mrs. Piper and the Society for Psychical Research* (New York: Scott-Thaw, 1904).

37. "Observations of Certain Phenomena of Trance," *Proceedings of the SPR,* 13 (1898), 526. For Hodgson's first reports on Mrs. Piper, see *Proceedings of the SPR* 6 (1890), 436–650; 8 (1892), 1–167; 13 (1898), 284–582.

38. For an example, see the account concerning Mrs. Thompson, *Proceedings of the SPR* 17 (June 1902), 61–244; of Mrs. Verrall, *Proceedings of the SPR* 20 (October 1906), 6–432; of Mrs. Holland, *Proceedings of the SPR* 21 (June 1908), 166–391.

39. Robert C. LeClair, ed., *The Letters of William James and Théodore Flournoy* (Madison: University of Wisconsin Press, 1966), p. 174.

40. Interview with Mrs. Piper in *New York Sunday Herald,* October 26, 1901.

41. "The Subliminal Consciousness," *Proceedings of the SPR,* 7 (1891–92), 298–355; 8 (1892), 333–404, 436–535; 9 (1893–94), 3–128; 11 (1895), 334–593. Myers, *Human Personality and Its Survival of Bodily Death* (London: Longmans, Green, 1903).

42. *Proceedings of the SPR* 7 (1891–92), 301.

43. "Symposium on the Subconscious," *Journal of Abnormal Psychology* 2 (June 1907), 63.

44. Myers, *Human Personality . . .* , vol. I, p. 72.

45. See the first lecture of James's *Varieties of Religious Experience.*

46. James, "Frederic Myers's Service to Psychology," *Proceedings of the SPR* 17 (May 1901), 17.

47. Ibid., pp. 16, 18; James, "Review of *Human Personality and Its Survival of Bodily Death," Proceedings of the SPR* 18 (June 1903), 26.

48. Quoted by James in "What Psychical Research Has Accomplished," *The Will to Believe and Other Essays in Popular Philosophy* (New York: Longmans, Green, 1897), p. 316.

49. "The Final Impressions of a Psychical Researcher," in Gardner Murphy and Robert O. Ballou, eds., *William James on Psychical Research* (New York: Viking Press, 1960), p. 324.

50. Letter from James to T. Flournoy, September 28, 1909, in *The Letters of William James and Théodore Flournoy* (Madison: University of Wisconsin Press, 1966), p. 224.

51. Alfred Binet, *Alterations of Personality* (New York: D. Appleton, 1896), pp. 325–329, 341.

52. Boris Sidis, *The Psychology of Suggestion* (New York: D. Appleton, 1911), pp. 2–3, 141 [first published in 1898].

53. Jastrow, *Fact and Fable in Psychology* (Boston: Houghton Mifflin, 1900), p. 56.

54. Ibid., p. 69.

55. Hall, "Philosophy in the United States," *Popular Science Monthly Supplement* (1879), 67.

56. Amy M. Tanner, *Studies in Spiritism* (New York: D. Appleton, 1910), p. xviii.

57. Ibid., p. xvi.

58. Théodore Flournoy, *Des Indes à la Planète Mars* (Paris: Alcan, 1900) [first English translation in 1900].

59. Tanner, *Studies in Spiritism.* Tanner's book began as a doctoral study under Hall.

60. Ibid., pp. 314, 379–380.

61. Prince, *Clinical and Experimental Studies in Personality,* p. 533.

62. Prince, *The Dissociation of a Personality: A Biographical Study in Abnormal Psychology* (London: Longmans, Green, 1906); *Clinical and Experimental Studies in Psychology,* pp. 305–23, 355.

63. Harlow Gale, "Psychical Research in American Universities," *Proceedings of the SPR* 13 (1897–98), 583–587.

64. H. Addington Bruce, *The Riddle of Personality* (New York: Moffat,

Yard & Co., 1908), p. xii. See also Alfred T. Schofield, *The Uncon-
scious Mind* (New York: Funk and Wagnalls, 1901), and C. G. Raue,
*Psychology as a Natural Science Applied to the Solution of Occult
Psychic Phenomena* (Philadelphia: Porter and Coates, 1889).

65. Hudson, *A Scientific Demonstration of the Future Life* (Chicago:
A. C. McClurg, 1895), p. 269. Also see Hudson, *The Law of Psychic
Phenomena* (Chicago: A. C. McClurg, 1893), and *The Evolution of
the Soul and Other Essays* (Chicago: A. C. McClurg, 1904).

66. Unless otherwise noted, the biographical information is from a
typescript "Autobiography" that is in the archives of the ASPR.
Hyslop dated the manuscript March 6, 1904.

67. Hyslop, *Psychical Research and the Resurrection* (Boston: Small,
Maynard and Co., 1908), p. 15, and *Science and a Future Life* (Boston: Herbert B. Turner, 1905), p. 237.

68. LeClair, ed., *Letters of . . . James and . . . Flournoy*, pp. 114–115.

69. James H. Hyslop, "History of the American Institute for Scientific
Research," *Proceedings of the ASPR* 1 (1907), 1–22.

70. *Journal of the ASPR* 1 (January 1907), 17, 22–23.

71. For the letters of endorsement see the *Proceedings of the ASPR* 1
(1907), 32–76.

72. Hyslop made no secret of the fact that he wished to keep the research of the ASPR out of the control of "laymen." In *Borderland of
Psychical Research* (Boston: Herbert B. Turner, 1906), p. 402, he
wrote: "Nature keeps her secrets in response to an inquisition that
only a few of the best trained minds can institute. . . ."

73. Letter from Funk to Hyslop, June 2, 1906. ASPR files.

74. Letter from Hyslop to Bayley, December 24, 1912, ASPR files.

75. Letter from Hyslop to Bayley, December 30, 1912, ASPR files.

76. In addition to the works already cited, see *Contact with the Other
World: The Latest Evidence as to Communication with the Dead* (New
York: The Century Co., 1919). In *Contact with the Other World* (p.
34), Hyslop wrote of the society: "Academic and scientific support,
probably on account of the avowed spiritistic sympathies of the
secretary, has been weak."

77. Hyslop, *Borderland of Psychical Research*, p. 408.

78. Nathan Hale, Jr., ed., *James Jackson Putnam and Psychoanalysis*
(Cambridge, Mass.: Harvard University Press, 1971), pp. 324–325.

79. Letter from Hyslop to Dorr, ASPR archives, February 15, 1906.

80. Hyslop, "The Doris Fischer Case of Multiple Personality," *Proceedings of the ASPR* 11 (1917), 13.

81. Hyslop, "The Subconscious and its Functions," *Proceedings of the*

ASPR 7 (1913), 39. In the same article Hyslop wrote (p. 46): "I do not see that we should show so close a connection between genius and hysteria with its congeners as Mr. Myers assumes."

82. Hyslop, "Apparent Subconscious Fabrication," *Journal of Abnormal Psychology* 1 (December *1906*), 213.

83. Hyslop, "A Case of Musical Control," *Proceedings of the ASPR* 7 (1913), 429–430.

84. "Preface to The Doris Case of Multiple Personality," *Proceedings of the ASPR* 9 (1915), 20.

85. W. H. Hamilton, J. S. Smyth, and James H. Hyslop, "A Case of Hysteria," *Proceedings of the ASPR* 5 (1911), 154, 170.

86. Hyslop, "The Subconscious and its Functions," p. 53.

87. Ibid., pp. 48–54.

88. Leonard T. Troland, "The Freudian Psychology and Psychical Research," *Journal of Abnormal Psychology* 8 (1913–14), 408.

89. Freud, "Psychoanalysis and Telepathy," in George Devereux, ed., *Psychoanalysis and the Occult* (New York: International Universities Press, 1953), p. 59. From a paper written in 1921.

90. Devereux, *Psychoanalysis and the Occult*, p. 108.

91. Freud made the remark in a letter to Hereward Carrington. See Ernest Jones, *Sigmund Freud: Life and Work* (London: Hogarth Press, 1957), vol. 3, pp. 419–420.

92. Carl Murchison, ed., *A History of Psychology in Autobiography*, (Worcester, Mass.: Clark University Press, 1930), vol. 1, p. 158.

93. Letter from Münsterberg to Hereward Carrington, November 16, 1909, Boston Public Library. Hugo Münsterberg, Theodore Ribot, Pierre Janet, Joseph Jastrow, Bernard Hart and Morton Prince, *Subconscious Phenomena* (Boston: Richard Badger, 1910), pp. 30–31.

94. Dunlap, *Mysticism, Freudianism and Scientific Psychology* (St. Louis: C. V. Mosby, 1920), pp. 7–8.

95. "Presidential Address of F. W. H. Myers to SPR. May 18, 1900," *Presidential Addresses to the SPR*, p. 119.

Chapter 6

1. *Preliminary Report of the Commission Appointed by the University of Pennsylvania to Investigate Modern Spiritualism in Accordance with the Request of the Late Henry Seybert* (Philadelphia: J. P. Lippincott, 1887). The acting chairman of the committee, Dr. Horace Howard Furness, was at the outset of the investigation leaning in favor of

the substantial truth of spiritualism. He quickly changed his attitude.

2. John Coover, *Experiments in Psychical Research at Leland Stanford Junior University* (Stanford: Stanford University Press, 1917). American parapsychologists later claimed that when Coover's experiments were lumped together, they did in fact furnish evidence of psi.

3. Biographical information taken from *Walter Franklin Prince: A Tribute to His Memory* (Boston: Boston Society for Psychic Research, 1935).

4. For Prince's assessment of Theodosia's cure, see his *The Psychic in the House* (Boston: Boston Society for Psychic Research, 1926), p. 6.

5. Carl Murchison, ed., *The Case For and Against Psychical Belief* (Worcester, Mass.: Clark University Press, 1927), p. 188.

6. Raymond Van Over and Laura Oteri, eds., *William McDougall, Explorer of the Mind: Studies in Psychical Research* (New York: Garrett Publications, 1967). His most controversial book prior to his coming to Harvard was *Body and Mind: A History and a Defense of Animism* (London: Methuen & Co., 1911).

7. Van Over and Oteri, *William McDougall . . .* , p.20.

8. Ibid., pp. 8–9, 13.

9. Ibid., p. 4.

10. Ibid., pp. 103–104.

11. Ibid., pp. 169, 218–219.

12. Ibid., p. 6.

13. *Journal of the ASPR* 57 (January 1963), 10–11. For an estimate of Troland's work see the review by F. C. S. Schiller, *Proceedings of the SPR* 31 (November 1920), 218–223. Later recipients of money from the Hodgson fund were Ernest Taves, Joseph Woodruff, and Gertrude Schmeidler.

14. Lodge, *Raymond* (London: Methuen & Co., 1916).

15. Reported in Doyle, *Our American Adventure* (London: Hodder and Stoughton, 1924) and *Our Second American Adventure* (London: Hodder and Stoughton, 1924).

16. Harry Houdini, *A Magician Among the Spirits* (London: Harper & Bros., 1924).

17. Matthew Josephson, *Edison: A Biography* (New York: McGraw-Hill, 1959), p. 439.

18. Van Over and Oteri, *William McDougall . . .* , p. 49.

19. Letter from Prince to George E. Carey, August 8, 1926, ASPR files.

20. Letter from Prince to Reverend Elwood Worcester, January 29, 1924, ASPR files.
21. *Scientific American* 127 (December 1922), 389.
22. For a popular account of the Margery case, see Thomas R. Tietze, *Margery* (New York: Harper & Row, 1973).
23. For a good depiction of Walter, see Hudson Hoagland, "Science and the Medium: The Climax of a Famous Investigation," *The Atlantic Monthly* 136 (November 1925), 681.
24. Carrington's defense of Palladino led to a furious quarrel with Hugo Münsterberg of Harvard. See Carrington, *Eusapio Palladino and Her Phenomena* (New York: Dodge, 1909). In 1909, Carrington asked Münsterberg to serve on a committee to investigate Palladino. Münsterberg did and published his negative conclusions in *Metropolitan*. Carrington, claiming that the article harmed him, then asked Münsterberg to pay $100 for the séances he had attended. An exchange of letters is in the Boston Public Library.
25. Tietze, *Margery*, pp. 56–63.
26. Part of the investigation was carried out on the third floor of Emerson Hall in a room loaned to Hoagland by the Harvard Psychology Department. A number of Harvard professors attended sittings.
27. Hoagland, "Science and the Medium," pp. 680–681. For a defense of Margery, see *Margery Harvard Veritas—A Study in Psychics* (Boston: Blanchard, 1925).
28. Letter from Bird to the board of trustees of the ASPR, January 29, 1931, ASPR files.
29. See generally the tributes in *Walter Franklin Prince: A Tribute to His Memory*.
30. See, for example, letter from Prince to Mrs. William M. Wood, February 8, 1926. ASPR files.
31. *Walter Franklin Prince: A Tribute to His Memory*, pp. 78–79.
32. Reverend Elwood Worcester, "Recent Developments in the Doris Case of Multiple Personality," ibid., pp. 82–87. Prince never committed himself in print to a spiritualist interpretation of "Sleeping Margaret," but see *The Psychic in the House*, pp. 37–41.
33. Prince, *The Case of Patience Worth* (Boston: Boston Society for Psychic Research, 1927).
34. Letter from Hoagland to Prince, May 10, 1928, ASPR files.
35. The idea for the symposium was suggested by Carl Murchison to McDougall and Houdini. The papers were published in Murchison, ed., *The Case For and Against Psychical Belief*.

36. Interview with Mrs. Laura Dale, February 2, 1971. The term "palace revolt" is commonly used in the literature of parapsychology to designate the 1941 events of the ASPR.

37. "Autobiography of Gardner Murphy," *Journal of Parapsychology* 21 (September 1957), 167.

38. Ibid., pp. 165–178. Also see "Interview: Gardner Murphy," *Psychic* 1 (January–February 1970), pp. 4–7, 32–39.

Chapter 7

1. Paul Allison, "Social Aspects of Scientific Innovation: The Case of Parapsychology," Master's thesis, University of Wisconsin, 1973, p. 32.

2. Letter from Rhine to McDougall, May 1, 1926, ASPR files. Rhine, *New Frontiers of Mind* (New York: Farrar and Rinehart, 1937), p. 51.

3. Letter from Rhine to trustees of the ASPR, July 15, 1926, ASPR files.

4. Letter from Rhine to Prince, August 15, 1927, ASPR files.

5. Letter from Rhine to Prince, November 23, 1927, ASPR files.

6. Raymond Van Over and Laura Oteri, *William McDougall . . .* , (New York: Garrett Publications, 1967), p. 84.

7. J. B. Rhine and Associates, *Parapsychology from Duke to FRNM* (Durham, N.C.: Parapsychology Press, 1965), pp. 6–8.

8. John F. Thomas, "An Evaluative Study of the Mental Content of Certain Trance Phenomena," Ph.D. dissertation, Duke University, 1933. An earlier version of the dissertation was rejected because it emphasized the spiritualist hypothesis too exclusively.

9. "Editorial Introduction," *Journal of Parapsychology* 1 (March 1937), 7.

10. Garrett and Rhine disagreed but remained on friendly terms for many years.

11. Aside from cards, a frequent type of test for telepathy involved attempts by subjects to imitate drawings that were hidden from their view. The disadvantages of such experiments were quickly recognized. It was very difficult to know when to score a hit or a miss. Moreover, even if a drawing was a perfect replica of the original, there was no clear way to apply the laws of probability to the case.

12. PK received official recognition from Rhine in 1944. See editorial, *Journal of Parapsychology* 8 (March 1944), 1–2. On precognition, see Rhine, "Evidence of Precognition in the Covariation of Salience Ratios," *Journal of Parapsychology* 6 (June 1942), 111–143.

13. For Rhine's first account of Linzmayer, see Rhine, *Extra-Sensory Perception* (Boston: Bruce Hamphries, 1934), pp. 80–91, and *New Frontier of the Mind* (New York: Farrar and Rinehart, 1937), pp. 86–95.

14. The library experiment was briefly mentioned in *Extra-Sensory Perception*, p. 116.

15. *Parapsychology from Duke to FRNM*, p. 12. As C. E. Hansel pointed out, Rhine's emphasis on the Pearce-Pratt series was rather late in coming. Critics have suggested that the experiment became more important in retrospect, after the other early work had been discredited. See Ian Stevenson, "An Antagonist's View of Parapsychology: a Review of Professor Hansel's *ESP: A Scientific Evaluation*," *Journal of the ASPR* 61 (July 1967), 259.

16. "Symposium: A Program for the Next Ten Years of Research in Parapsychology," *Journal of Parapsychology* 12 (March 1948), 18.

17. S. G. Soal and F. Bateman, *Modern Experiments in Telepathy* (London: Faber and Faber, 1953). The names of the two subjects were Mrs. Gloria Stewart and Basil Shackleton.

18. "Symposium: . . . Next Ten Years of Research . . ." p. 3.

19. Rhine became aware of the "decline effect" very early in his work. See *Extra-Sensory Perception*, pp. 185–186.

20. *New Frontiers of the Mind*, p. 108.

21. Gertrude Schmeidler and R. A. McConnell, *ESP and Personality Patterns* (New Haven: Yale University Press, 1958).

22. "It is independently established on the basis of this work alone that Extra-Sensory Perception is an actual and demonstrable occurrence." *Extra-Sensory Perception*, p. 222.

23. Letter from Prince to J. B. Rhine, February 28, 1934, ASPR files.

24. For some of the criticism made by parapsychologists, see Robert H. Thouless, "Dr. Rhine's Recent Experiments on Telepathy and Clairvoyance," *Proceedings of the SPR* 43 (1935), 24–37; and Correspondence from E. J. Dingwall, *Journal of the SPR* 30 (December 1937), 140–141, and 30 (March 1938), 188–189.

25. J. G. Pratt and Dorothy H. Pope pointed out some of the negative effects of tightened conditions in obtaining positive results: "There can be no doubt that as investigators have more and more planned their tests in the light of what the critics would think, they have so formalized the procedures that it has been increasingly difficult, if not impossible, to arouse a favorable type of interest in the tests." "The ESP Controversy," *Journal of Parapsychology* 6 (September 1942), 186.

26. See, for example, Kaempffert's article in the *New York Times Magazine,* October 17, 1937.

27. E. H. Wright, "The Case for Telepathy," *Harper's* 173 (November 1936), 586.

28. In this respect Rhine was comparable to Hyslop. See Rhine, *The Reach of the Mind* (New York: William Sloane, 1947); *New World of the Mind* (New York: William Sloane, 1953); *Parapsychology from Duke to FRNM.*

29. See the exchange between Sells and Rhine in *Journal of Parapsychology,* 5 (September 1941), 250–259. For the new editorial policy, see *Journal of Parapsychology* 6 (March 1942), 1–4.

30. "Editorial: Publication Policy," *Journal of Parapsychology* 14 (March 1950), 5.

31. The word "revolution" is sprinkled freely through all the literature of parapsychology. See chap. 1 of *New Frontiers of the Mind.* J. Gaither Pratt, one of Rhine's closest early associates, wrote that he became a "professional revolutionist" in 1936. Pratt, *Parapsychology: An Insider's View of ESP* (Garden City, N.Y.: Doubleday, 1964), p. 1. Also *New World of the Mind,* p. 6.

32. Allison, "Social Aspects of Scientific Innovation . . . ," p. 43; Rhine, *Parapsychology from Duke to FRNM,* p. 16.

33. In 1938, Lucien Warner and C. C. Clark conducted a mail survey of 603 full members of the APA. Of the respondents (58 percent of those polled), 9 percent viewed ESP as an established fact or a likely possibility, while 30 percent viewed it as a remote possibility; 89 percent considered ESP a legitimate scientific undertaking, and 79 percent thought that its study fell within the province of academic psychology. Allison, "Social Aspects of Scientific Innovation . . . ," p. 46–47.

34. Allison, "Social Aspects of Scientific Innovation . . . ," p. 42.

35. Christian Paul and Julia Heil Heinland, "Critique of the Premises and Statistical Methodology of Parapsychology," *Journal of Psychology* 5 (January 1938), 135–148; H. Rogosin, "Probability Theory and Extra-Sensory Perception," *Journal of Psychology* 5 (April 1938), 265–270; R. R. Willoughby, "A Critique of Rhine's Extrasensory Perception," *Journal of Abnormal and Social Psychology* 30 (1935), 199–207; Chester E. Kellogg, "The Problems of Matching and Sampling in the Study of Extra-Sensory Perception," *Journal of Abnormal and Social Psychology* 32 (October–December 1937), 462–479. Also see Harold O. Gulliksen, "Extrasensory Perception: What Is It?" *American Journal of Sociology* 43 (January 1938), 623–631.

36. J. B. Rhine, Burke Smith, Charles Stuart, and Joseph Green-

wood, *Extra-Sensory Perception after Sixty Years* (Boston: Bruce Humphries, 1940), p. 266–269, 287–289. William Birge and J. B. Rhine, "Unusual Types of Persons Tested for ESP: A Professional Medium," *Journal of Parapsychology* 6 (June 1942), 85–94.

37. Rhine, *New World of the Mind*, p. 128.

38. Allison, "Social Aspects of Scientific Innovation . . . ," p. 45–46.

39. Wundt, "Spiritualism as a Scientific Question. An Open Letter to Professor Hermann Ulrici," *Popular Science Monthly* 15 (September 1879), 582–583.

40. C D. Broad, "The Relevance of Psychical Research to Philosophy," *Philosophy* 24 (October 1949), 291–309.

41. *Extra-Sensory Perception after Sixty Years,* pp. 310, 325–326.

42. For a recent attempt to define the laws of parapsychology, see Joseph H. Rush, "Parapsychology's Century of Progress," *Parapsychology Today: A Geographic View* (New York: Parapsychology Foundation, 1973), pp. 213–214.

43. Rhine, *Parapsychology from Duke to FRNM,* pp. 107–108.

44. Ibid., p. 30.

45. Editorial, "Parapsychology and Dualism," *Journal of Parapsychology* 9 (December 1945), 225–228. Pratt, *Parapsychology . . . ,* pp. 289, 291.

46. For information on Lodge, see David B. Wilson, "The Thought of the Late Victorian Physicists: Oliver Lodge's Etherial Body," *Victorian Studies* 15 (September 1971), 29–48.

47. F. C. S. Schiller, "Some Logical Aspects of Psychical Research," in Carl Murchison, ed., *The Case For and Against Psychical Belief* (Worcester, Mass.: Clark University Press, 1927), p. 219.

48. *The Nature of the Physical World* (Cambridge, Eng.: Cambridge University Press, 1927); *New Pathways in Science* (Cambridge, Eng.: Cambridge University Press, 1935). Also *Science and the Unseen World* (London: G. Allen & Unwin, 1929).

49. Jeans, *The Mysterious Universe* (Cambridge, Eng.: Cambridge University Press, 1930); *The New Background of Science* (Cambridge, Eng.: Cambridge University Press, 1933); *The Universe Around Us* (Cambridge, Eng.: Cambridge University Press, 1929).

50. Upton Sinclair, *Mental Radio* (New York: Macmillan, 1962) [first published 1930].

51. Margenau, "ESP in the Framework of Modern Science," *Journal of the ASPR* 60 (July 1966), 214–228; Jordan, "Parapsychological Implications of Research in Atomic Physics," *International Journal of Parapsychology* 2 (Autumn 1960), 7.

52. Koestler, "The Perversity of Physics," in Allan Angoff and Betty

Shapin, eds., *Parapsychology and the Sciences* (New York: Parapsychology Foundation, 1974), p. 166.

53. Rhine's relative indifference towards physics and psychology is understandable, given his lack of training in those fields. His inattention to biology is perhaps more surprising in view of his background and the antimaterialist attitude of some biological writers. Rhine, however, did not expect psi phenomena to become related to any of the existing sciences without a rdical ajdustment of their theoretical concepts. Whatever others thought of the reorientation of scientific thought in the twentieth century, Rhine judged that it did not go far enough.

54. In his review of Rhine's *New World of the Mind*, R. H. Thouless criticizes Rhine for two assumptions: first, that there are no rational grounds for religious belief except those provided by scientific experiment; and second, that all statements of religious doctrine are in principle verifiable by scientific experimentation. Thouless thinks it necessary to remind Rhine that there may be more than one road to knowledge. *Journal of Parapsychology* 18 (March 1954), 47.

55. Rhine, *Parapsychology from Duke to FRNM*, p. 101.

Chapter 8

1. The best summary of Rhine's conclusions, based on work in the 1930s, is contained in Rhine, Burke Smith, Charles Stuart, and Joseph Greenwood, *Extra-Sensory Perception After Sixty Years* (Boston: Bruce Humphries, 1940). For work that bore his imprint during the 1940s, one had best go to the *Journal of Parapsychology*.

2. There is a good measure of disagreement among parapsychologists about whether they have achieved a repeatable experiment. Rhine certainly believes that his experiments have been duplicated in other laboratories, and the results of these experiments confirm his own findings. But most parapsychologists would argue that Rhine's card experiments are not repeatable in the same way as a process in chemistry. More often than not, duplications of Rhine's experiments produce no evidence of ESP.

3. See statement by George H. Hyslop, *Journal of the ASPR* 35 (Summer 1941), 113–14. Rhine, on the other hand, continued to argue that the question of life after death was not eligible for reinstatement as a major area of research: see *New World of the Mind* (New York: William Sloane, 1953), p. 308.

4. Lydia W. Allison, "Further Proxy Sitting with Mrs. Leonard," *Journal of the ASPR* 35 (October 1941), 196–225; "Cases," *Journal of the ASPR* 36 (January 1942), 29–42; S. Cox, "Some Unusual Experiences," *Journal of the ASPR* 37 (January 1943), 25–38; Gardner Murphy, "An Outline of Survival Evidence," *Journal of the ASPR* 39 (January 1945), 2–34. Roughly half of the material in the *Journal* was unsuitable for publication in the *Journal of Parapsychology,* even under the relaxed standards Rhine adopted in 1942.

5. Tyrrell, "Is Measurement Essential in Psychical Research?" *Journal of the ASPR* 39 (January 1945), 35–45.

6. *Journal of the ASPR* 38 (January 1944), 58–60.

7. Parapsychology and psychical research are used interchangeably in this manuscript. Rhine wanted the term "parapsychology" to be applied only to his own experimental branch of psychical research, but the distinction he meant to maintain was not adhered to. According to Rhine's terminology, the Parapsychology Foundation should have been called the Psychical Research Foundation.

8. *Ten Years of Activity* (New York: Parapsychology Foundation, 1965).

9. Eileen J. Garrett, *Adventures in the Supernormal: A Personal Memoir* (New York: Creative Age Press, 1949); *Many Voices: The Autobiography of a Medium* (New York: G. P. Putnam's Sons, 1968).

10. Burke M. Smith and Betty Humphrey, "Some Personality Characteristics Related to ESP Performance," *Journal of Parapsychology* 10 (December 1946), 269–289; Gertrude Schmeidler, "Rorschach Variables in Relation to ESP Scores," *Journal of the ASPR* 41 (January 1947), 35–64. Leo Eilbert and Gertrude Schmeidler, "A Study of Certain Psychological Factors in Relation to ESP Performance," *Journal of Parapsychology* 14 (March 1950), 53–74; Betty Humphrey, "Introversion-Extraversion Ratings in Relation to Scores in ESP Tests," *Journal of Parapsychology* 15 (December 1951), 252–262.

11. Garrett, *My Life as a Search for the Meaning of Mediumship* (London: Rider and Co., 1939), pp. 163–225.

12. Of course Garrett was not the first person interested in parapsychology to experiment with a drug. James not only experimented with nitrous oxide but called the attention of Americans to Benjamin Paul Blood. A. B. Child, a nineteenth-century American spiritualist, wrote extensively on the higher state of reality induced by hashish. See *BL,* January 22, 1859, and September 29, 1860.

13. Conference on "Parapsychology and Psychedelics," held in New York City, November 15–16, 1958. A second conference on para-

psychology and pharmacology was held in St. Paul de Vence, France, July 6–10, 1959.

14. *Ten Years of Activity*, p. 62.

15. Jan Ehrenwald, *Telepathy and Medical Psychology* (London: George Allen and Unwin, 1947). See contributions of Ehrenwald and Eisenbud to "Symposium: A Program for the Next Ten Years of Research in Parapsychology," *Journal of Parapsychology* 12 (March 1948), 6–12; 12 (June 1948), 83–86.

16. For a summary of research activity and the names of research centers, see Rhea A. White, "Parapsychology Today," in Edgar D. Mitchell, ed., *Psychic Exploration: A Challenge for Science* (New York: G. P. Putnam's Sons, 1974). Also William G. Roll, "Survival Research: Problems and Possibilities," ibid.

17. John G. Fuller, *The Great Soul Trial* (New York: Macmillan, 1969).

18. Rhine was perhaps more flexible than many of his critics realized, but his flexibility in most instances only raised further doubts about how seriously he took the demands of experimental rigor. Rhine's own writings were his worst enemy. For his assessment of the value of reports about spontaneous psi events, see "Research Aims for the Decade Ahead," *Journal of Parapsychology* 12 (June 1948), 101–107.

19. *Journal of the ASPR* 36 (April 1942), 49; *Journal of the ASPR* 40 (April 1946), 53–54.

20. See G. E. Hutchison, "Methodology and Value in the Natural Sciences," *Journal of Religion* 32 (1952), 175–187.

21. For a general survey of American academic support, see Frederick Dommeyer and Rhea White, "Psychical Research in Colleges and Universities," *Journal of the ASPR* 57 (January 1963), 3–31; 57 (April 1963), 55–105.

22. Whately Carington, *Matter, Mind, and Meaning* (New Haven: Yale University Press, 1949); S. G. Soal and F. Bateman, *Modern Experiments in Telepathy* (New Haven: Yale University Press, 1954); Gertrude Schmeidler and R. A. McConnell, *ESP and Personality Problems* (New Haven: Yale University Press, 1958).

23. Mitchell, "From Outer Space to Inner Space," in Mitchell, *Psychic Exploration*, pp. 25–50.

24. Carlson was on the board of trustees of the ASPR from 1962 until his death in 1968. The first psychical researchers were people of independent means. One English psychical researcher complained that Britain's postwar tax laws would wipe out psychical researchers along with the leisure class.

25. Lawrence LeShan estimated in 1974 that there were only twenty-

five full-time professional psychical researchers in the world. Le-Shan, *The Medium, the Mystic, and the Physicist* (New York: Viking Press, 1974), p. xiii.

26. As an example of this genre, see B. F. Skinner, "Card-Guessing Experiments," *American Scientist* 36 (July 1948), 456–462. G. R. Price, who charged parapsychologists with fraud in "Science and the Supernatural," *Science* 122 (August 26, 1955), 359–367, later apologized.

27. C. E. M. Hansel, *ESP: A Scientific Evaluation* (New York: Scribner's, 1966). Hansel's book raised a storm of protest from parapsychologists. A favorable review by Martin Gardner in the *New York Review of Books* (May 26, 1966) provoked replies from Bob Brier and J. G. Pratt. A second and unprinted reply from Pratt is in the ASPR Library (Pamphlet 240). Hansel's book gave parapsychologists like Pratt a chance to state publicly their dedication to a rigid scientific methodology.

28. See report in *New York Times,* August 20, 1974.

29. "The Role of Neurological Ideas in Psychology," *Journal of Personality* 20 (September 1951), 45.

30. See R. A. McConnell, "The Structure of Scientific Revolutions: An Epitome," *Journal of the ASPR* 62 (July 1968), 321–327. Also Joseph H. Rush, "Parapsychology's Century of Progress," in Allan Angoff and Betty Shapin, eds., *Parapsychology Today: A Geographic View* (New York: Parapsychology Foundation, 1973), 213–214.

31. Gardner Murphy, "Field Theory and Survival," *Journal of the ASPR* 39 (October 1945), 181–209.

32. Whately Carington, *Thought Transference: An Outline of Facts, Theory and Implications of Telepathy* (New York: Creative Age Press, 1946). For a summary of Carington's theory, see Margaret Pegram Reeves, "Whately Carington's Theory of Paranormal Cognition and Allied Phenomena," *Journal of the ASPR* 39 (April 1945), 95–112.

33. Jaffé, "C. G. Jung and Parapsychology," in J. R. Smythies, ed., *Science and ESP* (London: Routledge and Kegan Paul, 1967), 263–280. For summaries of some of the more important theories advanced about psi phenomena, see K. Ramakrishna Rao, "Consideration of Some Theories of Parapsychology," *Journal of Parapsychology* 25 (March 1961), 32–54.

34. Adrian Dobbs, "The Feasibility of a Physical Theory of ESP," in Smythies, ed., *Science and EPS,* 225–254.

35. H. H. Price, "Psychical Research and Human Personality," in ibid., 33–45.

36. Smythies, "Is ESP Possible?" in ibid., 1–14.

37. Broad wrote extensively on the subject of psychical research. See especially Broad, *Religion, Philosophy and Psychical Research* (London: Routledge and Kegan Paul, 1953). The debate over the physicality or nonphysicality of psi is an exceedingly confusing one. For guidance, see "Physicality and Psi: A Symposium and Forum Discussion," *Journal of Parapsychology* 25 (March 1961), 13–31. Also K. R. Rao, *Experimental Parapsychology: A Review and Interpretation (Springfield, Ill.: Charles C Thomas,* 1966); Allan Angoff and Betty Shapin, eds., *Parapsychology and the Sciences* (New York: Parapsychology Foundation, 1974); Laura Oteri, ed., *Quantum Physics and Parapsychology* (New York: Parapsychology Foundation, 1975).

38. Pratt, "Some Notes for the Future Einstein for Parapsychology," *Journal of the ASPR* 68 (April 1974), 133–155.

39. D. Scott Rogo, "The Crisis in Experimental Parapsychology," *Parapsychology Review* 3 (July–August 1972), 5–7.

40. Margenau, "ESP in the Framework of Modern Science," *Journal of the ASPR* 60 (July 1966), 214–228.

41. There was much less theoretical speculation about clairvoyance, precognition, or psychokinesis.

42. See Thouless's review of *New World of the Mind, Journal of Parapsychology* 18 (March 1954), 42–51.

43. Jule Eisenbud, "Psi and the Nature of Things," *International Journal of Parapsychology* 5 (Summer 1963), 245–268.

44. Murphy, "Lawfulness Versus Caprice: Is There a Law of Psychic Phenomena," *Journal of the ASPR* 58 (October 1964), 239.

45. Stevenson, "Review of Louisa Rhine's *Mind Over Matter," Journal of the ASPR* 65 (July 1971), 362.

46. Stevenson, "Some Implications of Parapsychological Research on Survival After Death," *Proceedings of the ASPR* 28 (May 1969), 33. For another criticism of the "behavioristic" direction of Rhine's research, see Charles Honorton, "Psi-Conducive States of Awareness," in Mitchell, *Psychic Exploration . . . ,* p. 619.

47. LeShan devoted an appendix to the question of why people refused to accept evidence of the supernormal. *The Medium, the Mystic, and the Physicist,* pp. 197–217. Also see Walter Franklin Prince, *The Enchanted Boundary: Being a Survey of Negative Reactions to Claims of Psychic Phenomena, 1820–1930* (Boston: Boston Society for Psychic Research, 1930).

48. *The Medium, the Mystic, and the Physicist,* p. 101–102.

49. Ibid., pp. 99–133.

50. *Walter Franklin Prince: A Tribute to His Memory* (Boston: Boston Society for Psychic Research, 1935), p. 52.

51. Rhine, "Why National Defense Overlooks Parapsychology," *Journal of Parapsychology* 21 (December 1957), 245–258.

52. Karlis Osis, for example, directed experiments dealing with meditation and drugs at the ASPR during the 1960s. His experimental approach was as cautious as that of anyone who had ever worked in the field of parapsychology. Some of America's leading parapsychologists worried openly about the kinds of activities being associated with parapsychology. See R. A. McConnell, "Parapsychology and the Occult," *Journal of the ASPR* 67 (July 1973), 225–243, and Rhine, "Is Parapsychology Losing Its Way?" *Journal of Parapsychology* 36 (June 1972), 170–176.

Chapter 9

1. "Responsibility in Parapsychology," *Parapsychology Review* 1 (November–December 1970), 13–19. Also "Is Modern Parapsychology a Science?" *Parapsychology Review* 3 (November–December 1972), 1–2, 23–26.

2. Science, Dingwall wrote, is "an organized attempt to find out how things work when they are viewed as causal systems." "Is Modern Parapsychology a Science?" p. 24. So, of course, is occultism.

3. *Psychic,* which began publication in California in the 1960s, was the most popular of the magazines devoted to the full range of supernormal and occult phenomena. For evidence of the concern, see Paul D. Allison, "Social Aspects of Scientific Innovation: The Case of Parapsychology," Master's thesis, University of Wisconsin, 1973.

4. Martin Marty, "The Occult Establishment," *Social Research* 37 (Summer 1970), 212–230. Also see Edward A. Tiryakian, ed., *On the Margin of the Visible: Sociology, the Esoteric, and the Occult* (New York: Wiley, 1974).

5. For a recent example, see D. H. Rawcliffe, *Illusions and Delusions of the Supernatural and the Occult* (New York: Dover, 1959).

6. Brittan, "Supra-Terrestrial Influences," *The Telegraph Papers* 1 (1853), 200.

7. Perhaps the best account of American Theosophy is contained in J. Stillson Judah, *The History and Philosophy of the Metaphysical Movements in America* (Philadelphia: Westminster Press, 1967). In addition, there is a wealth of information in Arthur H. Nethercot's two-volume biography of Annie Besant: *The First Five Lives of Annie Besant* (Chicago: University of Chicago Press, 1960) and *The Last Four Lives of Annie Besant* (Chicago: University of Chicago

Press, 1963). Unfortunately, there is never likely to be a reliable biography of Helen Blavatsky, but see John Symonds, *Madame Blavatsky: Medium and Magician* (London: Odhams Press, 1959) and
Gertrude Marvin Williams, *Madame Blavatsky: Priestess of the Occult* (New York: Alfred A. Knopf, 1946). Her lively qualities are evident in *Some Unpublished Letters of Helena Petrova Blavatsky* (London: Rider and Co., n.d.).

8. Letter from J. M. Roberts, *BL,* November 20, 1875.

9. Review of A.P. Sinnett's *The Occult World, BL,* June 3, 1882.

10. *BL,* October 16, 1875.

11. A. E. Newton, "Oriental vs. Occidental Spiritualism," *BL,* April 23,
1887.

12. Hinduism was introduced to an important segment of the American population during the Chicago Exposition in 1893. In that year
Swami Vivekananda attended the World Parliament of Religions
held in Chicago. He then launched national lecture tours that
lasted until 1895.

13. Quoted in Hardinge, *Modern American Spiritualism* (New York:
published by the author, 1870) p. 363. Hardinge, despite her opposition to occultism that was expressed in this volume, became
linked to the Theosophical Society. See her *Ghost Land. Or Researches into the Mysteries of Occultism* (Boston, 1876).

14. *Isis Unveiled* (New York: J. W. Bouton, 1877). Also see Blavatsky,
Key to Theosophy (London: Theosophical Publishing Society, 1890);
Secret Doctrine (London: Theosophical Publishing Society, 1893);
and *Modern Panarion* (London: Theosophical Publishing Society,
1895).

15. Henry Steel Olcott, *Old Diary Leaves: The True Story of the Theosophical Society* (New York: G. P. Putnam's Sons, 1895), pp. 98,
43–44.

16. Letter to Hiram Corson, March 22, 1876. In *Some Unpublished Letters of Helena Petrova Blavatsky,* p. 181.

17. Robert C. Galbreath, "Spiritual Science in an Age of Materialism:
Rudolf Steiner and Occultism," Ph.D. dissertation, University of
Michigan, 1970.

18. For some discussions of the historical tradition of occultism, see
Frances Yates, *Giordano Bruno and the Hermetic Tradition* (London:
Routledge and Kegan Paul, 1964); *The Rosicrucian Enlightenment*
(London: Routledge and Kegan Paul, 1972); Peter French, *John Dee:
The World of an Elizabethan Magus* (London: Routledge and Kegan
Paul, 1972); John Senior, *The Way Down and Out: The Occult in
Symbolist Literature* (Ithaca, N.Y.: Cornell University Press, 1959).

19. Harriet Whitehead, "Reasonably Fantastic: Some Perspectives on Scientology, Science Fiction, and Occultism," Irving I. Zaretsky and Mark P. Leone, eds., *Religious Movements in Contemporary America* (Princeton: Princeton University Press, 1974), p. 561.

20. Letter to Hiram Corson, March 22, 1876, and letter quoted in *BL*, April 21, 1877.

21. George Lawton, *The Drama of Life After Death: A Study of the Spiritualist Religion* (New York: Henry Holt, 1932), p. 577.

22. "The History of Occultism and its Relation to Spiritualism," *BL*, August 26, 1876.

23. Richard Hodgson was the chief architect of the report. See vol. 3 of the *Proceedings of the SPR*.

24. For a discussion of this point by two parapsychologists, see I. Stevenson and W. G. Roll, "Criticism in Parapsychology: An Informal Statement of Some Guiding Principles," *Journal of the ASPR* 60 (October 1966), 347–356.

25. See discussion in chap. 8.

26. C. G. Jung, *Memories, Dreams, Reflections* (London: Routledge and Kegan Paul, 1963). Aniela Jaffé, *Apparitions and Precognition: A Study of the Point of View of C. G. Jung's Analytical Psychology* (New Hyde Park, N.Y.: University Books, 1963).

27. Damon Knight, *Charles Fort: Prophet of the Unexplained* (Garden City, N.Y.: Doubleday, 1970), p. 206. Knight's book begins with an appreciative preface written by R. Buckminster Fuller.

Bibliography

I *Primary Sources*

The notes for the text adequately indicate the types of printed books and pamphlets used in piecing together the history of spiritualism and psychical research. I am further satisfied that readers can find in those notes the most important and most widely circulated publications generated by the controversy over both movements. To be sure, I have read and have been influenced in my thinking by a great many others that are not cited. But I have resisted the temptation to string together in the bibliography all the titles in my file boxes. My reason is simple: while running on to many pages, such a compilation would provide neither a definitive nor an exhaustive list of what has sometimes seemed to me an infinite number of tracts.

In finding concentrated collections of relevant material, I have been particularly rewarded by my work at the Widener and Houghton libraries at Harvard University, at the Sterling and Beinecke libraries at Yale University, at the American Society for Psychical Research, at the Society for Psychical Research, London, and at the New York City Public Library. Interested students should also be alerted to the special opportunities provided by the Harry Houdini collection at the Library of Congress and by the Harry Price collection at the Senate Library, University of London.

Archival and newspaper sources merit additional comments beyond what I have been able to say elsewhere. Manuscript collections relevant to a study of spiritualism and psychical research are scattered in depositories all over the country. Of the collections that I have been able to reach, I have found the following the most useful. The Wisconsin State Historical Society houses the valuable journals of John Shoebridge Williams, as well as some marvelous letters of Madame Blavatsky. The latter are in the papers of the ornithologist Elliott Coues, who was briefly in the Theosophical Society in the late 1880s. Also of interest at the Wisconsin Historical Society are the papers of Robert Schilling, Ada James, Zona Gale, and Ella Wheeler Wilcox. The letters of Sarah Helen Whitman at the Brown University Library contain many references to spiritualism (especially in correspondence with Horace Greeley). So do the letters of William Lloyd Garrison, Hugo Munsterberg, and Epes Sargent in the Boston Public Library. In the Regional History Collection at the Cornell University Library I found much useful material in the Charlotte Fowler Wells and the Fowler family papers. Also in the papers of the English professor Hiram Corson, Marcus M. Cass, and George Lucien Swift. The Robert Hare material at the American Philosophical Society was extremely important in writing the first chapter of this book. I found almost equally valuable the society's collection of letters and notes of the inventor Coleman Sellers. There are many collections at Duke University that pertain to spiritualism. The most helpful were the papers of John Armstrong Chaloner, Ella Gertrude Thomas, Flavius Joseph Cook, Godfrey Barnsley, and Paul Hamilton Hayne. The R. Heeber Newton papers at the New York Historical Society are disappointing with respect to the minister's psychic interests. But there are several interesting letters in the William Sidney Mount papers. With respect to psychical research and parapsychology, my greatest manuscript resource was the American Society for Psychical Research. The society possesses many interesting documents relating to its early history as well as letters to and from the leading figures connected with the movement in the United States and England.

As for spiritualist periodicals: most nineteenth-century newspapers and journals devoted to the spirits had brief lives, and it is exceedingly difficult to find surviving single issues, let alone complete runs, of many of them. The most important editor of the early movement was S. B. Brittan, whose name was associated successively with *The Univercoelum, or Spiritual Philosophy* (New York, 1847–49, instigated by people interested in Andrew Jackson Davis), *The Shekinah* (New York, 1852–53, absorbed by Joseph Rodes Buchanan's *The Journal of Man*), and *The Spiritual Telegraph* (New York, 1852–60, edited with Charles Partridge, as was *The Telegraph Papers*). But there were innumerable ephemeral enterprises begun in the 1950s by local societies in every part of the country. The most accessible to me were those edited either in New York City or in New England. Of particular note are LaRoy Sunderland's *Spiritual Philosopher* (Boston, 1850–51, name changed to the *Spirit World* in 1851), A. E. Newton's *New England Spiritualist* (Boston, 1855–56), R. P. Ambler and Apollos Munn's *Spirit Messenger* (Springfield, Mass., 1850–52), Joel Tiffany's *Tiffany's Monthly Magazine* (New York, 1856–58), and *The Christian Spiritualist* (New York, 1854–57, sponsored by the Society for the Diffusion of Spiritual Knowledge).

In 1857, Luther Colby began his long career as editor of the *Banner of Light*. The paper continued after his death and did not cease publication until 1907. The American Antiquarian Society has a virtually complete run of this important source. Of equal significance is *The Religio-Philosophical Journal* that Steven Jones founded in Chicago in 1865. It continued publication until 1905. For the later nineteenth century one might also consult *Facts* (Boston, 1882–87).

From its inception psychical research has also spawned great quantities of short-lived periodical literature. For example, from the early history of the American movement one can cite T. E. Allen's *Psychical Review* (Boston, 1892–94, published by the American Psychical Society). Indeed the original American Society for Psychical Research managed to publish only one volume of *Proceedings of the ASPR* (covering the years 1885–89) before it expired. But the ASPR founded by Hyslop has published a *Journal* and *Proceedings* (the latter irregular) since 1907. These can be supplemented by the *Proceedings of the Society for Psychical Research*, London (since 1882) and its *Journal* (since 1884). Also of a crucial nature are J. B. Rhine's *Journal of Parapsychology* (1937–   ), the *Bulletin of the Boston Society for Psychic Research* (1925–1936), the *International Journal of Parapsychology* (New York, 1959–68), and the *Parapsychology Review* (1970–   ). The last two are publications of the Parapsychology Foundation. For the connections between spirit voices, psychical research, and various brands of occultism in recent decades, consult the Parapsychology Foundation's *Tomorrow* (1952–73) and the San Francisco–based *Psychic* (1969–   ).

II. *Secondary Sources*

The early histories of spiritualism written by partisans of the movement are of course vital to the scholar. But the first account of the nineteenth-century movement written with any academic rigor is Frank Podmore, *Modern Spiritualism, A History and a Criticism*, 2 vols. (London: Methuen and Co., 1902). Podmore was once a spiritualist, and his book is exposé as well as history. But his firsthand contact with many of the subjects he discusses makes this an extremely valuable source. A rather less good account by a hostile observer is Joseph McCabe, *Spiritualism: A Popular History from 1847* (London: T. Fisher Unwin, 1920).

The first important account specifically about the American movement is George Lawton, *The Drama of Life After Death: A Study of the Spiritualist Religion* (New York: Henry Holt and Co., 1932). The book is provocative for the sociological and psychological interpretations that the author makes of the spiritualists he lived among at Lily Dale, New York. It is less useful as history and misleading, I think, in the degree of consistency it assigns to spiritualist religious beliefs. Also useful for the study of twentieth-century spiritualist religious practices is Charles Samuel Braden, *These Also Believe: A Study of Modern American Cults and Minority Religious Movements* (New York: Macmillan, 1949).

Two books primarily concerned with the history of spiritualism in England have been useful in this study. They are Katherine H. Porter, *Through a Glass Darkly: Spiritualism in the Browning Circle* (Lawrence: University of Kansas Press, 1958) and Geoffrey K. Nelson, *Spiritualism and Society* (London: Routledge and Kegan Paul, 1969). While narrow in scope the former is sensitive and altogether first-rate. The latter is finally disappointing as history and sociology, but it is virtually the first piece of recent scholarship to treat the subject in anything resembling an appropriately broad framework.

The first important history of the early American spiritualists is Ernest Isaacs, "A History of Spiritualism. The Beginnings, 1845–1855" (Master's thesis, University of Wisconsin, 1957). In 1975, Isaacs expanded the Master's thesis into a doctoral dissertation at Wisconsin. I have many quarrels with the author, mostly because I think that he has read too much of the early history of the movement (to which he has given the closest attention) into developments subsequent to 1855. I also find myself at odds with Isaacs over the importance he assigns various individuals. Nonetheless, his delineation of many leading figures in the movement is admirably done.

Much other recent work attempting a general assessment of nineteenth-century American spiritualism remains unpublished. Burton Gates Brown, Jr., "Spiritualism in Nineteenth-Century America" (Ph.D. dissertation, Boston University, 1973), provides the most detailed account of institutional developments within the movement. Mary Farrell Bednarowski, "Nineteenth-Century American Spiritualism: An Attempt at Scientific Religion" (Ph.D. dissertation, University of Minnesota, 1973) assesses the religious significance of spiritualism.

Also see Glen A. Gildmeister, "American Spiritualism, 1845–1855" (Master's thesis, Northern Illinois University, 1972).

There have been many recent popular accounts of spiritualism. Two of the better are Slater Brown, *The Heyday of Spiritualism* (New York: Hawthorn Books, 1970) and Herbert Jackson, Jr., *The Spirit Rappers* (Garden City, N.Y.: Doubleday, 1972). But much more useful to the student is Howard Kerr, *Mediums, and Spirit Rappers, and Roaring Radicals: Spiritualism in American Literature, 1850–1900* (Urbana: University of Illinois Press, 1972). His discussion of literary perceptions of the spiritualist movement was especially useful for my chapter on reform. Another fairly recent book that helped to frame the historical context of spiritualist ideas is J. Stillson Judah, *The History and Philosophy of the Metaphysical Movements in America* (Philadelphia: Westminster Press, 1967).

A number of people important to American spiritualism have been the subject of biographies. An especially excellent book is Richard W. Leopold, *Robert Dale Owen: A Biography* (Cambridge, Mass.: Harvard University Press, 1940). Unlike the biographers of many other prominent Americans affected by spiritualism, Leopold did not duck the issues posed by his subject's fascination with séances. A useful study of Swedenborg is Signe Toksvig, *Emanuel Swedenborg: Scientist and Mystic* (New Haven: Yale University Press, 1948). On Andrew Jackson Davis, see a series of articles that Robert W. Delp published from his Ph.D. dissertation: "Andrew Jackson Davis: Prophet of American Spiritualism," *Journal of American History* 54 (June 1967), 43–56; "Andrew Jackson Davis' *Revelations,* Harbinger of American Spiritualism," *New York Historical Society Quarterly* 60 (July 1971), 211–234; "American Spiritualism and Social Reform, 1847–1900," *Northwest Ohio Quarterly* 44 (Fall 1972), 85–99. Most of what has been written about the Fox sisters is careless and inaccurate. One must, for example, approach with considerable caution the biography by Earl Wesley Fornell, *The Unhappy Medium: Spiritualism and the Life of Margaret Fox* (Austin: University of Texas Press, 1964). Much more reliable is the biography of the man to whom Margaret Fox was romantically attached: see George W. Corner, *Doctor Kane of the Arctic Seas* (Philadelphia: Temple University Press, 1972). M. M. Marberry, *Vicky: A Biography of Victoria C. Woodhull* (New York: Funk and Wagnalls, 1967) is inadequate, as are all other books about this remarkable woman. In contrast, Madeleine B. Stern has written with skill on several people associated with spiritualism: *Heads and Headliners: The Phrenological Fowlers* (Norman: University of Oklahoma Press, 1971) and *The Pantarchy: A Biography of Ste-*

phen Pearl Andrews (Austin: University of Texas Press, 1968). Various other studies of American and English spiritualists include Neil Lehman, "The Life of John Murray Spear, Spiritualism and Reform in Antebellum America" (Ph.D. dissertation, Ohio State University, 1973); Jean Burton, *Heyday of a Wizard: Daniel Home, the Medium* (New York: Alfred A. Knopf, 1974); Trevor Hall, *The Spiritualists: The Story of Florence Cook and William Crookes* (New York: Helix Press, 1963); Alta L. Piper, *The Life and Work of Mrs. Piper* (London: Kegan Paul, Trench, Trubner and Co., 1929). On people who were once associated with spiritualism and recanted, see Herbert Schneider and George Lawton, *A Prophet and a Pilgrim* (New York: Columbia University Press, 1942); Robert Peel, *Mary Baker Eddy: The Years of Discovery* (New York: Holt, Rinehart and Winston, 1966); and Gertrude Marvin Williams, *Madame Blavatsky: Priestess of the Occult* (New York: Alfred A. Knopf, 1946).

There are many other books that influenced my interpretations of nineteenth-century spiritualism. I can mention here only those that touched most explicitly on my concerns. For background information I am indebted to Robert Darnton, *Mesmerism and the End of the Enlightenment in France* (Cambridge, Mass.: Harvard University Press, 1968); John D. Davies, *Phrenology: Fad and Science, A Nineteenth-Century American Crusade* (New Haven: Yale University Press, 1955); Whitney Cross, *The Burned-Over District: The Social and Intellectual History of Enthusiastic Religion in Western New York, 1800–1850* (New York: Harper & Row, 1965); and John B. Wilson, "Emerson and the Rochester Rappings," *New England Quarterly* 41 (June 1968), 248–258. On the subject of reform and spiritualism, the best commentaries are in Lewis Perry, *Radical Abolitionism, Anarchy and the Government of God in Antislavery Thought* (Ithaca, N.Y.: Cornell University Press, 1973); J. F. C. Harrison, *Robert Owen and the Owenites in Britain and America* (London: Routledge and Kegan Paul, 1969); Arthur Mann, *Yankee Reformers in the Urban Age* (New York: Harper & Row, 1966); Robert V. Hine, *California's Utopian Colonies* (New Haven: Yale University Press, 1966); and Scott Trego Swank, "The Unfettered Conscience: A Study of Sectarianism, Spiritualism, and Social Reform in the New Jerusalem Church, 1840–1870" (Ph.D. dissertation, University of Pennsylvania, 1970). Finally, my chapter on the spiritualist medium was influenced above all by the many fine articles of Ann Douglas and Carroll Smith-Rosenberg. I will not here repeat their contributions, which are fully cited in the notes. But I should mention two other works of a very different sort: Vieda Skultans, *Intimacy and Ritual: A Study of Spiritualism, Mediums, and Groups* (London: Routledge and Kegan Paul, 1974) and

Bonita Ann Freeman, "The Development of Spiritualist Mediums: Apprenticeship to a Tradition" (Ph.D. dissertation, University of Pennsylvania, 1974).

The starting points for secondary material on psychical research are Alan Gauld, *The Founders of Psychical Research* (New York: Schocken Books, 1968), and Frank Turner, *Between Science and Religion: The Reaction to Scientific Naturalism in Late Victorian England* (New Haven: Yale University Press, 1974). Both books deal primarily with England, but because of transatlantic intellectual connections both have much to say about America. Turner's focus is larger than Gauld's, and his book is excellent. A very useful study of the structure and institutions of professional parapsychology in America is Paul D. Allison, "Social Aspects of Scientific Innovation: The Case of Parapsychology" (Master's thesis, University of Wisconsin, 1973). Also see the excellent article by Michael McVaugh and Seymour Mauskopf, "J. B. Rhine's *Extra-Sensory Perception* and Its Background in Psychical Research." *Isis* 67 (June 1976), 161–189.

C. E. M. Hansel, *ESP: A Scientific Evaluation* (New York: Scribner's, 1966) professes to contain historical material, but it is better understood as belonging to the category of historical documents written in opposition to parapsychology. In fact virtually everything that has been written about parapsychology, other than what has been mentioned, is best left in the category of primary material.

I think that students of William James have generally underestimated his interest in psychical research. Less guilty of this than most studies is Gay Wilson Allen, *William James: A Biography* (New York: Viking Press, 1967). By far the best introduction to American psychology in the period during which psychical research was founded is Nathan Hale, Jr., *Freud and the Americans* (New York: Oxford University Press, 1971). See also Charles Rosenberg, "The Place of George M. Beard in 19th-Century Psychiatry," *Bulletin of the History of Medicine* 36 (May–June 1962), 245–259. Other than James, there are no adequate biographies of any American who contributed to psychical research, but see Raymond Van Over and Lauri Oteri, eds., *William McDougall, Explorer of the Mind* (New York: Garrett Publications, 1967). On Margery there is Thomas R. Tietze, *Margery* (New York: Harper & Row, 1973).

My attempts to understand how spiritualism and psychical research relate and do not relate to various occult traditions have turned my reading to subjects far afield from nineteenth- and twentieth-century American history. I have deliberately used the word "occult" in a more restricted sense than one can find in recent popular use of the word.

Occultism is based on traditions of esoteric mysticism and magic, but is not on that account synonymous with any weird fact or practice that has no ready scientific explanation. My ideas have been shaped above all by the writings of Frances Yates and some of her students. Of particular importance have been Yates, *Giordano Bruno and the Hermetic Tradition* (London: Routledge and Kegan Paul, 1964) and *The Rosicrucian Enlightenment* (London: Routledge and Kegan Paul, 1972) and Peter French, *John Dee: The World of an Enlightenment Magus* (London: Routledge and Kegan Paul, 1972). Other works important to my thinking on this confusing subject are John Senior, *The Way Down and Out: the Occult in Symbolist Literature* (Ithaca, N.Y.: Cornell University Press, 1959); Edward A. Tiryakian, *On the Margin of the Visible: Sociology, the Esoteric, and the Occult* (New York: Wiley, 1974); James Webb, *The Flight from Reason* (London: MacDonald, 1971); Arthur H. Nethercot, *The First Five Lives of Annie Besant* (Chicago: University of Chicago Press, 1960), *The Last Four Lives of Annie Besant* (Chicago: University of Chicago Press, 1963); Martin Marty, "The Occult Establishment," *Social Research* 37 (Summer 1970), 212–230; Robert C. Galbreath, "Spiritual Science in an Age of Materialism. Rudolf Steiner and Occultism" (Ph.D. dissertation, University of Michigan, 1970). Two other books particularly useful in explaining the interest taken in parapsychology by the student counterculture of the 1960s are Jacob Needleman, *The New Religions* (Garden City, N.Y.: Doubleday, 1970) and Irvine Zaretsky and Mark Leone, eds., *Religious Movements in Contemporary America* (Princeton: Princeton University Press, 1974).

Thomas S. Kuhn must by now be terribly weary of seeing his book cited in unexpected places. I do not suggest that *The Structure of Scientific Revolutions* (Chicago: University of Chicago Press, 1962) settles any problem about either the hostility or the indifference with which most scientists have treated the claims of parapsychology. But I know of no book more provocative of thought on the subject.

Index

Abbot, Francis Ellingwood, 60-62
Abolitionism, 70-71, 74-80
Adams, Couch, 139
Adams, Mrs. J. S., 121
Agassiz, Louis, 33
Allen, John, 97
Alpert, Richard, 206
American Association for the Advancement of Science (AAAS): and early opposition to spiritualism, 26; and recognition of Parapsychological Society, 209, 212, 221
American Association of Spiritualists, 66-67
American Institute for Scientific Research, 159-60
American Journal of Psychology, 153-54
American Psychological Association: and Rhine, 194-95
American Society for Psychical Research (ASPR), 153, 155, 164, 166, 169-72, 205, 214, 226; compared to English SPR, 143-44; financing of, 210; founding of (1885), 62, 142-44; founding of (1907), 150-60; palace revolt in, 183-84; and popular spiritualism, 161, 175-80, 186; professional standards of, 162, 174-75, 209, 236-37
Andrews, Stephen Pearl, 97n
Anthony, Susan B., 83
Anthroposophical Movement, 231-32
Anti-institutionalism: and spiritualist reform, 80-81
Anti-scientism, 215-16, 218-19, 239-43
Ayer, Marcellus S., 68

Baker, Rachel, 127-28
Baldwin, James Mark, 161
Balfour, Arthur, 139

308 INDEX

Spear, John Murray: and Association of Beneficents, 94; converts to spiritualism, 92-93; and free love, 97, 118; founds Harmonia Community, 94; New Motive Power of, 94; possible psychopathology of, 95, 98

The Spirit World, 13

Spiritual Fraternal Society (Boston), 68

Spiritual Philosopher, 13

Spiritual Telegraph, 13, 42; and Robert Hare, 32

Spiritualism: and antebellum reform, 70-71, 74-82; begins in Hydesville, 7-8; and Catholicism, 35, 43-44; characteristics of spirit messages in, 16, 21-22, 37, 48-49, 252-53 n; Christian spiritualism and, 14, 46, 49-50, 55; compared to other antebellum religions, 50-51; critics of, 17-18, 24, 27-36, 57-59, 72, 117-19; decline of, 64-69; distinguished from mysticism and occultism, 6-7, 23, 223-36; early appeal of and links to popular science, 7, 14-15, 19-24, 32, 35-39, 65; estimates of adherents of, 14, 41; and influence on religious liberalism, 49-50, 61-65, 68-69; and lack of wonder, 37-39; and late nineteenth-century reform, 72, 74, 82-90, 100-01; and materialism, 23-26; and morality, 34, 56-60, 81, 117-19; motivating psychology of, 1-7, 99-100, 102-3; non-

religious aspects of, 42-43, 45-46; organizations devoted to, 13-14, 66-69; precursors of, 8-12; prominent sponsors of, 3-5; Protestant opposition to, 28-29, 40-41, 44-49; publications of, 13; and revelation, 12, 22, 47-49; scientific investigation of, 27-35, 139-40, 165, 169-70, 177-79; as separate religion, 41-43, 66-69; standard interpretations of, 5-6, 102-3, 262n; theological views of, 51-60; and views of afterlife, 54-57; and women, 83-84, 103, 105-6, 110-17; and World War I, 175

Spiritualists: anti-institutionalism of, 13-14, 42-43, 68-69, 74, 76, 80-82; attitude toward evil of, 58-59, 79-81; attitude toward free will of, 82-83, 88; and feminists, 71, 83-84, 117-19, 259-60 n; motivations of, 1-7, 36-39, 43, 62, 98-100, 102-3; outsider mentality of, 74, 90-99, 106-8; persecution of, 99-100, 126-27, 254-55 n. *See also* Mediumship

Sprague, Miss A. W., 125

Stanford Research Center, 209-10

Stanford University: Thomas Stanford bequest to, 169-70

Stanton, Elizabeth Cady, 83-84

Starkweather, Ellen D., 107

Stebbins, Giles: emphasis on empiricism, 18; on reform, 84

Steiner, Rudolph, 231

Stevens, Abel, 31

Stevenson, Ian, 207, 210; and science, 217-18, 240-41